TWENTIETH CENTURY

CHINESE POETRY

AN ANTHOLOGY

*Translated and Edited
by Kai-yu Hsu*

Cornell Paperbacks

Cornell University Press

ITHACA, NEW YORK

This book is for Jean-Pierre, Roland, and Jeanne

FOREWORD

THE SELECTION of the poets represented in this volume has been guided by space limitation, personal preference, and an effort to include a fair cross-section of the works produced in this period. Wherever available, biographical data and dates are included. I find comfort in the thought that before too long a separate volume may appear to present Chinese poets outside of the mainland, who clearly deserve to be heard.

I have tried to keep the translations as close to the original Chinese as possible, but often I have had to depart from literalness in order to convey the meaning of a line or a stanza in clear English.

To J. and A. Axelrod, C. Birch, E. Breed, L. Cernuda, A. Freedgood, I. Lo, Ardath, Annie, and also the staff of the Chinese collection at Hoover Institution, I want to express my thanks for all their help.

Kai-yu Hsu

May 1962

CONTENTS

INDEPENDENTS AND OTHERS

INTRODUCTION

According to many students of Chinese literature, the best of Chinese poetry is poised in quiet beauty. It persuades without argument; it captures the significant through the insignificant; it creates a world wherein man loses his identity in nature, and together both nature and man find unity and meaning. All this is true of certain masterpieces of the T'ang Dynasty (618–906) which is generally regarded as the golden era of classical Chinese poetry, but the T'ang Dynasty is only one section in the stream of history.

Even in T'ang poetry divergent currents cross one another, and each current has its fountainhead in antiquity. Like all literatures, the Chinese had its early sources in primitive songs and dances. The most ancient Chinese verses preserve the images and myths that constituted the real, not just the conceptual, world of their singers. The image of a lord on high which stood for the supreme power, and the fish symbol which represented love and fertility in the 3000-year-old anthology, *The Book of Poetry* (*Shih Ching*); the myths of heavenly, earthly, and human spirits related in the 2300-year-old anthology, *The Songs of the South* (*Ch'u Tz'u*), were all important ingredients of daily life in ancient China. These two earliest Chinese anthologies also record the joy and sorrow, hope and aspiration, of the people who sang and listened to the songs. When these songs were first sung, the tradition of a great poetry was already taking shape.

The Chinese poetic tradition developed on three different planes. The first plane—and also the lowest in the eyes of tradition-bound Chinese poets—was the folk song. The folk song, in all its local variations and forms, has actually been the mainstay in the development of Chinese poetry and has remained one of its strongest rejuvenating forces. Whenever Chinese poetry exhausts its vigor as a result of too many restrictive influences, the folk song, with its genuine, robust power, returns to reinforce the formal poetry, and Chinese literature has witnessed a revival of creative energy. The only other force that has had as much effect on Chinese poetry as the folk song is foreign literature. As far back as the Han Dynasty (202 B.C.–A.D. 220), military tunes from the non-Chinese tribes in the north and northwest enriched Chinese poetry. And throughout the centuries, foreign verse forms and influences, like the indigenous folk song, have repeatedly brought fresh blood into the main artery of Chinese poetry. This process is still going on today.

Yet, however much his work actually benefited from the folk song, the traditional Chinese poet always relegated the folk song to an inferior position. He has refused to honor the folk origin and character of the exalted classics, *The Book of Poetry* and *The Songs of the South*, which have survived in their archaic language. This curious fact demands some explanation.

The traditional poets belonged to a social and literary elite whose ancestors had recorded the folk songs in these two classical works, edited them, and interpreted them for the benefit of posterity. The literary elite of China, commonly known as the *Wen-jen*, that is, the "literati," were the fortunate few who could afford the years of study necessary to master the elegant but archaic style of the Chinese written language. History tells us that most of them considered themselves followers of the Confucian doctrines; they literally monopolized the controlling positions in Chinese society, politics, and art, and dictated much of the cultural development of the country. With a zealous sense of responsibility, these "guardians" of Chinese culture went to work on the classics and gave them a moralistic interpretation which subsequently became accepted as orthodoxy. As a consequence, in later centuries the tradition-conscious Chinese poet would accept any of the love songs in *The Book of Poetry* as words of wisdom carrying a didactic message. At the same time he would dismiss a love song of his own time as vulgar, when in reality it was no more so than any one of the dozens of folk songs in *The Book of Poetry*.

The folk song was thus relegated to the level of entertainment literature, like the opera (which traditionally was not respected at all) and the stories and tales written for popular consumption. Poetry, according to the literati, was not for the unlettered populace. Kept outside the hall of formal poetry, the folk song nevertheless continued to grow as life went on and man never ceased to feel, respond, sigh, and sing.

A refined literary language known as "classical Chinese" was cultivated under the literati's tutelage. The child whose family was fortunate enough to be able to afford the services of a tutor started with *The Book of Poetry* at the age of five or six, went through the philosophical works of the Confucian era (c. 500 B.C.) as well as the scholarly commentaries on them written in a similar style, and often wound up with *The Book of Poetry* again at the end of his student career some twenty years later. The archaic style, particularly the prose style in the philosophical and historical works, was a terse, almost telegraphic language, suitable only for written communication. For centuries the literati accumulated historical anecdotes and literary lore until their special literary language became so allusion-laden that only the most erudite could feel completely at home with it.

At its best, the language through its rich imagery and metaphors could communicate a great deal in very few words. The two syllables, *chiang-nan* ("river south"), could bring to the mind of a cultivated reader the image of the land in eastern China south of the Yangtze River and the entire historical pageant of its development from the sixth to the thirteenth century: its rise to fame as the cultural and political center of China, the gaiety and glitter of its metropolises, the lush green of its countryside, and, above all, numerous lines of poetry written about these things by the great masters. Furthermore, since the schoolboy was always taught to chant and memorize the classical works as models for his own composition, his ear (or, more precisely, his pen) was attuned to the highly cultivated rhythm of this language when he grew to be an experienced writer. While his speech was the vernacular of his day, he would automatically write in the classical style. To be sure the history of Chinese literature is full of rebels who made a Wordsworthian effort to rejuvenate the classical language, and there were periodic movements to rid it of its obscure allusions. But the classical language in any form was an effective medium only among the literary elite, who remained a tiny minority in Chinese society.

In this classical language formal Chinese poetry developed on the second and more respected plane. For a theory about the essence of poetry, the literati turned to a dictum supposedly laid down by Confucius himself. It asserted that poetry was to "tell of a person's heart," which simply means "that one should tell whatever is in one's heart." The moralistic traditional poet, however, insisted on *his* interpretation of the dictum: that poetry was "to reveal one's mind," or rather "to reveal whatever one *should* keep in mind." To him poetry was a purveyor of wisdom and a mirror of the writer's moral self. Consequently poetry was included among the subjects for the imperial examination—the only road to civil service and social distinction. The poet was no longer a person who sang either to satisfy himself or simply to earn a living. He was the acme of man's achievement. He could be a statesman, a general, a scholar, and not infrequently an emperor, but almost never just a poet. Such exaltation of poetry made the writing of poems an aspiration of anyone who could read and write, regardless of the limitations of his poetic talents. Among the educated, poetry became a feature of daily life and a medium of social communication. Even a collection of platitudes might be considered a poem. The occasional poem was the order of the day. It was often written to commemorate a mandarin's spring festival banquet, or a prince's acquisition of a summer house. The degeneration of poetry on this plane reached its lowest depth when writing poetry became nothing more than a highly stylized exercise in linguistic dexterity.

Meanwhile the best of the poetic tradition, a refined appreciation of life and nature and a cultivated sensitivity to the musical essence of the language, continued to develop on a third plane. The prosodic motifs, enriched by non-Chinese tunes and folk songs, inspired the truly talented poets to perfect a variety of stanza forms during the T'ang Dynasty (618–906). The quatrain called "broken-off lines" (*chüeh chü*) and the eight-line verse called "regulated verse" (*lü shih*) were most popular and, by the end of the seventh century, had already become the backbone of classical Chinese poetry. Each line in these forms contained either five or seven syllables. In their embryonic stage these forms were found as basic units of earlier, longer songs. They were worked over and over until they proved to be the irreducibly compact and most versatile frames for the poetic language. Next to these two, the most influential stanza forms developed mainly during the ninth and tenth centuries (late T'ang and early Sung Dynasties) were known as *tz'u*, which made use of a good number of tunes each varying from sixteen to over a hundred notes in length. Unlike the broken-off lines or regulated verse, the *tz'u* contains mostly lines of irregular lengths which had to be fitted to different bars of music.

Analytical study of the sounds and tonal patterns of Chinese words had reached a high degree of sophistication during the Sui Dynasty (590–618), enabling later poets to balance rhythm and cadence according to strict rules in all these forms. Parallelism, a unique feature of the Chinese language which had its start in *The Book of Poetry* and *The Songs of the South* and was carried to an extreme in the elaborately descriptive prose poems called *fu* in the Han Dynasty, became an indispensable element in all T'ang poetry, particularly in the regulated verse. The use of parallelism requires a perfectly symmetrical contrast of images and words in a couplet. For instance, if the first line of a couplet refers to the mountain, the second line must refer to the river, or if the first line deals with the world of nature, the second line must deal with the world of man. Such rules may sound very rigid, perhaps too rigid to permit any full exercise of the poet's imagination, but it should be remembered that they were the result of many diverse experiments, and as such represented the crystallization of many great poets' experience.

The true feelings of man that found expression in *The Book of Poetry* and other ancient verses were again voiced, and loudly too, in T'ang and Sung poems. By the seventh century the images first used in *The Songs of the South* had acquired new evocative power. The search into the unknown and the quest for meaning beyond man's sensory existence had received an impetus from the importation of Indian Buddhism to China and the revival of native Taoism during the five hundred years from the first to the fifth century. The

cult of nature had been flourishing ever since the poet T'ao
Ch'ien (365–427) immortalized yellow chrysanthemums and
home-brewed wine. The T'ang and Sung Dynasties were
indeed the golden era of classical Chinese poetry, representing
the peak of the development of Chinese poetry on this plane,
rightfully recognized as the highest plane.

Highlighting T'ang poetry were the works of such famous
writers as Wang Wei (699–759), Li Po (701–762), and Tu
Fu (712–770). Their poems present an impressive array of
images, an infinite variety of nature's moods, and the full
grace of the epithetic classical Chinese language. What Wang
Wei evokes in a quatrain about mountains and woods

> On the uncluttered mountain, no one is seen,
> Yet voices are heard.
> The setting sun casts shadows in dense woods,
> And lights up patches of green moss.[1]

> > (from Hsü, *Annotated T'ang Poetry*, II, 32)

is a view of quiet beauty and a complete blending of man's
identity with nature.

Or take another poem by Wang Wei:

> In a bamboo thicket I sit alone,
> Plucking my lute and whistling a tune.
> No one knows this grove—so deeply hidden,
> Only the moon comes to shine on me.

> > (from Hsü, *Annotated T'ang Poetry*, II, 33)

[1] The original reads like this:

> > K'ung shan pu chien jen
> > Tan wen jen yü hsiang
> > Fan ching ju shen lin
> > Fu chao ch'ing t'ai shang

literally translated, word by word:

> > Empty mountain not see man
> > But hear man voice sound
> > Reverse view enter deep woods
> > Again (return) shine green moss on

Note the neat stanza form, uniform length of lines, and end rhymes.
The element of parallelism is not as pronounced here as it is in all
the "regulated verses" written by Wang Wei and other T'ang poets.
The regulated verse calls for exactly "parallel" couplets for its second
and third couplets in each eight-line poem.—Ed.

In this poem the moon appears as an understanding and sympathetic being sharing the poet's delight in tranquillity; and in turn, the poet's feeling is purified and elevated to the cool, calm, and peaceful joy of the moon. The language in which the poet communicates with the moon becomes almost audible to the reader, although no words are exchanged that are intelligible to the mundane ear. Poems like this anticipate the Japanese Haiku tradition.[2]

The Japanese Haiku, first developed in the thirteenth century and extensively practiced in the seventeenth century, is famed for its presentation of a natural mysticism, lofty and pure. It relates one form of life to another and registers man's

[2] Compare Wang's poem with a famous Haiku by Matsuo Bashō (1644–94):

Song of the cuckoo:	Hototogisu
in the grove of great bamboos,	o-take yabu-no
moonlight seeping through.	moru tsuki-yo

(from Harold G. Henderson, *An Introduction to Haiku*, 44)

The poems by Wang and Bashō are different in the stanza forms they use, but the worlds they create are very similar. Wang Wei's poem is a quatrain with five syllables in each line. A standard Japanese Haiku calls in all for seventeen syllables cast in definite prosodic schemes. However, several Chinese *tz'u* forms developed in the tenth and eleventh centuries appear to have anticipated the Japanese Haiku even in its prosodic structure. A sixteen-syllable *tz'u*, first used by Chang Hsiao-hsiang (active c. 1150) was adopted by many later Chinese poets. The woman poet, Wu Tsao, (c. 1800) wrote one:

> *Han*
> *Jen li hsi feng ts'ui hsiu tan*
> *Hsi yang mu*
> *Hua ying shang lan kan*

Literally translated, the poem reads:

> Cold
> Person stand west wind green sleeve thin
> Evening sun set
> Flower shadow climb railing

The sense of the poem seems to be:

> Chill—
> She stands in the western wind, her green sleeves thin.
> Evening sun sets,
> The flower's shadow ascends the balustrade.

The poem weaves the weather, the person, her costume, and the setting sun into a living and integrated whole. Movement in quietude is captured by the shadow of a flower. The whole poem fixes a

empathy with nature. Wang Wei seems to have done precisely this.

These are high-water marks of classical Chinese poetry. Some critics do not hesitate to say that they have never again been reached. This may be true if one considers subsequent developments in classical Chinese poetry which were mostly on the second plane. Trivia replaced exquisiteness; stereotype, originality. Perhaps classical Chinese poetry by the end of the nineteenth century had once again truly exhausted itself.

Whether or not it had, the change in Chinese poetry as seen in its latest works has certainly been dramatic. Here are two frequently quoted poems written in mainland China in 1958:

> In Heaven there is no Jade Emperor
> Nor is there a Dragon King in the sea.
> I am the Jade Emperor,
> I am the Dragon King.
> Hey, you Three Sacred Mountains and Five Holy Peaks,
> Make way!
> Here I come.

> We sing to the roaring river,
> It rises in thousands of waves.
> Of old, it followed along the mountain,
> Now we make it climb the hills.

> (from *The Songs of the Red Flag*, 6, 172)

These songs rank with the best of the literally millions of verses being composed today by bus drivers, lathe operators, buffalo herders, foot soldiers, and, of course, men of letters. The verses sing of the leadership of the Communist Party,

---

mood that induces the reader's meditative appreciation. Compare this poem with a Japanese Haiku by Taniguchi Buson (1715–83):
> Blossoms on the pear—
> and a woman in the moonlight
> reads a letter there.

(from Harold G. Henderson, *An Introduction to Haiku*, 105)
For further discussion on the influence of Chinese poetry on Japanese Haiku, see Asataro Miyamori, *One Thousand Haiku, Ancient and Modern* (Tokyo: Dobunsha, 1930), pp. 35, 181.—Ed.

according it the traditional reverence due one's father. They sing of the loving care that Mao Tse-tung showers on his peasant comrades in terms befitting a love duet in a folk song. Above all, they express the ecstasy of a people who for the first time have found expression for their simple but powerful sentiments.

In the crude lines of verse written by a peasant who has just finished his ten-week literacy course in the village night school, there is a cry of joy amounting sometimes to drunken frenzy. The cry may be terrifying, just as a war cry keeping time to the beat of a jungle drum is terrifying, but there is poetry in it also, as the following 1958 poem bears witness:

> One spade shaves off a thousand mountain tops,
> One load carries off two hills,
> One blast overturns a cliff of ten thousand fathoms.
>
> . . . .
>
> My two hands lift up the river,
> In a moment I hang it on top of the towering peak.
>
> (from *The Songs of the Red Flag*, 93)

The gusto parallels very well Li Po's wild fantasy written, as one of his friends said, after wine:

> One punch smashes the Yellow Crane Pavilion,
> One kick overturns the Parrot Island.

The difference between these two poems is that while Li Po's has always been recognized as an elegant fantasy of a bohemian poet, the modern poem has a savage beauty both serious and stirring. It is the difference between a traditional Chinese man of letters and a ditchdigger, between the allusion-laden classical language and the vigorous speech used by a villager in 1958, between the "higher" and the "lower" planes in the development of Chinese poetry. Mid-twentieth-century Chinese poetry is greeting a triumphal return of the folk song. In these latest verses there is no trace of the restraint, the subdued color, and the refined notes of T'ang poetry. The change is dramatic and needs to be viewed through an historical perspective.

* * * *

When the Chinese began to doubt the usefulness of their own tradition, including their literary tradition, in the second half of the nineteenth century, their skepticism was brought about by multiple forces at work in society. The literati as a group had been stubborn in their refusal to recognize a steadily widening world; they persisted in believing that China was the center of the universe. The Opium War (1839–42) rudely opened Chinese eyes to the material superiority of the Western world. The T'ai-p'ing Rebellion (1848–65) decisively illustrated the collapse of China's internal order. The subsequent unpleasant contacts with the Western powers, the "unequal treaties" signed with them and the "concessions" yielded to them, shocked the educated Chinese, discouraging some and infuriating the rest. Feverish moves were made to find a remedy. Some Chinese intellectuals advocated total Westernization, which, unfortunately, was conceived merely as a technological revolution. Others urged reform but failed to carry it beyond superficial adjustments in the administrative system.

As the situation continued to worsen, culminating in the occupation of Peking by Western troops in the aftermath of the Boxer Rebellion (1900), the social and intellectual atmosphere in China was chaotic and desperate. So many things and formulas had been tried, and China was showing no improvement. Out of desperation the educated Chinese grabbed at anything that promised salvation. Someone said the Manchu imperial government was to blame; a revolt immediately got underway to abolish the monarchy. Another suggested doing away with China's cultural tradition because it was responsible for the national crisis: almost overnight the echo of "Down with the Confucian Temples" resounded through the country. The main current of these intellectual agitations was the drive to make Chinese youths adopt an entirely new attitude toward life. The movement was spearheaded by several professors in the University of Peking who appealed to their students to accept the validity of modern science and democracy. The students were urged to change their retiring attitude to purposeful aggressiveness, and to abandon useless metaphysical abstraction for practical knowledge.

It was in such an atmosphere that the "literary revolution" started in 1917 when Hu Shih (1891–1962) offered an eight-point program to rejuvenate Chinese literature. He suggested replacing the terse, allusion-laden classical language with modern vernacular (*pai-hua*), and in 1918, the journal published by the intellectual leaders in the University of Peking actually made the changes. Many publications followed suit, and the movement spread like a brush fire in spite of persistent and rancorous opposition. Soon a number of small literary coteries sprang up to find new directions for their creative energy. Only a few of them were principally concerned with poetry, but all of them were embroiled in political polemics as they had to declare and defend their views on literature.

The views expressed covered a wide spectrum, ranging from the extreme left to the extreme right. The Society for Literary Studies founded in 1921 advocated "literature for life," stressing the inseparable relationship between literature and the real life of man. Later the position of this Society shifted its motto from "literature to describe life" to "literature to improve life." The Creation Society founded in 1920 started with a dedication of itself to the "creation of beauty," and soon changed its emphasis to the "destruction of evil." The Sun Society founded in 1928 was consistent and persistent in its promotion of a "revolutionary literature." Several opposition groups rallied under the banner of "art for art's sake," but these groups were fighting a losing battle. Foreign encroachment upon China's interests and dignity was increasing. The young people became steadily more restless. From May 4, 1919 to May 4, 1937, there were twenty-one major clashes between the police and student demonstrators protesting against certain government policies and actions. The Communist movement, beginning as an organized effort in 1921, was winning the ideological struggle as the refined notes on the Muse's harp were drowned in a socialist trumpeter's blare. "Revolutionary literature" became the order of the day in the 1930s.

The development of poetry during this period reflected fully the complexity of the war of ideas. Each of the several groups of poets that sprang up had its own position at the beginning, but gradually all converged upon social realism—treating the conflict among men only in its social context. The first of these groups pioneered the use of the vernacular in poetry.

The Pioneers

The literary pioneers were understandably preoccupied with the ugly physical reality in which they lived. The change of seasons, the pain of parting, reminiscences of the past, and the serenity of the natural universe were no longer the immediate subjects of the poet's concern. They had become too remote and irrelevant. It was the ricksha pullers laboring under a scorching sun, the tears of a child-bride married to a total stranger three times her age, the silent protest of an abused boy-apprentice, the misery of a peasant family unable to sell their homespun cloth for food that aroused sympathy in the new poet, Liu Ta-pai (1880–1932), who wrote in 1920:

> My brother's wife weaves cloth,
> My brother sells it.
> But there is no cloth
> To mend my worn pants.
>
> . . . .
>
> When he took the cloth to town
> At the city gate he was stopped.
> He had no money to pay duties
> The guards confiscated his cloth.
> Take the cloth then, but why
> Take in my brother also?

(from *Selected Contemporary Chinese Poems*, 47–50)

The newly acquired Western concept upholding the dignity of the individual human being, together with some knowledge of Western poetry, emboldened the new Chinese poets to write about love between man and woman. Wang Ching-chih (1903–   ) was, for a while, a controversial writer severely criticized by those who considered themselves guardians of social morals, but all Wang did was to write a number of poems like the following:

When I go to bed I see you on the ceiling;
When I drink tea you are in my cup;
When I read, I see no words but you in the book

(from *Compendium*, 144)

His critics perhaps did not anticipate that their attacks were to make Wang famous, popular, and even worshipped by many youthful readers. He found words for many other young people who felt the same way but did not know how to express it or did not dare.

Love for one's mother, a tradition-honored theme, remained popular but appeared in a much greater variety of metaphors than ever before. If Ping Hsin (1902–   )[3] had been born twenty years earlier, she would not have found the "paper boat" in her poem written in 1923:

Mother, if you see a tiny white paper boat in your sleep,
Do not wonder how it has entered your dream.
It was folded by your loving daughter, with tears in her eyes,
Who begs it to carry home her love and sorrow, over the
endless mountains and waters.

(from *Compendium*, 134)

The pioneer poets, of course, were also tempted to ponder on what was lastingly real and true, when they had a moment of peace and quiet. Vestiges of the ancient nature myth lingered among them. Tsung Pai-hua (1900?–   ), for instance, retained a simple faith in life, an infinite sympathy for all things animate and inanimate. He held all things in nature as dear and near to him as members of his own family, and he proclaimed:

The universe in my heart,
The reflection of mountains and rivers in a crystal-clear mirror.

(from *Compendium*, 268)

Ping Hsin, given to contemplation of birds, grass, and the sea, found the relation of infinite time to infinite space disturbing. She wrote:

[3] Regarded as the first woman poet to write in the vernacular. The history of Chinese literature records many women poets, some dating as far back as the Han Dynasty.—Ed.

The flowers and rocks beside the railroad tracks!
In this instant
You and I
Chance to meet among the infinite beings,
Also bid our last farewell among the infinite beings.
When I return,
In the midst of the myriads of our kind,
Where can I ever find you again?

(from *Compendium*, 136)

Others in this group went even further away from tradi-
tional Chinese ideas. Hu Shih (1891–1962), a philosopher
trained at Columbia University, admired John Dewey so
much that he wrote verses arguing for the validity of sci-
entific empiricism. In one of his experimental poems, he as-
serts that mind is superior to matter because "thought trav-
els faster than sound or light."

He called his verses experimental because they were ex-
periments in using modern daily speech as his poetic me-
dium. He was not always successful, and his fellow pioneers
at times fared even worse. In the beginning, the search for a
new poetic language resulted merely in a juxtaposition of old
linguistic conventions with elements taken from modern daily
spontaneous speech. As Hu Shih himself admitted, the lan-
guage used in his modern poems moved as awkwardly as the
suddenly unbound feet of an old-fashioned Chinese woman.
With the exception of Ping Hsin, almost all these early writers
were criticized for the awkwardness of their language. A
serious concerted effort to establish a suitable modern poetic
form and to analyze its texture had to await the appearance
of another group of poets known as the Crescent group.

The Crescent Group

In 1923 a group of young writers gathered around Hsü
Chih-mo (1895–1931) and formed the Crescent group. The
name may have been chosen because the members admired
the Indian poet and mystic, Tagore, whose *Crescent Moon*
and *Stray Birds* had already found quite a following in China.[4]

[4] Some of these literary groups chose their names quite without any
reason. One (mainly interested in prose) actually got its name after

Ping Hsin, though she admitted to having been inspired most strongly by Tagore, was not considered one of his group. The Crescent writers declared that the mind and spirit of the Chinese people must be freed, and that the liberation could come only when its expression had been found in the arts and in poetry. These writers rightly recognized the rush of ideas and creative urge after the dam of tradition had been broken, and they regarded it as their duty to create new forms and new rhythms that would be proper vessels for new ideas.

Wen I-to (1899–1946), a highly respected literary critic and a leader of the Crescent school, championed the use of measured prosodic units in the vernacular language to achieve a musical effect similar to, and perhaps better than, the best of the classical works. His extensive training in painting and other graphic arts led him to perceive and defend the interrelationship between poetry and the other arts, like Gautier, whom he admired. He also saw an intrinsic indentification of essence with form. A truly beautiful woman could not but have a golden heart, he almost said, and artistic immortality could be achieved only when the carving was as flawless as the gem itself.

Putting his own theories into practice, Wen I-to pointed in his work to a new direction for poetry, and the effect was electrifying. The seriousness of the Crescent poets toward their work, toward every word and every line they wrote, has left a lasting influence on modern Chinese poetry.

The Crescent poets demonstrated that balanced phrases and cultivated metaphors can produce an unforgettable effect with any theme the poet selects. Consider, for example, these exquisite lines that Wen wrote in memory of his daughter who died in early childhood:

> Forget her, as a forgotten flower,
> As a dream in the wind of spring,
> As in a dream, a bell's ring.
> Forget her, as a forgotten flower.

. . . .

one of its founders opened a book at random and pointed his finger at a word without looking. Hence its untranslatable name, Yü Ssu.—Ed.

> Perhaps you hear earthworms turning dirt,
> Perhaps you hear grassroots sucking water.
> Perhaps prettier than man's cursing voice
> Is this kind of music you now hear.
>
>   (from Wen, *Complete Works, Ting,* 12–15)

He also could weave a vision, an ideal man must stretch himself to reach, into a verse with a breathlessly forward-rushing cadence:

Never have I sought the red of fire, nor the black
Of the Peach Blossom Pool at midnight, nor the plaintive
        tune of a lute,
Nor the fragrance of roses. Never have I loved the proud
        dignity of a leopard.
The tenderness I longed for, no white dove could offer.
I never wanted these things, but their crystallization,
A miracle ten thousand times more miraculous than them all!

            (from Wen, *Complete Works, Hsin,* 650)

In working out their theory, the Crescent poets were guided by an attitude toward love, life, and beauty which had much in common with that of the Western European Romantic writers. Wen I-to never ceased to praise Keats, and Hsü Chih-mo, Wen's close friend, always respected Byron as "that beautiful devil, that glorious rebel." To them not only must beauty be true but the true must be made beautiful by the poet, and the meaning of life lies in the relentless, intense effort to create beauty, to turn one instant into eternity:

. . . . Have no fear for me, as
No gusty wind can extinguish the lamp of the soul. To have
        this
Body turned into ashes is nothing because that is precisely
My one moment of eternity. . . .

            (from Wen, *Complete Works, Hsin,* 651)

Dedication of life to this ideal did not, however, reduce this group of poets to working exclusively in *émaux* and *camées*, to carving concentric ivory spheres according to the design of the poet's inner vision with no reference to the outside world of reality. Their ideals, particularly Wen I-to's, were subject to modification along with the changing intellectual climate. A naive but noble sympathy with one's fellow men, which provided the earlier experimental poets with much of their emotional identity, also took hold of the Crescent poets.

Though British-educated Hsü Chih-mo was as familiar with Wordsworth as he was with the Bloomsbury group (under whose influence he fell during his Cambridge days), he wrote about a beggar who had nothing in common with his Cumberland predecessor. Hsü's beggar groans:

> I am but a pile of black shadows, trembling,
> Lying like a worm on the frontage road of humanity;
> I wish only a bit of the warmth of sympathy
> To shelter what's left of me, after repeated carving.

> (from *Selected Works of Hsü Chih-mo*, 73–74)

Wen I-to shed tears for his compatriots doing laundry work in America as well as for the youthful recruit who, too sick to march under the guard's whip toward the front, was left to die on the roadside. How could beauty reside in such ugly reality, Wen asked himself, and his own answer was:

> Here is a ditch of hopelessly dead water—
> a region where beauty can never reside.
> Might as well let the devil cultivate it—
> and see what sort of world it can provide.

> (from *Dead Water*, 39–41)

Because the China he saw was not what his poetic imagination had led him to visualize,

> I've come, I shout, bursting out in tears of woe,
> "This is not my China—Oh, no. No!"
> I've come because I heard your summoning cry.
> Riding on the wind of time, raising a torch high,
> I came. I knew not this to be unwarranted ecstasy.
> A nightmare I found. You? How could this be!

> (from *Dead Water*, 58–59)

Without in any way directly relating itself to the leftist movement, which quite rapidly gathered momentum toward the end of the 1920s in Chinese literary circles, the Crescent group at that time shifted its attention to the urgent social ills and the national crisis. Wen I-to reidentified his ideal beauty with the essence of Chinese culture which was threatened, and he dedicated anew his life, effort, and poetry to restoring the validity of Chinese culture. The romantic longing for the perpetually beautiful remained the bedrock of the Crescent poets' basic commitment to poetry, but harsh reality forced them to channel their creative energy toward the building of a state myth to take the place of the classical nature myth. In this new myth, as in the old one in earlier eras, the poet found his world of beauty.

Not all the Crescent poets followed Wen I-to's path in their intellectual development, but the same degree of fervent dedication to life's purpose continued to ring loud and true in most of their works written during the 1930s, which are judged to be superior to their earlier verses. There is a strong element of stoicism in their determination to face reality and to offer their lives, but their stoicism is accompanied by a sense of fatigue. The vicissitudes of life and the chaos in society had continued too long; the burden of the poet's commitment weighed steadily heavier as the road appeared longer each day. As Sun Yü-t'ang (1905?–   ) put it:

Carrying two baskets of iron, one sack of sand, I trudge on
    the dust of the ancient road,
Cross a valley, and circle a mountain, with stars shining
    above.
The depth of the night, the silence of old pines, where
    dewdrops mourn the fallen petals;
The long, long road—when will it lead me home?

                (from *The Precious Horse*, 69–70)

The old horse, be it ever so strong and sturdy, cannot avoid feeling a bit weary of life. Along with the weariness come resignation and the secret hope for deliverance. Is this the return of the old Buddhist influence?

The Metaphysical Group

Concentration on the search for a rational explanation of life was the purpose of the Metaphysical Group of poets, who, in the main, subjugated their hearts and turned to their minds. They treated emotions coolly and gazed at life calmly. They scrutinized the world around them, including themselves; even personal love was to them a phenomenon to be analyzed and metaphorized with an equal degree of detachment. They tried to define reality and the relation of man to the universe. What Feng Chih (1905–   ) saw in the acquiring and losing of a form revealed to him a bit of the secret about substance and existence:

From a pool of freely flowing, formless water,
The water carrier brings back a bottleful, ellipsoid in shape,
Thus this much water has acquired a definite form.
Look, the wind vane fluttering in the autumn breeze

Takes hold of certain things that cannot be held.

(from *The Sonnets*, 55)

Pien Chih-lin (1910–   ) read on a blade of grass the pattern of life and death and the inability of man to comprehend it or to do anything about it:

A patch of dying sun at five o'clock,
Half a ring of lamplight at six.
Just think, there are people who spend all their days
Dreaming a little and watching the wall a little,
While the grass on the wall grows tall and then yellow.

(from *The Han Garden*, 176)

In the same blade of grass Feng Chih saw the grandeur of humility; he saw what was most lasting in the impermanent:

Often as I ponder on the life of man,
I feel compelled to pray to you,
You, a cluster of pale-white weeds,
Never failed to deserve a name:
And yet you elude all possible names
To lead a life, insignificant and humble.

(from *The Sonnets*, 9)

In an infinite variety of images, these poets stated their metaphysical belief. The metaphors are forever poetic and challenging, but the ideas, as T. S. Eliot once commented, perhaps cannot exceed a limited number. We can quite readily detect the ingredients in their ideas—the basic components of their conceptual world—as consisting of certain assumptions about the existence of the soul, the dichotomy of form and matter, ultimate reality and primary cause. These are mainly Western in their origin. In addition, from the indigenous ideas of China these poets took the Taoist assumption of a universal essence of which the essence of man is but a part, and the Taoist treatment of nature, which, being the most impressive manifestation of the universal essence, comes closest to the universal essence itself. In their poetry, the Buddhist challenge to the phenomenal world was also continually recognized and supplied inspiration for poems about the futility and illusiveness of life.

The Symbolists

The reliance on metaphor to express a metaphysical idea, as exemplified by Feng Chih and Pien Chih-lin, gave support to Li Chin-fa and his friends, who have come to be recognized as the symbolists in modern Chinese poetry. Li Chin-fa (1900?–   ) has acknowledged his debt to Verlaine and Mallarmé, but in his effort to deal with life only through symbols and images, he appears to have gone even farther than his French mentors. He seems to have assumed that outside of the world of impressions, which he captures with his symbols, no meaning exists. He presents a series of pictures, without so much as a string to thread them together for the benefit of the reader. If the reader fails to integrate the fragmentary pictures—some brilliant, some dull, some utterly incomprehensible—into a meaningful whole, Li declines responsibility by saying that life and reality are themselves fragmentary. There is an "Expression of Time" in his anthology:

> Wind and rain on the ocean,
> Dead deer in my heart.
> Look, autumn dream has left on spread wings,
> Only this dejected soul remains.

> I pursue abandoned desires,
> I mourn discolored lips,
> Ah, on the shadowy grassland,
> The moon gathers our silence.
>
> (from *Compendium*, 211)

Sometimes Li and his friends appear to be demanding a supersensitivity of their readers; at other times their poems require a high degree of psychic insight in order to penetrate their meaning. The difficulty of these symbolist works does not stem principally from their unusual associations of ideas with concrete images and sensory reality, or from their frequent omission of certain links in the chain of association. It is the studied departure from linguistic conventions, both new and old, both written and spoken, which only partly ruined the works of earlier experimenters, that at times renders Li's poems hopelessly esoteric. The music of the language, its spontaneous rhythm and melody, seems to have been purposely sacrificed in order to stop the reader—and to force him to reread the same line several times over for its intended effect, which is often very different from the first impression.

Not all Li Chin-fa's fellow symbolists sacrificed the familiar melody and rhythm in the language that spoke effortlessly to the Chinese ears of the 1920s. Tai Wang-shu (1905–1950?), a follower of Valéry, has chosen to let a smooth cadence carry his images and thus make them come closer to the reader. The symbolic suggestions in Tai's verses are sketched in more definite lines, with a thinner veil shrouding them, and because of this, his lines, like the following, are better remembered:

> Light rain fell on your unkempt hair:
> So many little pearls sprinkled in black kelp,
> So many dead fish tossed about on the waves,
> With a mysterious, sad gleam.
>
> (from "A Sonnet," *Compendium*, 219)

Tai seems to prefer the plainer symbols that can easily be summoned to the mind of any reader while taking a walk in the rain or along a creek on a chilly autumn day. Even when he deals with the sounds and forms fancied at midnight, or a

lovelorn sigh, he maintains lively pace. This virtue has en-
abled him to share Li Chin-fa's fame but spared him the
criticism. Color is also Tai's concern, and he uses it with great
care so that it harmonizes with the entire mood of the poem.
This is another feature that sets him apart from Li Chin-fa.
Tai later turned away from symbolism to write short lyrics on
single observations snatched from an undramatic and un-
eventful existence. These have turned out to be possibly his
best poems.

A third member of this group, Mu Mu-t'ien (1900–   )
went from Manchuria to France. He has admitted his indebt-
edness to Laforgue and, like him, strives for uncommon
musical effects in his lines. It is his belief that graphic devices
can also be used to suggest the cadence of sound in Chinese
poetry, as in "The Pale Temple Bell" (1926):

Pale   bell sounds   decadent   and blurred
Diffuse   in the exquisite   but desolate   misty   vale
—Dried weeds   thousands   of layers—
Listen   the perpetually   fantastic   ancient bell sounds
Listen   the thousands   of strokes.

(from Compendium, 236)

A general feeling of dejection prevails among the symbolists
of this period. They seem to prefer the blurred, the decaying,
and the indescribable. Their lines are shot through with mel-
ancholy, however stoically viewed. Even Wang Tu-ch'ing
(1898–1940), whose works have been admired for their By-
ronic pageantry, is too often drenched in despair. When he
walked out of a Parisian café, his poetic sensitivity was im-
mediately turned away from the animated conversation he
had just had with Anatole France on social revolution, and
all he could think of was:

> Silently
> Walking alone,
> Feeling inside
> The sorrow of a homeless man
> About to lose his country . . .
> Ah, the quiet and chilly streets
> At dusk, under rain.

(from Selected Works of Wang Tu-ch'ing, 68–69)

There was enough in the reality surrounding these symbolists to complete a *fin de siècle* atmosphere for them, and they turned to the dying and decadent for that flicker of beauty that they paint in intense blue like the will-o'-the-wisp caught in a graveyard. Especially when they returned to China, the ugly chaos they found there left them in despair and blinded them to the existence of any truly hearty laughter in this world. Small wonder that Li Chin-fa moaned that life appears to him withered and faded. He sees it only as a smile on the "lips of Death." These Chinese symbolists worship Mallarmé, and they have imitated Valéry with considerable success. What they have failed to do is to present an ecstasy about life after shedding tears over the suicide of Narcissus.

The Independent Poets

Other modern Chinese poets have emerged who share many experiences in common with their fellow writers already described, but who have created their own worlds that do not quite fit any of the identified schools of poetry. Some critics refer to these poets as the Independent Group.

Many of the poems of Tsang K'o-chia (1910?–   ) written in the 1930s capture a fleeting moment in life, like a flash of lightning in its striking intensity. His images are sharp, and the structure of his verse is meticulously concise. In such stanzas as the following he shows his peculiar success in integrating a character with his background, with the man always in the center:

A sad wail trails him from door to door,
But tonight the wail brings out nobody from the houses.
Behind the gates everyone tightly locks up a warm autumn,
Every face, like a spring blossom, blooms toward the bright
      moon.
The western wind follows him, the moon follows him,
To the old temple as he mounts the steps.
He wants no chilly light to hang on his tatters, and with a
      shrug
Disappears in the shadowy depths of a shrine.

                 (Midautumn Festival, 1934, *The Canal*, 3)

The comfort, and even gaiety, of the people celebrating the traditional Moon Festival behind their securely locked gates are here made insignificant in contrast to a disappointed beggar's nocturnal rounds ending at a desolate temple. The beggar's life assumes all the importance in the world of the poet at the moment, and nature is intimately meshed with it. Tsang K'o-chia can never view life in abstraction. His lines cling to the human being with such force that at times, as he himself has made clear, it becomes actually painful to him. Perhaps this is a clue to the secret of his later shift to feverish songs about the tears and joys of people—particularly those in lower walks of life.

In sharp contrast to the intensity of Tsang K'o-chia stands the poetry of Ho Ch'i-fang (1911–   ). Ho sketches his images gently in monochrome. Even when he occasionally uses colors, they are only subdued pastels, as in his "Prophecy":

It has finally arrived—that heart-throbbing day.
The sound of your footsteps, like the sighs of the night,
I can hear clearly. They are not leaves whispering in the wind,
Nor the fawns darting across a lichened path.
Tell me, tell me in your singing voice of a silver bell,
Are you not the youthful god I heard about in a prophecy?

(from *The Han Garden*, 4)

At times Ho perpetuates the best tradition of classical "occasional" poems. The year's end, a time for reminiscing about a far-off friend, inspires him to write:

> When a dried pine cone falls,
> And the wings of low-flying birds rustle by,
> You pause in your solitary stroll in the woods;
>
> . . . .
>
> When winter's white frost seals your window,
> Hiding yourself in a long spell of illness
> Do you still think of your house in the north?

(from *The Han Garden*, 26–27)

But there is a lingering flavor about these lines that goes beyond the merely pleasant rhythm and sounds of the classical occasional poems. It is the ultrasensitivity of the poet

that enables Ho, or his close associate, Li Kuang-t'ien
(1907–   ), to grasp the poetic significance of a "Nocturnal
Bird," a gaping "Window in Autumn," a "Trumpet," a "Visit"
to a friend, who, it so happened, was away (which reminds us
of Wang Wei's famous lines), and a walk "Across a Bridge."
Ho and Li see the gravity and importance in what is seem-
ingly trivial. Their poems are like Chinese green tea which
tastes so plain and yet lasts and lasts on the discerning palate.
They are the writers able to fix permanently the essential
quality of a seemingly insignificant detail. At the same time,
they do not yield to the temptation of stressing the meta-
physical meaning of the deceptively trivial. They may hint at
certain abstractions, but they never state them. No wonder
they could and did maintain an enduring association with
such a "metaphysical" writer as Pien Chih-lin.

Or we may turn to the lines of Cheng Min (1924?–   ),
a relatively young writer whose commentary on life shows a
remarkable degree of sophistication. She does not portray the
intense moments of life as Tsang K'o-chia does, nor does she
record the ordinary moments of reality as Ho Ch'i-fang and
Li Kuang-t'ien do. Her eyes scan the horizon of life, the urban
and the rustic, and she reflects on it—as, for example, in
"Quiet Night":

Those pursuing reality behind their counters
Now count their day's gain from reality, and then go to bed
With their unstable joy and unshakable regret, letting
Reality turn into void, into doubt, in their tired bodies.

Under the roof, the self-satisfied lovers
Secretly feel an emptiness in the midst of self-conscious
    happiness.
They embrace each other tightly, hoping to crush the space
    between them,
"We are not discontented, God, but a bit lost. . . ."

(from *The Poems*, 178)

When trying times with their shaken traditions and changing
values forced themselves upon her, as they had upon all her
compatriots since the beginning of the twentieth century,

how could she fail to echo the "Heart Beat" of Wen I-to? As she does here:

Ah, China, your destiny, with so many obstructing forces,
     every bit of your history a hindrance!
It appears as hundreds and thousands of nightmares to
     haunt us ceaselessly,
Hiding in every corner, even in our very blood—that
     dreadful enemy!
Every time after it feigned death to get from us a
     bloodbath,
It looms up again at a distance, just as we are about to lay
     on it a wreath.

(from *The Poems*, 160)

And, in a weary but desperate plea,

Time and time-nurtured civilization, and the self-respect that
     grew from civilization,
All vanished. This drooping eyelid is a quieted battlefield,
Ah, mankind, if one day you exchange your rifle for a magic
     flute,
Your surrender will be your most glorious victory.

(from *The Poems*, 181)

Wartime Trends

Cheng Min, did not see a battlefield, but in the early 1940s when she wrote, many writers in China did. Even those who never actually spent an hour in a field trench were living constantly under the shadow of war. Enemy bombers were overhead almost daily; calm reflection was impossible and serenity non-existent. The metaphysicists, no longer able to brood in silence, added their voices to the anguished cries of those who had been painting life in its objective reality or focused on its most pressing, sensuous immediacy. In Tsang K'o-chia's writings the plaintive wail of a beggar on the eve of the Midautumn Festival gives way to the angry protest of an injured people, and the quietly sympathetic Western wind and moon are now equally enraged and bitter after an air raid:

In the shadow of death
Some men stirred.
Some quickened their steps toward the city,
Training their eyes on the smoke columns
Guessing, in their sinking hearts,
The location of their houses.

· · · ·

The volcanic mouth in the roof roared,
Human flesh hung on tree tops.

· · · ·

A procession of bodies carried off to the countryside,
Leaving a train of bloody tears behind.

(from *The Mud Puddle*, 36–39)

With civilization lying in ruin, all that is left to symbolize man's progress in the twentieth century is the means of wanton destruction under which moonlight turns ghastly pale and spring blossoms look pitifully futile. No poet can retain a heart to sing of either. Any abstraction seems too irrelevant. Man turns to the stubbornly robust, and even primitive, for hope, and red-tasseled spears bathed in blood become the most appealing poetic image. The lusty cry of the peasants fighting as guerrillas, inspired by the savage instinct for survival, becomes the high note in the poet's music. The Muse has dropped her lyre for a bugle, and the drumbeat has drowned out the soft melody of a jade flute. Now we hear the two-beat, simple, tense rhythm ringing loud from a war dance—like that recorded by T'ien Chien (1914–   ):

Look!
Their
Vengeful
Force,
Their
Vengeful
Blood,
Their
Vengeful
Songs.

(from Wen, *Complete Works, Ting*, 236–37)

This is indeed a return to the primitive, but the poets who
turned to folk songs for inspiration could easily recall the folk
origin and simple four-beat rhythm in *The Book of Poetry*,
the earliest extant poetic anthology in Chinese, accepted by
all as the fountainhead of Chinese poetry. The circle closes
once again. The thesis that Chinese poetry periodically re-
turns to the common people to rejuvenate itself, expounded
by Wen I-to and by Chen Shih-hsiang (now teaching at the
University of California), finds support in another historical
process.

Narrative poems, similar to the folk ballads which sing of
the lives and loves of legendary characters and historical fig-
ures, have also experienced a popular revival. The stories and
heroes are born of the war; the mountains and marshes where
the bitterest struggles against the enemy took place provide
the most celebrated geographical settings: the T'ai-hang
Mountain Range, the Hung-tse Lake region, the dense woods
of Manchuria, and the loess dunes of Shansi and Shensi. K'o
Chung-p'ing (1910?–   ) writes of the Border Zone Militia
in a 750-line poem, and of the Peiping-Hankow Railway
workers who organized themselves to resist the approaching
Japanese troops in 1938. The second poem, with only its
first section completed, already runs over 2000 lines. Ai
Ch'ing (1910–   ) devotes many thousands of lines to the
soldiers fallen in action, of whom one "died a second time":

> It all happened so suddenly
> Allowing no time even for a fleeting thought
> Or for a flashing question of surprise and wonder.
> As a burning bullet
> For the second time—also, ah, for the last time—
> Pierced his body.
> His life
> Having been through this world (so they say),
> Fell
> Like a tree at the stroke of a gigantic ax.
>
>   (from *Selected Poems of Ai Ch'ing*, 238)

These poets sing of the peasant turned guerrilla, the coun-
try girl who volunteered to nurse a wounded soldier, the
child risking his life to deliver a war message, the bugler, the

solitary sentry, the ammunition carrier, the living who clenched their teeth in anger, and the dead with an undying curse on their lips. They cannot avoid using the weapons of satire and sarcasm and even boisterous accusation against what they believe to be out of step: the continuing civil strife among the war lords, the Kuomintang, and the Communists, the wartime profiteering, the heartless indifference—in a word, against everything that looked treasonous in view of the dying soldiers and against the backdrop of a war-ravaged country. Tsang K'o-chia (1910?–   ) writes of his disappointment with the delegates who congregated in Chungking in the fall of 1946 to argue about a provisional constitution at such a time. He also tells how the police in the rear area used the pretext of security to check on the people's associations and reading, and how earlier some of the best troops were ordered to march toward the Communist base in the north instead of against the Japanese front. His lines on these subjects are not polished verse; they are blunt and direct; occasionally they scream, but they never cease to speak for a disturbed generation.

Throughout the war the military, political, and literary fronts were parallel. While the battle was joined between the Chinese and the Japanese, the ideological and power struggle between the Communists and the Nationalists never ceased. In Yenan, the Communist headquarters in the 1940s, leftist writers gathered together to re-examine the direction in which literature was developing. They agreed that waging war against a foreign enemy was the writers' duty, but that beyond this the writers should follow the road to social realism by learning from workers, peasants, and soldiers. Though this notion had first been brought up by the Creation Society's Kuo Mo-jo in the early 1920s, it was in 1942 that the dictum was officially pronounced in Yenan by none other than the Communist leader, Mao Tse-tung (1893–   ), who is himself a skilled writer of classical-style verse. "Social realism" has since become the official Communist policy that has guided the new regime in directing the nation's literary activities, including the few purges in literary circles. Poetry, however, could not be legislated into being, and it was left for the poets to find themselves in a rapidly changing society.

After 1949

Where could these poets go after 1949, after the end of the open war with the Japanese and the Kuomintang? Soldiers and guerrillas were no longer dying on the front line, but the battle was by no means over. Order had to be born out of chaos, and a purpose in life restored to the populace. The sense of urgency had not departed, but a breathless demand to rebuild had been added to the urgency of survival. Activities became ever more feverish in postwar China. The poet had no chance to return to tranquil contemplation. Organized political forces dictated against any such return. The general intellectual atmosphere veered away from all traditional values except one: life, the physical existence of man. To insure this existence in the world of today, man must fight for his group. The poet who has been nurtured in this atmosphere tends to identify his ideal with the interests of his fellow men. He may occasionally allow his imagination to roam on a wider intellectual horizon, but these are rare occasions nowadays. The pressure of the pace of life is ruthless. Probing the deeper meaning of life, of truth and beauty in any form of abstraction, will continue to seem irrelevant in China for a long time to come. Meanwhile, who is the hero that deserves the poet's praise? The answer is, of course, he who has changed his sword for a plow or for a pair of wrenches. Listen to the songs of the laborers in a steel plant, at a growing dam, or on a newly communized farm. Only yesterday, many of these same hands were digging the trenches on the battlefield. It is of them that the poets are singing now.

Thus Ho Ch'i-fang who twenty years ago recorded his feelings upon visiting a friend who was not at home, now hears the majestic singing of dike-workers that overpowers the rumble of the river itself:

> I seem to be standing in the river with you,
> Completely forgetting cold and danger,
> I hook my arm with yours
> Bracing the dike with our bodies.
>
> (from *Selected Poems of 1953.9–1955.12*, 309)

And the metaphysical turn of Rilke yields to the romantic ecstasy of Goethe in that diligent student of German poetry, Feng Chih, when he sings of the Anshan Steel complex near Mukden:

I sing of Anshan steel.
Because of many wishes, I sing of Anshan steel.
When the train reaches the riverside, we wish for a bridge;
When the survey team arrives in wild mountains, it seeks
     deeper ore deposits;
For all these wishes, I sing of Anshan steel.

> (from *Selected Poems of 1953.9–1955.12*, 93)

The younger poet, T'ien Chien, who won acclaim by giving voice to the drumbeat of war a few years before, sees another kind of heroic mobilization aimed at an equally great challenge:

"MOBILIZATION"

Towering mountains are a brass gong.
Strike it up now! Listen, our motherland is cheering.
At the ringing of the picks in the air
Life advances a step forward.

> (from *Selected Short Poems of T'ien Chien*, 132)

A new vision looms up in his eyes when men start planting trees on a stretch of dessicated land:

> We plant this tree
> To crown the desert with a jewel.

> Jewels may return to dust, but
> The green tree will remain forever jade green.

> (from *Selected Short Poems of T'ien Chien*, 137)

Just as everything inconsistent with the war effort a decade before was denounced and satirized, the poems written during the early 1950s mirrored the waves of political and social tides that swept away the remnants of the old order—bad as well as good. The Korean War episode revived, for a spell, the wartime themes, but the main trend carried on, beating the drums of reconstruction. The dynamite blasts of the road builders silenced individual voices.

A strange and perhaps terrifying phenomenon is sweeping the literary front in China today. We have been following the development of modern Chinese poetry through the works of a few well-established poets. The post-1949 era has witnessed the rise of a large number of young poets with very diverse backgrounds. The new leaders in China seem determined to see every front "blossom" at the same rate in the same direction; the rate of dam construction and production increase must be made proportionate to the increase in literary output. Consequently, with every drive to increase the production of steel there has been a comparable effort in the publication of poems. Teams of cultural workers, including inexperienced college students as well as seasoned writers, have been visiting the countryside, the factories, the farms, and the frontier areas. Like their counterparts in technological fields, these cultural workers encourage the farmers and laborers to learn reading and writing, and urge them to tell their stories and compose or recite their folk rhymes. The rhymes are then recorded, and, after various degrees of polishing, are published. Literally thousands upon thousands of these verses have appeared in recent years. And along with these verses a new crop of poets has emerged whose names have become familiar in publishing circles and to readers.

The future of Chinese poetry rests in the hands of these younger writers. They are applying themselves to the task with a set of convictions that are extensions of a historical continuum in Chinese literature. The political pressure driving them to go "to the soldiers, farmers, and workers" is by no means the only force guiding their creative energy. As Kuo Mo-jo said with vigor in the early 1920s, many writers of twentieth-century China are genuinely convinced that only by going back to the common people can fresh blood be injected into literature. In a variety of ways the same theme has been re-emphasized by many literary leaders since Kuo Mo-jo. Tsang K'o-chia, for instance, wrote in 1947, in his preface to *The Zero Degree of Life*, "After fifteen years of polishing my verses, now I realize the beauty of simplicity. Breaking away from my own little circle, I happily face the boundless field of poetry." And he rededicated himself to "expressing the truest hatred and love in the simplest terms —expressing them deeply, forcefully, and beautifully." Clearly there has been a reorientation in the aesthetic sense of the modern Chinese poet, and it is futile to try to surmise how much of it has been a conscious effort, or how much of the present result has been sincerely accepted. Without dismissing the political pressure under which Chinese poets are working today, the re-orientation must be faced by any student of modern Chinese poetry as a fact.

The poet who goes to the villages to record folk rhymes remembers another age-old tradition in Chinese poetry. Many emperors in Chinese history maintained an official bureau to collect folk songs as a gauge of public reaction to the administration. Many of the folk songs thus collected have lived on in China's poetic heritage. Some of the songs and verses recently collected from the frontier areas, such as the long story poem *Ashima* of Yunnan origin, have a disarming charm. Even imitations of these folk verses have achieved a good measure of the frontier atmosphere and flavor. Wen Chieh's "Love Song of Turfan," is representative:

> Young lad under the apple tree,
> Please don't, don't sing any more;
> A girl is coming along the creek,
> Her young heart throbs in her bosom.
> Why is her heart throbbing so,
> So violently, even skipping beats? . . .

(from *Selected Contemporary Chinese Poems*, 202)

The effort to preserve genuine local speech and the question of what is the appropriate amount of literary polishing are in conflict—a conflict that has yet to be solved. Until it is, the reader of the latest poems from mainland China may find them disconcertingly crude. Can this be avoided? One wonders. The process of developing an effective new language for Chinese poetry, which started at the beginning of the century, is still continuing, and its destination is still very uncertain. What appears to be quite certain is the momentum which is at present sustained by the overwhelming enthusiasm of a storyteller or a folk singer who has just learned to write a handful of words. There is no doubt about the fertile imagination of the Chinese, or about the richness and expressiveness of their spoken language. The unleashing of this rich store of creative energy has just begun. The controlled, written vocabulary that illiterate country people in mainland China are being taught to read and write has been sufficient to generate an ecstasy among the laborers and farmers—now that they too can write poetry! They have been initiated into a new world from which they will never want to retreat. This is the ecstasy we hear in:

> Hey, you Three Sacred Mountains and Five Holy Peaks,
> Make Way!
> Here I come.

Or in the voice of a laborer greeting the first seamless steel pipe:

> The old foreman rubbed his eyes,
> With his calloused hands
> He touched the pipe again and again,
> A drop of hot tear fell on it.

Or even in the panegyrics in honor of Mao Tse-tung, to which most readers outside mainland China (and inside mainland China as well, some say) react with nausea. In these poems Mao is compared to the sun, the east, hope, salvation, and light. The exaltation of his name is comparable to the traditional clichés reserved for the emperor, except that the language is colloquial.

* * * *

Certain dominant trends in modern Chinese poetry are discernible as one looks back at the path trod by the writers included in this anthology. The experience has been an unrelenting search—a search for man's emotional identity, for a rational explanation of life, and for a new and more effective medium of expression. The search will continue. The poet is, first of all, a man. His sensitivity being superior to that of his fellow men, he is always the most forlorn when an accepted meaning of life is challenged. When events demand a redefinition of man's ideal, the poet is the first to set out in quest of it. The modern Chinese poet inherited certain ideals from his own cultural tradition, of which the most powerful is a combination of Confucian utopianism and the Mahayanist sense of self-sacrifice. He has held the belief that the true value of man lies in his effort to bring order and peace to the entire universe, and he has been impressed by Buddha's selflessness and compassion that will not let him rest until every creature is saved. These ideals permeate the Chinese mind, and the modern Chinese does not have to be a diligent student of Confucian classics or Mahayanist sutras to become imbued with them.

The nineteenth century unloosed the floodgate of Western ideas on China. Various combinations of Chinese and Western ideas have produced many unexpected fruits. The most vital fusion, however, seems to be of the traditional Chinese ideals and the Byronic variety of romanticism. The Byronic romanticist strives to live intensely, not to pluck the ripe plum while one may, but to get "something done" before the sands run out. The national pathos of twentieth-century China welcomes this variety of romanticism. So much needs to be done, and there is so little time. This may explain the otherwise strange shifts of position among modern Chinese thinkers and poets. The "romantic" Chinese poets of the 1920s followed Byron and Goethe; they searched for pure Beauty as an abstract ideal, and in this search they found meaning for their lives. Their attitude was no different from that of a devout Buddhist who sees beauty only in a transcendental calm and who dedicates his life to its pursuit. The increasing harshness of physical reality during the 1930s and 1940s drove the sensitive poet to reidentify his ideal, and he reverted, at least partly, to the traditional values of China. He now finds the meaning of his life only in giving life to his fellow men, and the symbol of state as the identity of his compatriots' collective life takes hold of his imagination. One cannot fail to detect this awesome note when Wen I-to cried out in 1928, "This is our China" and described her as "You, the untamable beauty!" Or when, in 1947, Cheng Min stated, with pain, "Ah, China. . . . You are bearing the birth pang for the sake of a more thorough rebirth." Or when a printing plant worker, in 1954, exclaimed upon lifting up a new map from his press:

This land, over 950,000 square kilometers in its length and
        breadth,
Every bit of it draws and holds my gaze, like a magnet
Pulling my heart to soar over it.

              (from *Selected Poems of 1953.9–1955.12*, 53)

Behind these lines a state myth has taken shape, and in these voices there is a note that has come very close to religion.

HU SHIH (1891–1962)

On February 24, 1962, the man who did the most to stir things up in twentieth-century Chinese literature collapsed and died at a podium in Formosa where he had just given a speech. Death came to him in a manner befitting his career as teacher, author, and thinker, whose contributions dot the entire course of the development of Chinese vernacular literature.

Educated at Cornell and Columbia, Hu Shih introduced Russell and Dewey to the Chinese and championed scientic empiricism; re-examined classical Chinese literature and encouraged objective historical research. He held a series of exalted posts in and outside the government, which was perhaps wrong for him; for the busy life of a scholar-statesman kept him from finishing his *History of Chinese Philosophy* (only Volume I was completed) and his *History of Modern Chinese Literature*. His theory about the Chinese Renaissance remained the same as it was when he first expounded it in the early 1930s, and his study of Chinese Buddhism, brilliant though it was, was truncated.

Leftist critics have been particularly castigating in their comments on Hu's record. They say that he never quite understood the nature of the "literary revolution" he is supposed to have started, and that he withdrew from the intellectual battlefield shortly after his return to China in 1917.

But whatever his critics may say about his lack of thoroughness and originality, he remains the first to have started a serious drive toward elevating the use of vernacular to a truly literary level.

The vernacular had found its way into some Chinese poems prior to Hu Shih, but it remained for Hu to articulate a conscious effort to use the daily speech in writing poetry. This resulted in his *Experiments* (first edition, 1920). Clearly these are not inspiring poems, but as Hu himself explained, they do indicate something about the possibilities of turning the vernacular into good poetry. "Dream and Poetry," included here, is one of Hu's declarations that has produced infinite arguments and criticism. Chu Hsiang in his *Chung shu chi* calls this poem nonsense and concludes that the entire volume of *Experiments* is insipid in content and puerile in technique.

DREAM AND POETRY

It's all ordinary experience,
All ordinary images.
By chance they emerge in a dream,
Turning out infinite new patterns.

It's all ordinary feelings,
All ordinary words.
By chance they encounter a poet,
Turning out infinite new verses.

Once intoxicated, one learns the strength of wine,
Once smitten, one learns the power of love:
You cannot write my poems
Just as I cannot dream your dreams.

September 10, 1921
Experiments, 91–92

Author's note: This is my "Poetic empiricism." To state it simply: even a dream has to have its basis in experience, not to speak of poetry-writing. Nowadays a great trouble with many people is that they like to write poetry without a basis in experience. One poet of Peking said:

"Pang tzu noodles
Line by line
Stuffed into his mouth."

Another great name in poetry from Shanghai said:

> "Yesterday the silkworms had their first molt
> Today they have their second molt
> Tomorrow, their third molt.
> The worms sleep but not men."

Eating noodles and raising silkworms are indeed the easiest things in the world. But those without such experiences are not qualified to talk about these things; therefore, how much truer is it about writing poetry.

[Hu Shih here refers to the fact that *Pang tzu* noodles are never eaten string by string, and silkworms never molt that fast.—Ed.]

OLD DREAM

> From the green foliage below the hill
> Emerges a corner of flying roof.
> It awakens an old dream, and causes
> Tears to fall within me.
>
> For it I sing a song of old,
> In a tune no one understands,
> Ah, I am not really singing,
> Only reviewing an old dream.

> July 4, 1927
> *The Crescent Monthly*, Vol. I, No. 6

LIU TA-PAI (1880–1932)

LIU TA-PAI was one of several teachers of Chinese literature at the Chekiang High School when the school was racked by controversy over the "new literature" in the early years of the century. Liu advocated the use of the vernacular language in literary writings. His opponents said that this was because he was incapable of using the old classical language, despite the fact that he had won a high degree in the old imperial examinations. The school prepared to dismiss Liu, and was stopped only by a petition composed and signed by Liu's students, which, as it turned out, was an elegant piece of prose written in the elevated classical style.

Liu was thoroughly trained in classical Chinese poetry. Even in his vernacular poems, the dexterous use of prosody reveals his classical discipline. Fired by the revolutionary zeal that motivated many of his contemporaries, Liu once declared in Peking, then still under the last Manchu monarch, that he was going to assassinate the emperor with a dagger:

A dagger on my belt,
A cup of wine in hand.
When the cup is drained, the dagger leaves its sheath,
And down falls my enemy's head.

· · · ·

As I pour a cupful to toast my dagger,
My singing splits the evening clouds.

Liu lived a successful life, culminating in a term as Vice Minister of Education in the Republican government, yet remained an untamed soul in his poetry, which was collected in seven volumes published between 1924 and 1935. The most touching of his poems were written when his sweetheart, Wu Fu-hsia, left him; they are in the classical *tz'u* style, like the following:

The moon is full
And by chance people meet together.
The moon is the same as of old,
But are people the same also?
Much of the bygone surges in my heart:
I dread the approach of midnight
And yet midnight has long passed again.

. . . .

A WHOLE SHEET OF SOLITUDE

A whole sheet of solitude,
Under the dripping rain,
Shattered
Into drips and drops.

Soon,
Solitude follows the rain to the pond,
Again returning to a whole sheet.
Solitude returns in a whole sheet.

Shao-hsing, September 28, 1922
Compendium, 82

CH'ENG-HU IS NOT DEAD

Ch'eng-hu,
It has been a year now,
Perhaps your body has completely rotted away.
But your heart can never decompose,
As it throbs, full of life, in the bosoms of countless farmers.

If the innumerable farmers' bodies rotted away together with
        yours,
The landlords would have long run out of things to eat:
If the hearts of the countless farmers died along with your
        body,
The landlords could then eat in peace forever.
Yet, that can never be!

For one more year the landlords have been eating in peace;
Nobody can be sure how many more years they will do so.
The death of your body is the landlords' good luck,
But your undying heart that defies your dead body
Spells out the doom of the landlords.

> Hangchow, January 24, 1923
> *Selected Modern Chinese Poems*, 45

THE SPIRIT OF SPRING

A little open-top boat
Floats on warm spring water:
A man, barefoot and in a short jacket
Stands astern, rowing an oar.
A woman wearing ordinary clothes but no powder or rouge,
Paddles in the middle of the boat;
In her arm is a child, dressed in red and green.

The cadence of their oars, one in front and one behind,
  Their merry chatter
   And unrestrained laughter,
And the child looking left and right,
  Listening with his eyes wide open,
   And gurgling . . .
A little open-top boat
Sails along to the cadence of the oars, of the chatter and
  laughter, and of the songs.

The boat
Is loaded with love
And life,
Which overflow the boat.
Their love
And their life
Also fill the sky and the water:
The spirit of spring thus better captured than by the blossoms
  and willows.

> In a boat at Hsiao-shan, March 29, 1923
> *Selected Modern Chinese Poems*, 46–47

ON A RIVER IN LATE AUTUMN

A homing bird,
Though tired,
Still carries a load of setting sun.

A flip of the wings
Spills the sunset on the river;
The hoary-haired reeds
For a moment appear in a coat of rouge.

Shao-hsing, October 30, 1923
Compendium, 84

QUIET NIGHT

A dream rises;
In it my soul soars, directionless.
Ah, it's better awake than having a dream!

A window full of moon,
Several lines of flowers' shadows,
Silence reigns in the room and outside all around.

Never so lonesome before,
A picture none can paint,
A world no dream can match.

Past midnight, now only shortly before dawn,
From far away comes a rooster's crow,
Shattering this world of quietude.

Chiang-wan, March 29, 1924
Selected Poems of Liu Ta-pai, 84–85

THE LONE TREE AND OTHERS

I

The lone tree, isolated from its crowd,
Stands facing me.
Clearly in silent words it says,
"We have no companion, you or I."

II

Western wind, blowing all night long,
Even the autumn forest over there has grown thin.

III

To voice all the grief of man,
Autumn rains wail and
Autumn winds issue their angry howl.

> Chiang-wan, September 3, 1926
> *Selected Poems of Liu Ta-pai*, 108

CHU TZU-CH'ING (1898–1948)

THE SELECTIONS from Chu Tzu-ch'ing's poems are meager, but no anthology of twentieth-century Chinese poetry would be complete without a mention of his share in it, even more as an authoritative interpreter and critic than as a poet.

The short lyrics he wrote in the vernacular in the early 1920s were fresh, delightful, and original. His language was somewhat weak, even puerile at times, but as he later pointed out, in his astute critical judgment of Chinese literature, the written vernacular language of the period was still feeling its way. It needed time to mature, and its innovations needed time to gain acceptance. "Destruction," his long poem published in 1923, had a wide circulation and was a great influence on the fledgling modern poetry.

After 1925 he turned to prose and rarely returned to poetry. He remained, however, always a diligent observer of the development of the new poetry, and his commentaries guided many young poets during the critical years of transition.

When he edited an anthology of modern Chinese poetry in 1935, summing up its development from the turn of the century to that point, he was quite neutral. He observed the progression from the "free verse" school to the "rigid form school" to the "symbolist" school, recognizing the contributions of each, but not naming his own preference. Without making any direct admission, he considered his own contribution in the early days as belonging to the "free verse" movement—the drive to free poetry of the structural restrictions imposed by the classical form.

By 1935, he had already been teaching in the Tsing Hua University for ten years. He had published two collections of essays and a number of studies on classical Chinese literature, which established him as a prose stylist and scholar. Yü Ta-fu, a leading figure of the Creation Society, considered Chu's prose beautiful, second only to that of Ping Hsin. One of his prose collections was the result of a trip to Europe in 1931–32, and many of the essays in it immediately became standard selections in high school and college readers.

In 1935 he still saw room for both the almost esoterically aesthetic symbolists and the realists who insisted on using the language of the peasant in the future of Chinese poetry. In 1940, however, he began to recognize the great promise in bringing poetry closer to the ordinary reader, and he stressed the importance of reading poetry aloud to determine its quality. The war also strongly affected his feeling about literature. He produced an authoritative statement on "patriotic verse" and later urged his fellow intellectuals to recognize the value and beauty of "slogans" in poetry as long as they were judiciously used to reflect the true feeling of the poet and his reader. But he drew a clear distinction between popularization and vulgarization and continued to work for the former.

Shortly before his death in 1948 he was still exhorting poets to realize that the world of poetry was always large enough to accommodate a rich variety of themes and forms. The last words he wrote were a reaffirmation of his belief that literature cannot be divorced from life, and that life in the China of the late 1940s demanded the broadening of the individual's private life to include some of the political life of his group. The pronoun "I," he said, must be understood as "We" in modern Chinese poetry because poetry always follows its time, and also marches ahead of it.

THE LITTLE GRASS

After a long sleep, the tiny blades of grass
Now come awake.
They stand in the sun
Yawning, and rubbing their eyes.
         Once withered and yellow, the tiny blades of grass
Now turn green.
Bobbing in the soft breeze,
Facing each other with smiles.

      Once lost, the tiny blades of grass
Now sprout everywhere.
The cheery chirp of the birds:
"Friends, it has been a long time!"
      Ah, so strong is the feeling of spring!
Lovable little blades of grass, our friends.
Did spring bring you here?
Or did you bring her?

                    Peking, March 18, 1920
                    The Snowy Morning, 3–4

from DESTRUCTION

      Sauntering on the road,
Down crested and dejected,
That's me, that's me.
The infinite colors
And patterns
Arrayed in display so near me:
These, so pleasing to the eyes;
And those, so flattering to the ears.
What I smell is the strong fragrance,
And a strong flavor lingers on my tongue;
What I can touch
And feel,
Are all so smooth,
So fluffy and soft.
As if floating,
Why such feeling of floating?
Pushed,
And dragged,
Forever in my bending and stretching,
Have I ever for a moment been master of myself?
I've been in a dream,
And on a sick bed,
I miss only having a moment with my mind all clear.
I find myself in the cloud
With the winds blowing in all directions;

I find myself in the depth of the sea
Where the undercurrent churns without stop.
Only on the good earth, so dark green,
Have never been imprinted, however faintly, my footsteps.
I drift along,
And along I drift.
I reach and reach on my tiptoe,
But cannot tread on the land of my country.
Growing old in the wind and dust,
Declining in the wind and dust,
I have only this feeble body remaining,
And several clusters of dark shadows.
The beginning of disintegration this is,
I think and think:
"So very dear, though so hazy
My homeland—my homeland.
I must go home, go home."

．　．　．　．

Although there may be profound words
Painting a picture of heavenly blossoms falling like rain,
　　　　Displayed before my eyes
Is a vision, misty as if behind a gauze.
It pulls me on to soar and soar
All the way to the thirty-third heaven.
Enshrouded in the colorful clouds
Beneath my feet lies the gray world
That grows smaller and smaller,
Receding, almost beyond my thought.
The gusty winds below
Roar in a gyrating pool,
Cutting into the fiber of my flesh.
If I, rocking back and forth,
Fell down,
I'd be like a deflating balloon,
Trodden under people's feet,
Leaving behind only the sound of the escaping air.
And the churning gusty wind
Would be like a knife with three points
Cutting apart my flesh.

I shall be dismembered in the clouds of many colors,
Or even changed to a whiff of smoke,
Disappearing slowly.
With a shiver, I
"Think of the infinity of heaven and earth . . ."[1]
Let me go home, let me go home.

. . . .

Hangchow, September 1922
The Selected Works of Chu Tzu-ch'ing, 34–48

[1] From a poem by Ch'en Tzu-ang (656–98); quotation marks are the author's.—Ed.

YÜ P'ING-PO (1899–   )

Yü P'ING-PO like Chu Tzu-ch'ing was a distinguished literary critic and teacher of literature as well as a pioneer poet in the vernacular. They even collaborated in publishing one of the earliest vernacular verse anthologies, *The Snowy Morning* (1922). Yü followed this with three collections of his own verse, *The Winter Night* (1922), *Returning West* (1924), and *Reminiscence* (1925), all of which reveal an excellent discipline in classical poetry brought to bear on new experiments. Wen I-to regarded Yü as the only poet who really contributed music to the new poetry through his "refined, distilled, and exquisite prosody."[1]

Later Yü concentrated on literary research and criticism. His study of *The Dream of the Red Chamber*, first published in 1923, remained a standard reference until 1954 when the leftist and Communist critics attacked it as an anti-materialistic, bourgeois, and unpatriotic work. Yü is still, however, a professor of literature in mainland China.

RETURN TO THE NORTH

The baked-bun peddler,
Midnight, in the biting wind,
Slowly calls.
I hear it, I know "I have come home."

> December 1, 1921
> *Compendium*, 30

[1] Wen, *Complete Works*, Ting, 142.

CASUAL LINES

What is that all over the world?
A laugh, a tear drop,
A sad and cold smile,
But everyone is silent.
What is that all over the world?

1921
The Snowy Morning, 59

PING HSIN (1902–   )

THE SEASHORE of Cheefoo on the Shantung Peninsula, with its surging surfs and visiting boats in the harbor, nurtured the love of nature and solitude in a precocious child, Hsieh Wan-ying.[1] The wind, water, and bugle calls from the ships were her constant companions. She liked them and rebelled against her reading lessons until she discovered that books offered her an inexhaustible source of stories which her uncle and nurse were too busy or too tired to tell. At the age of seven she had already groped her way through a large number of full-length novels, skipping many difficult passages, but getting the stories.

She took pride in telling the sailors these stories when her father took her to visit the boats. The sailors, in turn, rewarded her with their storybooks; thus she rapidly acquired a sizable library and repertoire. She even began to try writing stories, or paraphrasing those she had read, in semi-classical language. Through her uncle-tutor she also had access to the latest journals and newspapers. She hungrily read them all. The only novel she did not enjoy was *The Dream of the Red Chamber*.

The job of tutoring her passed from the first to a second uncle who led her toward poetry when she had barely passed her tenth birthday. During the 1911 revolution her family moved south to join their relatives in Fukien where, for the first time, she was weaned from her early tomboy life and became acquainted with hairdos and rouge, the favorite subjects among her numerous cousins there. At about the same time she started her education in modern schools.

Her high school education was completed in Peking, at the Pei Man Girls' School, an institution sponsored by a Christian mission which cast the shadow of the Cross across her forma-

[1] Ping Hsin is her pen name.

tive experience. Together with the sea and the sand, this experience laid the foundation for what she herself has described as her "philosophy of love."

Her first attempt at writing in the vernacular was not verse but essays which she published in the *Peiping Morning News*. They were journalistic commentaries on current events that she wrote as secretary to the Girl Student Association of Yenching University. This was in the wake of the May Fourth incident of 1919, and the students were all up in arms. Her essays had a facile style and were quite well received. Then she turned to short stories, making use of her childhood impressions of the sea and the sailors.

Tagore's *Stray Birds*, which she read in 1920, and her own fondness for toying with fragments of images prompted her to write *The Stars* in 1921 and *Spring Waters* in 1922. She denied that these short stanzas were poetry. She said later, in 1932, "I don't understand the new poetry; I suspect it and dare not try it myself." And she recalled that when the first few stanzas of *The Stars* were submitted to her cousin who edited the *Peiping Morning News*, he telephoned her, asking, "What is this?" Embarrassed, she replied, "Just something in the line of miscellaneous thought." Yet it was these "miscellaneous thoughts" that launched her as a poet.

Her songs evoked echoes in the hearts of many teen-agers, who in the 1920s were beginning to recognize the significance of their own feelings as against the feelings of their parents and elders. Some of them actually left home and plunged into the dramatically changing society where loneliness was frightful. Ping Hsin's words gave them comfort and reassured them of the warmth in man's life that is lasting:

> Mother,
>> Throw away your sorrow;
>>> Let me sleep soundly in your lap,
>>>> Only with you my soul can rest.
>>> (from *The Poems of Ping Hsin*, 116)

From 1923 to 1926 she attended Wellesley College and addressed her writings to young readers back in China. Among them she found her best and most appreciative readers; she also found herself. Occasionally her poems still appear in mainland Chinese publications. Her metaphors reflect the late political and intellectual atmosphere, but her style has not changed greatly.

from THE STARS

2

Ah, Childhood!
It's the true in a dream,
And a dream among the true,
And the tearful smile in reminiscence.

12

Mankind,
Let us love one another.
We are all travelers on a long journey
Heading for the same destination.

34

The builder of continents
Is not the surging billow
But the tiny grains of sand down beneath.

48

Fragile blades of grass,
Be proud!
Only you so impartially adorn the entire world.

52

The flowers and rocks beside the railroad tracks!
In this instant
You and I
Chance to meet among the infinite beings,
Also bid our last farewell among the infinite beings.
When I return,
In the midst of the myriads of our kind,
Where can I ever find you again?

1921
The Poems of Ping Hsin, 102–80

from THE SPRING WATERS

11

The south wind stirs
Bringing here the smiles of spring
From that country of ripples.

12

The sound of strings nears,
The blindman is here.
But as the sound fades into the distance,
Do the fates of the benighted souls
Also depart with it?

23

Plain is the water in a pond,
But with a touch of sunset,
It turns into a sea of gold.

24

Ah, jewel-like little isles,
How can you show your rugged strength
When countless of your summits
Are submerged in water?

25

In shaping the snow into blossoms—
The north wind is tender after all.

28

All beings are deceived by light and shadow.
Beyond the horizon—
When did the moon ever wax and wane?

33

Blossoms in the corner of the wall!
As you appreciate your solitary beauty,
The universe becomes rather small.

42
The lonely sail on the edge of an evening glow
Unknowingly
Completes nature's picture.

43
Spring has no words.
But her quiet latent power
Has already
Made the world tender for me.

60
The falling star—
Shines only when crossing the sky of man;
It darts out from darkness,
And flees into darkness again.
Is life also so unaccountable?

65
It's only a lonely star!
But in the infinite darkness
It has written up all the solitude of the universe.

66
Extreme quietude—
Is it Easter or mere loneliness?
Only the city wall stands frozen,
And the willow twigs, snow-clad.
What matters the chill?
Let me walk out into a picture of total whiteness.

74
In this hazy world,
I have forgotten the first word,
Nor will I ever know the last.

83

Beneath the temple gate, under a light rain,
The steps are moist.
Only I, standing alone,
And a few fleeting clouds—
Are we to grasp the profound dharma together?

105

O, Lord—
If in life eternal
Is allowed only one happiness extreme,
This would be my earnest plea:
"Let me be in my mother's lap,
Let mother be in a tiny boat,
And that boat float on a moonlit sea."

118

Wisteria blossoms fall in the pond.
In the arbor
There is not a single soul all day long,
Only the rustling leaves in the breeze.

146

The flower of experience
Bears the fruit of wisdom,
But the fruit of wisdom
Is impregnate with a seed of sorrow.

168

Under a misty moon,
In the corridor winding around a quiet courtyard,
If the ethereal chime did not disrupt the silence,
One could hear
The falling petals.

169

When the infant before birth,
From outside the sphere of life,
Gazes through life's window,
He has already seen, dimly, at a distance,
The cavern of death.

176

Tiny blossoms on the battlefield,
I adore you for your love most profound
That, braving the rain of bullets,
Comforts the fresh bones.

182

Fare you well,
Waters in Spring,
I thank you for your murmuring flow, all season long,
That has carried away many thoughts of mine.

I wave at you,
Bidding you flow gently to the sea of humanity.
I want to sit near your sources
Quietly to await the echoes.

1922
The Poems of Ping Hsin, 181–271

DELIVERANCE

Moonlight, clear as water,
I pace the ground under a tree
In deep, deep thought.
Deep in thought, I pick up a fallen twig
To tap, with a sigh, my own shadow
On the moonlit ground.

Life—
Everybody treats it as a dream,
A blurred dream.

My friend,
As you try to find clear lines in the blurred world,
Your life's suffering
Thus begins!

You may treasure life's snow-white robe,
Yet life has to cross
The immense sea of darkness.
My friend,
The world does not abandon you,
Why should you abandon the world?

Let life stand alone and noble like a stork,
Free as a cloud,
And pure and calm as water,
Even if life were a dream,
Let it be a clear dream.

In deep, deep thought—
Deep in thought, I throw away the fallen twig.
Quietly and calmly I gaze at my shadow
On the moonlit ground.

                    February 5, 1923
                    The Poems of Ping Hsin, 49–51

T'IEN HAN (1898–   )

BETTER KNOWN as a dramatist, T'ien Han, from the central Chinese province of Hunan, became one of the founders of the Creation Society in 1920 upon his return from Japan. A leader of the new drama movement in China, he also contributed to the experiments in poetry in the early 1920s. His book of verse, *Spring in Edo*, was published in 1922.

EVENING

On the horizon
   at the corner of the house,
    in the woods,
Not quite like flying dust,
   nor fog,
    nor smoke.

Evening breeze
   blows at wild trees
    sobbing gently
In the wilderness
   insects
    chirping.

My love,
   please sing me
    a new tune
—soft as
   a gossamer
    in the air—

"Whisper
in the silver gray
starlight.

Sleep
among the whirling
pearly dew drops."

1926 (?)
Compendium, 126

KUO MO-JO (1892–   )

THE BOUNDLESS creative energy of Kuo Mo-jo has taken him through many areas of literary and scholastic endeavor. He started out at the age of twenty-seven as a poet writing in the vernacular, and became a short-story writer, a playwright, a historian of ancient China, a specialist in ancient Chinese script, and a translator of Japanese, English, and German literature. He is still writing poetry today.

The voluminous output of his pen is matched by his politically active life. He founded many magazines, organized literary coteries, served in the government, participated in the revolutionary army, and was several times a political exile.

His hometown, Lo-shan (also known as Chia-ting in Szechwan Province), is an old, provincial town located at the scenic conflux of two rivers in western China. A son of a fairly well-to-do family, he received his early education in Chinese classics and was already quite well trained in Chinese poetry before he entered a modernized school. He was not impressed by his teachers there who appeared to know little more about Chinese literature than he. This, and his reputation as an incorrigible prankster who plagued his schoolmates as well as his teachers, made him unwelcome, and he never stayed long enough in any high school to complete his studies. Full of wild dreams, he went to Japan in 1914 to study medicine at the Kyushu Imperial University, but instead of medical books, his favorite reading was Western literature. He particularly liked Heine, Goethe, and Shelley. Among his numerous translations, *Faust* became very successful in China.

Somewhere around 1919 Walt Whitman's works suggested to Kuo Mo-jo the possibility of using modern language in poetry, and from the autumn of 1919 to the following summer he wrote poems every day. He was like a young boy with his senses newly awakened to the grandeur and beauty of the

world as he wrote one of his early poems, "I Sound the Bugle
on the Edge of the Earth,"

White clouds surge angrily in the sky,
Ah, what a breath-taking view of the Arctic on a sunny day!
The unlimited Pacific tries to overthrow the earth with
     all its strength.
Ah, the rolling billows rush toward me!
Ah, the ceaseless destruction, ceaseless creation, and
     ceaseless effort!
Ah, the force! What force!
The picture of force, the dance of force, the song, poetry,
     and rhythm of force!

                 (from *The Works of Kuo*, I, 62)

Not only was nature full of wonder for him, but also the
things created by man. He saw the smoke rising from a fac-
tory chimney as a "black peony," an "illustrious flower of the
century." Everything was impregnated with beauty, strength,
and meaning. Even death and decay fascinated him: they,
too, represented a phase of the manifestation of nature's
mystery and wonder and one aspect of man's creative power.
He took to pantheism and adopted as his mentors, Chuang
Tzu, one of the earliest writers on Chinese Taoism; Spinoza;
and the fifteenth-century Indian mystic, Kabir.

Ideological tides were surging in early twentieth-century
Japan even more tumultuously than in China. Most of the
Chinese students in Japan had there their first exposure to
Darwin, nineteenth-century English Romanticism, the Marx-
ist doctrine, and other theories and views. Kuo Mo-jo rapidly
gravitated toward the position of a romantic who sought to
lead a social and intellectual crusade to save the world, partic-
ularly its poor and downtrodden. Thus when Kuo published
his first book of poems, *The Goddess*, in 1921, he prefaced it
with a declaration:

Ah, *Goddess!*
You go to find those who come into sympathetic vibration
     with me,
You go to enter the bosoms of my youthful brothers and
     sisters,
To pluck the chords of their hearts,
And kindle their lights of wisdom.

In this declaration he describes himself as a proletarian who, like so many other young intellectuals in those days, regarded the label of Communist a badge of honor without necessarily understanding what Communism really meant in theory and practice.

The Creation Society that Kuo founded shortly after his return to China in 1918 was, at the beginning, dedicated to a romantic quest for beauty in literature. Kuo wrote an essay, "Our New Literary Movement," to express the Creation Society's unreserved dedication to literature, "to the creation of the most beautiful, the capture of the most true, and the recording of the most touching," and for a brief period he followed this dictum quite faithfully. He edited literary publications in Shanghai and wrote short poems on his life and observations. As he became involved in the incessant polemics on literature and political revolution, he found the first position taken by the Creation Society more and more untenable; there was really not much beauty in the life of Shanghai at that time. As he reviewed his poetry written during 1920–22 and collected in his second book, *The Starry Sky* (1923), he found that the stars were not quite the same as he had seen them:

> Ah, the fitfully blinking stars!
> Some of you are bloodstains, still fresh and red,
> And some, glistening drops of tears—
> In your pitiably feeble light
> There is hidden so much depressing frustration.
>
> (from *The Works of Kuo*, I, 152)

Kuo had married a Japanese girl. His family, including his young child who had yet to learn Chinese, shared a dingy apartment with Ch'eng Fang-wu, another founder of the Creation Society. The two men struggled to maintain a daily, a monthly, and a quarterly when publishing was not a lucrative business anywhere in China. Kuo lived in very reduced circumstances.[1]

Kuo's next book, *The Vase* (written in 1925 but published

---

[1] Hsü Chih-mo visited Kuo on October 11, 1918, in the latter's very unimpressive apartment, and wrote a revealing account in his diary. See Liang Shihch'iu, *About Hsü Chih-mo*, 25–26.

in 1927) is the only group of love poems that he ever wrote
and shows a higher degree of polish than *The Goddess*. But
it reflects merely a brief interlude in Kuo's poetic life. He had
already started an intensive study of the Marxist theory of
literature, and toward the end of 1924, he began to talk about
a "total destruction" of evil forces: "Before the phoenix can
be reborn, it has to commit its old remains to a consuming
flame." He put fifteen rather radical poems together in a new
volume, *The Vanguard*, which was published in 1928, suggest-
ing that they were the vanguard of the voice of revolution.
The earliest of the fifteen was written in 1921, but most of
the others were completed in 1923.

One of the poems describes an imaginary conversation be-
tween the Yellow and Yangtze Rivers. It tells of the social
evils witnessed in China, ending in a call to action:

Fellow human beings, wake up, wake up, wake up!
If you don't do what the American War of Independence did,
And stand up, refuse to pay taxes . . .
Never will you have the chance to change your destiny.

                              (from *The Works of Kuo*, I, 300)

Kuo himself has said that in 1925 he was already deter-
mined to embrace Marxism. In the same year he went to
Canton to accept a post in the Sun Yat-sen University. When
Chiang Kai-shek was readying his troops for the Northern
Expedition against the warlords in 1926, Kuo joined the army
staff in the political training department and traveled with
the army for a few months. Many other leftists were also in
the Kuomintang army at that time. The 1927 coup that
spelled the first and final split between the Kuomintang and
the Communists caused the death of many Communists
and left-wingers, and sent still more of them into exile. Kuo
fled Shanghai, intending to go to Russia, but he went to
Japan instead.

Before his departure for Japan, he completed twenty-four
poems which were collected in *Recovery* (1928). In these
poems Kuo expresses his disappointment at the failure to
change China's social order immediately:

Yesterday this world seemed to be collapsing,
Today this world has returned to chaos before the lull;
All around me is impenetrable darkness,
And I might just as well be sitting in an iron prison.

(from *The Works of Kuo*, I, 379)

But he appears not to despair, for he says:

Friends, do you think it's too depressing now,
This is but the eve before the birth of a new world.

And he dedicates himself to this task:

I have prepared a toast with bright red wine,
Friends, this is the warm blood filling my breast,
I shall brew a storm of strife tonight
To fight for that newborn sun, that newborn universe.

(from *The Works of Kuo*, I, 381)

From 1928 to 1937 he remained in Japan, translating over a dozen major works of Western European and American literature, writing several historical novels and several volumes of autobiography, and completing the study of ancient Chinese history that has earned him a name among scholars, but writing no poetry. It was not until the Kuomintang and the Communists, at least on the surface, reunited to resist increased Japanese aggression that Kuo returned to China. He resumed his 1926 job in the Kuomintang government and during the next eight years produced a number of successful historical plays and participated in all important literary and political activities.

In 1938 he published twenty-one poems in a volume called *The Sound of War*. In these poems he championed China's cause against Japan and criticized the indifference he had seen upon his return to China. Several poems are in the classical language and style.

Immediately after V-J Day, the struggle between the Kuomintang and the Communists re-emerged. The leftists were again in physical danger. Kuo went to Russia. After the Peking regime was established in 1949, he was appointed Vice Premier and has remained a top leader in China's cultural affairs ever since.

The Turmoil (1948) includes his poems written during 1939–47, commenting mostly on current events that had involved him in dramatic political activities. In his own preface, he declares that this volume should be read as current history rather than poetry. The poems he has written since 1948 mostly praise the glory of the new order.

Wen I-to in June, 1923, spoke of Kuo as the only truly "modern" Chinese poet who grasped "the spirit of the time." In *The Goddess*, Kuo is unrestrained in his use of what was very new and modern in the Chinese world and introduces many Western images. He was among the first to start the fad in vernacular Chinese literature of using expressions in Western European languages. This was fresh and fashionable for a while, but, as Wen I-to also pointed out, it was nonsense to replace Confucius with Socrates or Hsi Shih (a famous beauty in Chinese history) with Venus, when neither Socrates nor Venus meant much to the average Chinese reader in the 1920s. Kuo's recent poems have been using more and more of the folk-song vocabulary adapted to the classical prosodic schemes of five-syllable and seven-syllable quatrains.

NEW AULD LANG SYNE

1

I sit alone on a rock ledge near the sea,
Waiting to send off the early summer sun to the west.
Water in the immense sea dances under my feet,
Reaching up countless arms to embrace the sun.
The sun, wearing a brilliant robe of golden clouds,
Is about to visit its kin in the west.
Its lustrous eyes, unblinking, stare at me.
Are you asking me to go with you, Sun?

2

I sit alone on a rock ledge near the sea,
I'm sending off the early summer sun to the west.
Rosy clouds rise on the horizon where the sea touches the sky,
With a column of black haze in their midst, like a battle
     scene.

Ah, Sun, you are a burning grenade!
I want to watch you explode into blossoms, red as blood.
Your lustrous eyes, unblinking, stare at me,
And I also wish to go with you, Sun.

3

I sit alone on a rock ledge near the sea,
I have already sent off the early summer sun to the west.
I turn my head to inspect the sky all around me,
Banners of clouds are unfurling in all directions.
Water in the immense sea has been dyed thoroughly red.
A band of Bacchuses are prancing before my eyes.
Are your lustrous eyes, unblinking, still staring at me?
I wish I had been able to go with you, Sun.

1920
The Works of Kuo, I, 90–91

THE CREMATORY

This confounded head of mine
Is the burner in a crematory;
It has burned up my soul long ago!
Ah, where did this cool breeze come from?
It blows out of the crematory,
A blade of spring grass.

1919 (?)
The Works of Kuo, I, 120

THE SINGING CICADA

The cicada's singing, ceaseless.
Ah, autumn! The sound wave of the tide of time
Fades away, note after note. . . .

1919 (?)
The Works of Kuo, I, 122

A MISANTHROPE'S SERENADE

Ah, the sky and the sea, unlimited!
A bubble on liquid silver!
A splashing galaxy above,
And below, a sweep of boiling molten crystal,
Everything living is sound asleep.
I, alone, with a cape of white peacock feathers on my
      shoulders,
Gaze at the sky, from the bow of an ivory boat,
Far far away.

Ah, if I were to be a mermaid shedding tears of pearls,
Living a weeping existence on the bottom of a dark ocean,
I'd rather vanish forever in the "infinite,"
Like a falling star
Trailing a light of destruction,
Across these ethereal rays of silver.
Go on, and on, and on!
Let not the moon ahead shine in vain.

> November 23, 1920
> *The Works of Kuo*, I, 125

AN IMPRESSION OF SHANGHAI

I was shocked out of my dream!
      Ah, the sorrow of disillusion!

Idle bodies,
      Sensual and noisy flesh,
Men wearing long robes,
      Women, short sleeves,
Everywhere I see skeletons,
      And everywhere, coffins
Madly rushing,
      Madly pushing.
Tears well up in my eyes,
      And nausea, in my heart.

I was shocked out of my dream.
Ah, the sorrow of disillusion!

April 4, 1919 (?)
The Works of Kuo, I, 139

NEAR THE WEST LAKE

A stroll on the curved path by the lake,
In misty rain,
My clothes weigh a little heavier.

April 10, 1919 (?)
The Works of Kuo, I, 145

THE SOUTHERN WIND

A breeze stirs from the south across the sea,
Whiffs of smoke rise above the pinewoods.
Several women in blue, each wearing a white shawl,
Are carefully sweeping up the pine needles.

What a picture of classic grace,
Tempting me to halt my steps, and
Reminding me of the younger years of humanity—
That quiet, unhurried, antiquity.

October 10, 1921
The Works of Kuo, I, 168

A WINTER SCENE

The sea hugs a dead globe,
Her tears dance around the corpse.
White cloud angels flee into the space,
Only hungry buzzards come to the funeral.

From the corpse emerges a cluster of maggots,
Excitedly staging a game of war.
I wonder if I should sing a battle hymn,
Or a sad dirge.

1921 (?)
The Works of Kuo, I, 186

EARTHQUAKE

The earth has come to life!
All beings are astir!
But only for a wink's time
And then all quiet again—

The quiet after commotion,
A quiet like death.
The sun smiles at the children,
Smiling at those once frightened.

I recall in my childhood,
Mother saying it's a crocodile blinking its eyes;
Was there really a crocodile under the earth?
I saw it, yes, in my young mind.

Now that the crocodile is dead:
I know the earth swings its way through space,
I know it's because of a fault or a volcano,
But does that make me a mite wiser?

1922 (?)
The Works of Kuo, I, 192

from THE VASE

"There was a girl some years ago,
  Who went to the Ling Mountain one day,
  The mountain was full of plum blossoms
  And she picked five of them.

"She threaded the blossoms on a pin
And sent them to a poet.
The poet, ah, he was a fool,
He swallowed them and died.

"Since the death of that poet,
Several years have gone by. Then
From his grave on the Ling Mountain
Appeared a cluster of plum trees.

"Spring again! The girl came
To tend his grave; the flower
Buds were already swelling,
Though grass was still asleep.

"Before the grave the girl stood,
Strumming a few notes on her lute;
At the sound of her music,
The blossoms began to bloom.

"Sweet scent hovered above the tree,
And below it rang the chords of her lute.
Suddenly came a gust of wind, and
The girl vanished in the air.

"When the wind stilled, a carpet
Of fallen petals covered the tomb;
No longer was the girl there, but
Her lute played in the grave."

EPILOGUE

Ah, if I were to have that moment, really,
I could die right now. And if you
Could forgive my silly request,
Hurry up and bury my humble remains.

February 3, 1925
The Works of Kuo, I, 245–47

HE WHO PURSUES FORCE

Farewell, melancholy thought!
Never again disturb the white hot flame burning in my heart.
If you try it, you, pitiful moth,
Shall die immediately.

Farewell, delusive beauty of nothingness!
Never come again to knock on the iron door of my heart.
You, pitiful wretch of the street,
Go and seek out those money bags.

Farewell, the reluctant and the negative;
Farewell, delicate embroidering pins!
I will seize a Koran in my left hand,
And in my right hand, a gleaming sword.

> June 27, 1923
> *The Works of Kuo*, I, 308

THE TERROR SPREADS LIKE FIRE

White spreads before us as far as our eyes can see,
But we are not afraid of its terror.[2]

We have already accepted death as homecoming,
And we take long strides on the road we've chosen.

If you want to kill, go ahead and kill!
For each one of us killed, one hundred will rise.
We all have on us the hair of the Sacred Monkey
That makes numerous ourselves when we blow on it.[3]

[2] After the 1927 "coup," the leftists described the Kuomintang policy as the "white terror."—Ed.
[3] Refers to the legend of the magic monkey as told by the sixteenth-century writer, Wu Ch'eng-en.—Ed.

White spreads before us as far as our eyes can see,
But we are not afraid of its terror.
When we kill one we warn a hundred of his like,
Our terror spreads like fury and like fire.

January 7, 1928
The Works of Kuo, I, 359

"IRON VIRGIN"

The Iron Virgin was found in Medieval Europe,
A really cruel torture was she.
Her inside was just a box with sharp nails,
But her outside showed the image of Holy Mary.

The Holy Lady was the door of the box,
From behind her breast a spike protruded.
The victim was put inside, and the door, closed,
The long nail thus pierced the victim's chest.

In Manchuria the Japanese had a new invention,
Sharp nails were lined up on the inside of a barrel.
With the victim in it, and both ends sealed,
The barrel was left in the streets to be kicked around.

The torture had no kind looks of the Holy Lady,
But was equipped with such iron breasts as the Virgin's.
The Japanese, they say, just named it Nail Box,
Ah, they surely are good at imitation.

August 31, 1937
The Works of Kuo, II, 27

ON KUAN SHAN-YÜEH'S PAINTING[4]

Laughable are the lutists who know no music at all,
Yet in public try to talk about "the stringless lute."
Such mad Chan has led astray many a good youth, and
Has for hundreds of years ruined the art of painting.

A revolution in painting must first depart from ancient
    elegance.
Folk style values what is true to life and realistic.
If the image is not realistic, it is then false,
And the vulgar, when really driven home, is naturally the
    divine.

1945 (?)
The Works of Kuo, II, 96–97

WATCHING ICE SKATING[5]

Waves of snow interweave with the swallows in the cloud,
Sky stretches on top of the water.
The pairs of skate-blades, tiny icebreaker boats:
People fly by like shooting stars—
What infinite joy!

All these young people, spreading out as far as you can see,
All racing forward.
"The Unrestricted Travel" is now rewritten.[6]
Paradise on earth now a reality,
So very soon!

January 23, 1957
The Works of Kuo, II, 262

[4] The author's note explains that Kuan Shan-yüeh's painting is naturalistic realism expressed through traditionally Chinese techniques. Kuan has since become a popular artist in mainland China. These are two of the original six stanzas written in the traditional quatrain form with seven syllables to each line.—Ed.

[5] This poem is written in the traditional *tz'u* form. The author's note states that he was attempting to match a poem by Mao Tse-tung with the same rhyming scheme.—Ed.

[6] The reference is to the title of a chapter in the famous Taoist book, *The Chuang Tzu* (c. third century B.C.).—Ed.

WANG CHING-CHIH (1903–   )

> I brave people's adverse criticism at every step
> To turn back to look at my sweetheart,
> How happy and scared I am at the same time!
> (from *Three Memoirs in Chinese Literature*, 77)

THIS IS an excerpt from a poem by Wang Ching-chih which created a storm in 1922. The response to its publication was immediate. Many critics said it was indiscreet and condemned the author as a bad influence on the morals of the youth. Chou Tso-jen, one of the leading men of letters well versed in both classical Chinese and Western European literature, defended Wang Ching-chih, saying that there was nothing immoral about a boy loving a girl. And Hu Shih praised the poem as a breath of fresh air in Chinese poetry.

Wang came from Anhwei Province in eastern China. His courage in violating literary taboos won him great popularity, and early success made him overconfident. When he taught at the Chi-nan University in Shanghai, he clashed with the university administration by insisting that vernacular works be included among the reading materials for the students.

He published two volumes of poems: *Orchid Winds* (1922) and *The Lonely Country* (1927). His friends said that after these poems Wang never studied much of anything, or wrote much. Among his many idiosyncrasies were his habit of cutting off the margins of his books to save shelf space and a blind respect for modern science, which he did not understand at all. When his child was an infant, he insisted on raising him according to a book of modern child-care. The infant lost weight and became very sickly. Wang's mother-in-law intervened and took the baby home to raise according to the old, unscientific method. A few weeks later the child regained his health. Despite this experience, Wang never changed his opinion.

Wang's poems are simple and direct, and there is a youthful charm about them in spite of their naïveté.

THE WIND'S ARROWS SHOOT CEASELESSLY

>The wind's arrows shoot ceaselessly,
>>Every arrow hits my heart:
>Why must they shoot me?
>>They are after my hope.

>The sun is an iron wheel revolving,
>>Every day it rolls over my head;
>Why must it crush me?
>>It's trying to destroy my youth.

>>>>*Compendium*, 146

TIME IS A PAIR OF SCISSORS

Time is a pair of scissors
>And life, a bolt of brocade.
Section by section the brocade is cut;
When the last section is done,
>The scraps are committed to a bonfire.

Time is an iron whip,
>And life, a tree full of blossoms.
One by one the flowers are lashed off;
When the last is gone,
>The fallen petals are trampled into the dirt and sand.

>>>>Autumn 1925
>>>>*Compendium*, 146

UNTITLED

Sorrow is the unbounded sky,
  And happiness, the stars.
My love, you and I are
  The bright moon in the starry sea.

The deep roots are sorrow,
  And the green foliage, joy.
My love, those blooms growing on top
  Are you and I.

Water in the sea is joy,
  The unbounded sea itself, sorrow.
The fish swimming in the sea
  Are you and I, my love.

Sorrow is the countless bee hives,
  Joy, the sweet honey:
My love, you and I are the bees
  Working so busily.

      Hangchow, autumn 1923
      Compendium, 147–48

WEN I-TO (1899–1946)

"Often do I heave long sighs
  To hide my tears, silent tears,
  Sorrowing for the lives of my people
  That are so full of grief and fears!"

WEN I-TO inscribed these lines, by the third-century B.C. poet, Ch'ü Yüan, on a friend's paper fan only about a month before he died on July 15, 1946. It was a politically benighted year, and he died a victim of assassination.

The old poem spoke Wen's mind. Poet, artist, and scholar, Wen was also a sturdy warrior. His imagination was fired by the suffering of the people and by political abuse. He came, after a tortuous detour in his search for the higher values of life, to the conclusion that the entire political and social order of China must be changed before the common citizen's lot could be improved. What he said and the way he said it were not tolerated. The forces that were hurt by his criticism silenced him.

The path of Wen's intellectual development is the one that most Chinese intellectuals have traveled since the beginning of the century. Born in Hupeh Province, he was given an excellent traditional education in the Chinese classics by his parents and tutors, and wrote quite good poetry in the classical style until his exposure to Western literature as a student at Tsing-hua College (the only Western-supported college in China) prompted him to try the vernacular.

All his life Wen oscillated between his love for the cultural tradition of his country, and his genuine appreciation of the good elements in Western cultures. At first he admired Western literature and art, but after a number of years at Tsing-hua College, he became critical of America and defensive about things Chinese. Then he came to America. From 1922 to 1925 he studied painting at the Art Institute of

Chicago and Colorado College, and later at the Art Students
League in New York, but his interest was steadily veering
toward poetry. In Chicago he met Harriet Monroe, Carl
Sandburg, and Amy Lowell. But it was John Keats, whose
poetry satisfied Wen's love for beauty as well as his respect
for abstract ideas, who became his poetic mentor, and Wen
the Romanticist remained throughout his life committed to
the search for an ideal marriage between Truth and Beauty.

Wen the poet grew homesick in America, and in his poetic
imagination China became a symbol of everything noble, ex-
alted, and warm. Wen the patriot was pushed further in his
dislike of the United States when he visited American China-
towns and felt the stings of racial discrimination. He recorded
his reaction in his famed "Laundry Song," an imitation of
Thomas Hood.

His adoration of his fatherland, however, was not without
reservations. He remembered certain things in the old society
of China that rankled. One of these was the situation of ab-
solute parental authority. Wen married early. The bride was
selected by his father. The marriage, fortunately, was a happy
one, despite the intellectual distance between them. Wen
sent his wife a long poem from America, the fourteenth
stanza of which reads:

> I am sending these verses to you;
> It matters not if you cannot read them all.
> Just rest your fingertips on these words . . .
> The throbbing you feel will pulse
> In unison with your own heart.

The letter containing this poem was intercepted by his
parents, and she never saw it until it was published much
later. Wen's father disapproved of his son's writing to his
wife from America. This act made Wen an avowed crusader
against the tyranny of old social conventions and ignorance.
Homeward-bound in 1925, he carried with him no Ph.D.
diploma, but a small library of Western poetic works and a
sense of mission to spearhead an intellectual revolution that
would save his country—with art and poetry.

The China he found upon his return, as he recorded in
"Discovery," was disappointing. There was no lack of tension

in Shanghai and Peking, but it was not easy to carry out a
literary revolution. Even getting a job was a problem. His
domestic affairs were also disturbing. He had been unhappy
with the arrangement of leaving his wife in his parents' house
while he was in America; now he was further grieved over the
death of his four-year-old daughter, which he blamed on his
parents' old-fashioned ideas. A series of political events re-
minded him that he had agreed to start a drive with a num-
ber of his friends to revive the nationalistic spirit of his fel-
low countrymen. So while teaching in Peking, in 1925–26, he
was active in trying to organize his intellectual friends to de-
velop a program of political action. But his heart was not in
politics, and he soon found himself turning toward the pub-
lication of a literary journal. And it was in his studio apart-
ment that the Crescent group of poets was formed. Hsü
Chih-mo, recalling the founding of the Crescent Society, has
written:

> I heard that the house of Wen I-to was the paradise of
> poets. . . . Last Saturday I went there. The three studio
> rooms were decorated with unusual taste. He had painted
> all the walls black, highlighting them with a narrow gold
> strip. The effect was like a naked African beauty wearing
> only a pair of gold bracelets and anklets. In one of the
> rooms a niche was carved in the wall, in which was placed,
> naturally, a sculpture of Venus de Milo about a foot high.
> . . . Against the totally black backdrop, the soft and warm-
> colored marble statue was rich in dreamy suggestiveness.

In this atmosphere, with his friends, Wen I-to worked out
his theories about poetry and experimented with them in his
own verse. His was not an extreme position of the "art for
art's sake" principle, but under his and Hsü Chih-mo's leader-
ship the Crescent school of poetry ran counter to the main
literary current, which was drifting toward social and political
literature. Always sensitive to the inequities of life, Wen felt
that the nation needed something more than poetry. At the
same time he was not prepared to contribute more directly
to the nation's salvation. Frustrated, he retreated to the Chi-
nese classics to restudy what he had read in his young student
days, both because he wanted to prove to his colleagues teach-

ing Chinese literature that he also had scholarly command in this field, and because he was sincerely convinced that true value and wisdom could be found in them. He became a distinguished authority on Ch'ü Yüan, the author of the third-century B.C. anthology, the *Ch'u-tz'u.*

The war did not permit him to remain "buried in the old papers" long. He had to flee Peking when Tsing-hua University was moved to Changsha in Hunan Province, and lost most of his books. In 1938 when the college had to move again, farther south to Kunming in Yunnan Province, he led an exodus of several hundred students, walking through the mountains of central China for sixty-eight days before they arrived in Kunming. The situation continued to worsen. Japanese troops pressed closer every day, and every day some of his students would leave to join either the Communist or the Nationalist army. When Wen realized that these young people were dying in a civil war, he was infuriated. He protested against the government then in power, the Kuomintang. His expressions appeared to be more and more in sympathy with the left, and his death warrant was sealed.

Wen I-to's contribution to modern Chinese poetry lies chiefly in his theory about rhyme, form, and imagery. He believed that the Chinese language offered an unusually rich range of rhymes of which the Chinese poet ought to take advantage. While accepting the vernacular language as a promising poetic medium, he criticized the indiscriminate use of colloquialism in poetry. He objected to Hu Shih's interpretation of "natural rhythm," and urged poets to distill the poetical and musical elements from the plain speech. He himself wrote vernacular verse with a metrical cadence to show that it could be effectively done, constructing a new prosody for the new language. "If we compare poetry to the game of chess," he said, "we can easily understand why poetry without form, like a game of chess without rules, must be such a meaningless thing!" He admitted that there was form in nature, but maintained that any form copied intact from nature could not be perfect; perfection in form was achieved only after much patient chiseling. He quoted Goethe's letter to Schiller, and the words of the seventh-century Chinese man of letters, Han Yü (768–824), to support his theory that "The greater the artist, the more he enjoys dancing in fetters." Wen's own poems, which observe all these tenets, have a sculptured structural beauty.

CHAMPION

O my love, you are a champion;
But let's play a game of chess.
My aim is not to win,
I wish only to lose to you—
My body and soul,
Both in their entirety.

1921
Wen, *Complete Works, Ting,* 79

DEATH

O, my soul's soul!
My life's life!
All my failures, all my debts
Now have to be claimed against you,
But what can I ask of you?

Let me be drowned in the deep blue of your eyes.
Let me be burnt in the furnace of your heart.
Let me die intoxicated in the elixir of your music.
Let me die of suffocation in the fragrance of your breath.

Or may I die ashamed in front of your dignity,
Or frozen in your unfeeling chill,
Or crushed between your merciless teeth,
Or stung by your relentless poison-sword.

For I shall breathe my last in happiness
If my happiness is what you decree;
Otherwise I shall depart in endless agony
If my agony be your desire.

Death is the only thing I beg of you,
And to you I offer my life, my supreme tribute.

1921
Wen, *Complete Works, Ting,* 75

AUTUMN COLORS[1]

Water in the creek
As purple as ripe grapes
Rolls out golden carp's scales
Layer upon layer

Several scissor-shaped maple leaves
Like crimson swallows
Whirling and turning, rising and dipping
On the water.

Thick and fat like bears' paws,
Those dark brown leaves
Scattered on the green.
Busy, timid squirrels
Scurry out and in among the leaves,
Gathering food for the approaching winter.

Chestnut tree leaves, now of age,
Complained to the western wind all night long,
Finally win their freedom.
With a deep blush on their dry faces,
They giggle and bid farewell to the ancient branches.

White pigeons, multi-colored pigeons,
Red-eyed silver gray pigeons,
Raven-like black pigeons,
With a golden sheen of purple and green on their backs—
So many of them, tired of flying,
Assemble beneath the steps.
Their beaks buried in their wings,
Quietly they take their afternoon nap.

[1] In earlier editions, the title was "Autumn Forest."—Ed.

Crystalline air, like pure water, fills the world;
Three or four pert children
(In orange, yellow, and black sweaters)
Dart through the clove bushes,
Like goldfish cavorting among the seaweeds.

Aren't they a forest of masts on the Huang-p'u River?
Those countless ascetic poplars
Stand piercing the slate-blue sky in stony silence.
That aspen stands like a gallant youth,
Draped in a gold-embroidered cape.
Resting one hand on his hip,
He gazes at the jade-green pool,
Admiring his own reflection.

As they lean on the zig-zag crystal balustrades,
The morning sunbeams smile at the world.
From their smile flows liquid gold—
Yellow gold on the oaks,
Red gold on the oaks,
White gold on the barks of the pines.

Ah, these are no longer trees,
But tinted clouds—
Of amber, of agate,
Fanned by sensitive winds and kindled by the sun.
These are no longer trees,
But exquisite, bejeweled clouds.

Ah, these are no longer trees,
But a palace in the Forbidden City—
Yellow-glazed tiles,
Green-glazed tiles;
Story upon story, pavilion on pavilion—
The silvery songs of the birds
Imitate the chimes under the flying eaves.
These are no longer trees,
But an imperial capital in full regal splendor.

You, majestic, festooned autumn trees!
Neither brocades of Lord Ling-yang,
Nor carpets from Turkey,
Nor the rose window of Notre Dame,
Nor the frescoes of angels by Fra Angelico,
Can rival your colors and brilliance.

You, majestically garbed autumn trees!
I envy your romantic world,
Your bohemian life,
And your colors.

I'll ask T'ien Sun to weave me an embroidered robe[2]
So that I may wear your colors;
Or press you from grapes, oranges, and kaoliang
So that I may drink your colors!
And from Puccini's *La Bohème*,
And from the seven-jeweled censer of Po-shan,
I will listen to your colors,
And inhale your colors.

Ah, how I long to lead a life of colors,
As dazzling as these autumn trees!

1922
Wen, *Complete Works, Ting,* 106–10

THE DREAMER

If that blue ghost light
Is the sparkle bursting from the dream
Of the entombed,
What fear have I of death?!

1922
Wen, *Complete Works, Ting,* 113

2 T'ien Sun is the star Weaving Maid, who resides across the
Milky Way from the Ox Herd.—Ed.

THE LAST DAY

The dewdrops sob in the roof-gutters,
The green tongues of banana leaves lap at the window panes.
The four white walls seem to back away from me:
I alone can not fill such a big room.

A brazier aflame in my heart,
I quietly await a guest from afar.
I feed the fire with cobwebs, rat dung,
And snakeskins in place of split wood.

As the roosters urge time, only ashes remain;
A chilly breeze steals over to caress my mouth.
The guest is already right in front of me;
I close my eyes and follow him away.

>   1926
>   Wen, *Complete Works, Ting,* 15–16

THE LAUNDRY SONG

(One piece, two pieces, three pieces,)
Washing must be clean.
(Four pieces, five pieces, six pieces,)
Ironing must be smooth.

I can wash handkerchiefs wet with sad tears;
I can wash shirts soiled in sinful crimes.
The grease of greed, the dirt of desire . . .
And all the filthy things at your house,
Give them to me to wash, give them to me.

Brass stinks so; blood smells evil.
Dirty things you have to wash.
Once washed, they will again be soiled.
How can you, men of patience, ignore them!
Wash them (for the Americans), wash them!

You say the laundry business is too base.
Only Chinamen are willing to stoop so low?
It was your preacher who once told me:
Christ's father used to be a carpenter.
Do you believe it? Don't you believe it?

There isn't much you can do with soap and water.
Washing clothes truly can't compare with building warships.
I, too, say what great prospect lies in this—
Washing the others' sweat with your own blood and sweat?
(But) do you want to do it? Do you want it?

Year in year out a drop of homesick tears;
Midnight, in the depth of night, a laundry lamp . . .
Menial or not, you need not bother,
Just see what is not clean, what is not smooth,
And ask the Chinaman, ask the Chinaman.

I can wash handkerchiefs wet with sad tears,
I can wash shirts soiled in sinful crimes.
The grease of greed, the dirt of desire . . .
And all the filthy things at your house,
Give them to me—I'll wash them, give them to me!

> 1925 (?)
> Wen, *Complete Works, Ting,* 28–30

FORGET HER

Forget her, as a forgotten flower—
      That ray of morning sun on a petal
      That whiff of fragrance from a blossom—
Forget her, as a forgotten flower.

Forget her, as a forgotten flower,
      As a dream in the wind of spring,
      As in a dream, a bell's ring.
Forget her, as a forgotten flower.

Forget her, as a forgotten flower.
    Listen, how sweetly the crickets sing;
    Look, how tall the grass has grown.
Forget her, as a forgotten flower.

Forget her, as a forgotten flower.
    No longer does she remember you.
    Nothing now lingers in her memory.
Forget her, as a forgotten flower.

Forget her, as a forgotten flower.
    Youth, what a charming friend,
    Who makes you old overnight.
Forget her, as a forgotten flower.

Forget her, as a forgotten flower.
    If anyone should ask,
    Tell him she never existed.
Forget her, as a forgotten flower.

Forget her, as a forgotten flower.
    As a dream in the wind of spring,
    As in a dream, a bell's ring.
Forget her, as a forgotten flower.

                  Winter 1926
                  Wen, *Complete Works, Ting,* 13–14

CONFESSION

Let me not deceive you, I am no poet,
Even though I adore the integrity of white gems,
The blue pines and immense ocean, the sunset on crows'
    backs,
And the dusk woven with the bats' wings.
You know that I love heroes and towering mountains,
And our national flag unfurling in the wind . . . all these
From saffron to the antique bronze of chrysanthemums.
Remember, my food is a pot of bitter tea.

But, aren't you afraid?—In me there is yet another man,
Whose thought follows a fly's to crawl in the garbage can.

> 1926–27
> Wen, *Complete Works*, Ting, 5

A CONCEPT

You, a perpetual myth, a beautiful tale,
A persistent question, a flash of light,
An intimate meaning, a leaping flame,
A distant call . . . what are you?
I don't doubt; the law of causality is ever so true.
I know: the sea is always faithful to its sprays.
Being the rhythm one complains not against the song.
Ah, you, tyrannical deity, you've subdued me;
You've conquered me, you dazzling rainbow—
Memory of 5000 years, please hold still.
I only ask how to embrace you tightly,
You, such an untamable spirit, such a beauty.

> 1927
> Wen, *Complete Works*, Ting, 21

DISCOVERY

I've come, I shout, bursting out in tears of woe,
"This is not my China—Oh, no! No!"
I've come because I heard your summoning cry.
Riding on the wind of time, raising a torch high,
I came. I knew not this to be unwarranted ecstasy.
A nightmare I found. You? How could this be!
This is terror, a bad dream over the brim of an abyss,
But not you, not what my heart continues to miss!
I ask heaven, ask the winds of all directions.
I ask (my fist pounding the naked chest of the earth)
But there is no answer. In tears I call and call you
Until my heart leaps out—ah, here you are!

> 1927
> Wen, *Complete Works*, Ting, 21–22

YOU SWEAR BY THE SUN

You swear by the sun, and let the wintry geese on the
    horizon
Attest to your faithfulness. Fine, I believe you completely,
Even if you should burst out in tears I wouldn't be
    surprised.
Only if you wanted to talk about "The sea may dry up and
    the rocks may rot . . ."
That would make me laugh to death. Isn't this moment
    while my breath lasts
Not enough to get me drunk? What need is there to talk
    about "forever"?
Love, you know my desire lasts only the duration of one
    breath,
Hurry up then and squeeze my heart, hurry, ah, you'd better
    go, you go . . .
I have long guessed your trick—no, it's not that you've
    changed—
"Forever" you have long promised someone else, only the
    dregs are my lot.
What the others get is your essence—the eternal spring.
So you don't believe me? But if one day Death produced
    your own signature,
Will you go? Yes, go to linger in His embrace and only
Talk to Him about your undying loyalty.

1927 (?)
Wen, *Complete Works*, Ting, 6

I WANTED TO COME HOME

I wanted to come home
While your little fists were like the orchids yet to open;
While your hair still remained soft and silken;
While your eyes shone with that spirited gleam;
I wanted to come home.

I did not come home,
While your footsteps were keeping cadence in the wind;
While your little heart was beating like a fly against the
          window pane;
While your laughter carried that silver bell's ring,
          I did not come home.

I should have come home,
While a spell of blur covered your eyes;
While a gust of chilly wind put out a fading light;
While a cold hand snatched you away like a kite;
          I should have come home.

1927
Wen, *Complete Works, Ting,* 18–19

THE DESERTED VILLAGE

Where did they go? How has it come to pass?
On stoves squat frogs, in ladles lilies bloom;
Tables and chairs float in fields and water ponds;
Rope-bridges of spiderwebs span room on room.
Coffins are wedged in doorways, rocks block windows:
A sight of strange gloom that rends my heart.
Scythes lie rusting away in dust,
Fishing nets, abandoned, rot in ash-piles.
Heavens, even such a village cannot retain them,
Where roses forever smile, and lily leaves grow as big as
          umbrellas;
Where rice sprouts are so slender, the lake so green,
The sky so blue, and the birds' songs so like dew-pearls.
Who made the sprouts green and the flowers red?
Whose sweat and blood is it that is blended in the soil?
Those who have gone left so resolutely, unhesitatingly.
What was their grievance, their secret wish?
Now, somebody must tell them: "Here the hogs
Roam the streets, ducks waddle among the pigs,
Roosters trample on the peony, and cows browse on vegetable
          patches."

Tell them: "The sun is down, yet the cattle are still on the
    hills.
Their black silhouettes pause on the ridge, waiting,
While the mountains around, like dragons and tigers,
Close in on them. They glance about and shiver.
Bowing their heads, too frightened to look again."
This, too, you must tell them: "These beasts recall days of
    old
When evening chill approached and poplars trembled in the
    wind,
They only needed to call once from the hilltop.
Though the trails were steep, their masters would help them,
And accompanying them home there would be the scent of
    hay.
As they think thus, their tears fall.
And they huddle together, jowl against jowl . . ."
Go, tell their masters, tell them.
Tell them everything, do not hide anything.
Ask them to return! Ask them to return!
Ask them why they do not care for their own cattle.
Don't they know that these beasts are like children?
Poor creatures, so pitiful, so frightened.
Hey, where are you, messenger?
Hurry now, tell them—tell Old Wang the Third,
Tell the Eldest Chou and all his eight brothers,
Tell all the farm hands living around the Lin-huai Gate,
Tell also that red-faced blacksmith Old Li,
Tell Old Woman Huang and all the village women,
Tell them all these things, one by one.
Tell them to come back, come back!
My heart is torn by this sight of gloom.
Heavens, such a village cannot retain these people,
Such a paradise on earth without a man!

                  1927
                  Wen, *Complete Works, Ting,* 24–26

QUIET NIGHT

This light, and the light-bleached four walls,
The kind table and chair, intimate as friends,
The scent of old books, reaching me in whiffs,
My favorite teacup as serene as a meditating nun,
The baby sucking contentedly at his mother's breast,
A snore reporting the healthy slumber of my big son . . .
This mysterious quiet night, this calm peace.
In my throat quiver songs of gratitude,
But the songs soon become ugly curses.
Quiet night, I cannot accept your bribe.
Who treasures this walled-in square foot of peace?
My world has a much wider horizon.
As the four walls cannot silence the clamor of war,
How can you stop the violent beat of my heart?
Better that my mouth be filled with mud and sand,
Than to sing the joy and sorrow of one man alone;
Better that moles dig holes in this head of mine,
And vermin feed on my flesh and blood,
Than to live only for a cup of wine and a book of verse,
Or for an evening of serenity brought by the ticking clock,
Hearing not the groans and sighs from all my neighbors,
Seeing not the shivering shadows of the widows and orphans,
And the convulsion in battle trenches, mad men biting their
          sickbeds,
And all the tragedies ground out under the millstone of life.
Happiness, I cannot accept your bribe now.
My world is not within this walled-in square foot.
Listen, here goes another cannon-report, another roar of
          Death.
Quiet night, how can you stop the violent beat of my heart?

1927
Wen, *Complete Works*, Ting, 20–21

A REPLY

Shining glories I dare not accept;
No halos to crown my head.
Banners and drums are not my share;
No yellow earth for the path I tread.

Let not pride plate me in gold,
I decline a visit from "success."
With both hands grappling busy strife,
I guess the dawn, without looking.

Give to others the pomp of silken robes;
For me, only hard labor—a joy so real.
To make me temper songs of plain tunes
God has promised me a will of steel.

But please, no banners and drums for me.
No yellow earth for the path I tread.
Shining glories I dare not accept;
No halos to crown my head.

1928
The Crescent Monthly, Vol. I, No. 2

PRAYER

Please tell me who the Chinese are,
Teach me how to cling to memory.
Please tell me the greatness of this people
Tell me gently, ever so gently.

Please tell me: Who are the Chinese?
Whose hearts embody the hearts of Yao and Shun?
In whose veins flow the blood of Ching K'o and Nieh Cheng?
Who are the true children of the Yellow Emperor?[3]

[3] All legendary and historical heroes and sages of China.—Ed.

Tell me that such wisdom came strangely—
Some say it was brought by a horse from the river:
Also tell me that the rhythm of this song
Was taught, originally, by the phoenix.

Who will tell me of the silence of the Gobi Desert,
The awe inspired by the Five Sacred Mountains,
The patience that drips from the rocks of Mount T'ai,
And the harmony that flows in the Yellow and Yangtze
      Rivers?

Please tell me who the Chinese are,
Teach me how to cling to memory.
Please tell me the greatness of this people
Tell me gently, ever so gently.

> 1927
> Wen, *Complete Works, Ting,* 22–23

ONE SENTENCE

There is one sentence that can light fire,
Or, when spoken, bring dire disasters.
Don't think that for five thousand years nobody has said it.
How can you be sure of a volcano's silence?
Perhaps one day, as if possessed by a spirit,
Suddenly out of the blue sky a thunder
      Will explode:
  "This is our China!"

How am I to say this today?
You may not believe that "the iron tree will bloom."
But there is one sentence you must hear!
Wait till the volcano can no longer be quiet,
Don't tremble, or shake your head, or stamp your feet,
Just wait till out of the blue sky a thunder
      Will explode:
  "This is our China!"

> 1927
> Wen, *Complete Works, Ting,* 23–24

PERHAPS (A DIRGE)

Perhaps you are too tired of crying,
Perhaps you want to sleep awhile.
Then I'll tell the owls not to cough,
Frogs to hush, and bats to stay still.

I'll not let the sunshine pry your eyelids,
Nor let the wind your eyebrows sweep.
Nobody will be allowed to awaken you,
I hold a pine umbrella to shelter your sleep.

Perhaps you hear earthworms turning dirt,
Perhaps you hear grassroots sucking water.
Perhaps prettier than man's cursing voice
Is this kind of music you now hear.

I'll let you sleep, yes, let you sleep—
Close your eyes now, tightly.
I'll cover you gently with yellow earth,
And tell paper ashes[4] to fly lightly.

> 1927 (?)
> Wen, *Complete Works, Ting*, 12–13

DEAD WATER

Here is a ditch of hopelessly dead water.
No breeze can raise a single ripple on it.
Might as well throw in rusty metal scraps
or even pour left-over food and soup in it.

Perhaps the green on copper will become emeralds.
Perhaps on tin cans peach blossoms will bloom.
Then, let grease weave a layer of silky gauze,
and germs brew patches of colorful spume.

[4] From the paper money burned for the dead.—Ed.

Let the dead water ferment into jade wine
covered with floating pearls of white scum.
Small pearls chuckle and become big pearls,
only to burst as gnats come to steal this rum.

And so this ditch of hopelessly dead water
may still claim a touch of something bright.
And if the frogs cannot bear the silence—
the dead water will croak its song of delight.

Here is a ditch of hopelessly dead water—
a region where beauty can never reside.
Might as well let the devil cultivate it—
and see what sort of world it can provide.

1927 (?)
Wen, *Complete Works, Ting,* 16–17

THE NIGHT SONG

A toad shivered, feeling the chill,
Out of the yellow earth mound crawled a woman.
Beside her no shadow was seen,
And yet the moon was so very bright.

Out of the yellow earth mound crawled a woman,
And yet no crack showed itself in the mound,
Nor was a single earthworm disturbed,
Nor a single thread of a spider web broken.

In the moonlight sat a woman;
She seemed to have quite youthful looks.
Her red skirts were frightful, like blood,
And her hair was draped all over her back.

The woman was wailing, pounding her chest.
And the toad continued to shiver.
A lone rooster crowed in a distant village,
The woman disappeared from the yellow earth mound.

1927 (?)
Wen, *Complete Works, Ting,* 19–20

MIRACLE

Never have I sought the red of fire, nor the black
Of the Peach Blossom Pool at midnight, nor the plaintive
      tune of a lute,
Nor the fragrance of roses. Never have I loved the proud
      dignity of a leopard.
The tenderness I longed for, no white dove could offer.
I never wanted these things, but their crystallization,
A miracle ten thousand times more miraculous than them
      all!
But, this soul of mine being so famished, I simply cannot
Let it remain without food. So, even trash and dregs
I have to beg for, don't I? Heaven knows I am not
Willingly doing this, nor am I too stubborn, nor too stupid.
Only I cannot wait for you, wait for the approach of that
      miracle.
I dare not let my soul go unsustained. Who doesn't know
How little these things are worth:
A tree full of singing cicadas, a pot of common wine.
Even the mention of misty mountains, valleys at dawn, or
      glittering starry skies,
Is no less commonplace, most worthlessly commonplace.
      They do not deserve
Our ecstatic surprise, our effort to call them in touching
      terms,
Our anxiety to coin golden phrases to cast them in song.
I, too, would say that to burst into tears because of an
      oriole's song
Is too futile, too impertinent, too wasteful.
Who knows that I *have* to do it: this heart is too hungry,
Forcing me to make believe, to use coarse cereals for fine
      viands.

I am ready to confess, the moment you—
The moment that miracle occurs, I shall at once abandon the
      commonplace
Never again will I, gazing at a frostbitten leaf,
      dream of the glory of a spring blossom.

Never will I squander the strength of my soul in peeling the
     stubborn rocks
In vain search of the sheen of jade; just give me a miracle,
I shall never again whip the "ugly" for the meaning
Of its opposite. In truth, I have long been tired
Of these doings, these brain-wracking implications.
I only ask for a plain word, jewel-like, radiating
Luster. I ask a whole, positive beauty.
Not that I am so stubborn or stupid that I cannot imagine
The angelic face behind the fan when I see a fan.
So—

I will wait for no matter how many incarnations—
Since a pledge has been made, also an unknown number of
Incarnations ago—I'll wait, without complaint, only quietly
     wait
For the arrival of a miracle. There must be such a day.
Let thunderbolts strike me, volcano blast me, the entire hell
Turn over to crush me . . . Afraid? Have no fear for me, as
No gusty wind can extinguish the lamp of the soul. To have
     this
Body turned into ashes is nothing because that is precisely
My one moment of eternity—a divine fragrance, a most
     mystifying
Silence (the sun, the moon, and all the stars are halted in
     their
Revolutions, even time stands still), a most perfect
     peace . . .
I hear the sound of a door latch, suddenly,
And from afar comes the rustling of a skirt—that then is the
     miracle—
In the half-opened golden gate, there you are, crowned with
     a halo.

1930
The Selected Works of Wen I-to, 89–92

HSÜ CHIH-MO (1895–1931)

"What do you think of it, Moon,
                As you go?
   Is Life much, or no?"
"Oh, I think of it, often think of it
                As a show.
"God ought surely to shut up soon,
                As I go."

                                    Thomas Hardy

"A little while and we die; shall life not thrive
                as it may?
   For no man under the sky lives twice, outliving
                his day."

                                    A. C. Swinburne

"O love, my love! If I no more should see
Thyself, nor on the earth the shadow of thee,
         Nor image of thine eyes in any spring—
How then should sound upon Life's darkening slope
The ground-whirl of the perished leaves of Hope,
         The wind of Death's imperishable wing?"

                                    D. G. Rossetti

THESE LINES find clear echoes in the poems of Hsü Chih-mo, the leader of the Crescent school, who is generally recognized as the greatest Chinese poet of his generation. He read them, translated them into Chinese, and molded his own thought around them. In the barely ten years of his productive (and prolific) life, he championed a total liberation of man's soul, a complete realization of man's pursuit of beauty, and an unreserved surrender of oneself to love. His burning anxiety to seek life's utmost fulfillment in defiance of any restriction was

prompted largely by Swinburne's impressionism; his exalta-
tion of love is close to Rossetti's erotic mysticism; but in his
praise of love and life seen in their most beautiful moments,
Hsü Chih-mo time and again betrays his feeling of futility
about both—and with a sigh sinks back to find comfort in
Hardy's stoic pessimism.

The talented and ebullient son of a Hsia-shih banker (in
Chekiang Province), Hsü acquired his faith in love, freedom
and beauty in a peculiar way. He had had adequate training
in the Chinese classics before he was exposed to the curricu-
lum of a Western-style college in Shanghai, had acquired a
facile command of classical Chinese, and had become one of
the favorite students of Liang Ch'i-ch'ao, (1873–1929), the
great patriarch of Chinese scholars at the turn of the century
and a man credited with ushering Chinese thought into the
modern era. Family background and influence conditioned
Hsü's early ambition to become a Chinese Hamilton. The
vision of a Rockefeller or Carnegie who built up an empire
charmed him, and he set out to study social science at Clark
University in Massachusetts in 1918. Later he transferred to
Columbia University. While en route to the new world, Hsü
wrote a long message on board the ship, expressing in a very
elegant classical language his determination to serve his coun-
try.[1] He addressed his pledge to do so to his parents and
friends at home. There is no doubt that he meant everything
he said in that message because the attitude he expressed is
the cornerstone of his basic philosophy of life—"The central
meaning of life," as he said in his credo later, "lies in sub-
jecting one's soul to endless adventures."[2]

It is not surprising that life in the United States did not
satisfy his restless soul. Having observed the ugly reality in his
native country, he now felt that he could not learn or "experi-
ence" enough in America. He believed in the spiritual su-
periority of man's soul and the existence of certain perpetual
truths which he wanted to find. As he declared in his "Fallen
Leaf," "We cannot let utilitarianism crush the soul of man

[1] Liang Shih-ch'iu, *About Hsü Chih-mo*, 19–22.
[2] In "Marching Forward," written in April, 1926. *Selected Works
of Hsü Chih-mo*, 163.

. . . or the superstition of the time (either religion or science) choke to death the unchanging value in the universe." This romantic longing for something to satisfy his inner anxiety could have driven him to the mountains of India, had it not been for his other equally strong belief in living an intense life. He went instead to England.

The poet, Mu Mu-t'ien, said of Hsü that his poetry is "but a reflection of the adventures of his soul."[3] This is true, but Hsü did not find his voice until the atmosphere of aristocratic idealism at Cambridge helped him to cultivate his poetic sensitivity. Hsü confessed in his "The Cambridge I Know": "My eyes were opened by Cambridge, my appetite for knowledge was stimulated by Cambridge, my concept of 'self' was nursed by Cambridge. . . ." From Thomas Carlyle he accepted the motto of "Everlasting yea," which strengthened his determination to "declare war against one's destiny." The kind of starry-eyed idealism he embraced was expressed in his almost childlike faith in the validity of absolute individualism: to assert oneself, to realize oneself, to find oneself, and to express oneself. He continued to search for the sublime and the ecstatic; something above the ordinary yet not of the other world. He was too committed to the Western this-world outlook on life. He said in his "Notes Written on the T'ien-mu Mountain," "We who acknowledge the baptism of the Western view of life are prone to take life very positively, to seek vigorously our involvement in this world and be unwilling to retreat. We thrust our burning hot bodies into the grindstone of life, and we do not want to save even one drop of blood unspent." It was in this spirit that he viewed the heroes of the East and the West. He praised the Christian martyrs and the Russian revolutionaries in the same breath, because he himself sought to "free" his own soul and imagination from all restrictive forces.

From Swinburne Hsü acquired a taste for the alliterative cadence of verse, and from the Bloomsbury group suggestions on the use of various new images. He met Katherine Mansfield and her associates. They and the peaceful beauty of Cam-

[3] *Selected Works of Hsü Chih-mo,* 2.

bridge decided him on a literary career. What he owed to
Cambridge he acknowledged in a farewell poem:

> I still take pride in having maintained the purity
> Of my soul in a culture of skyscrapers and fast cars,
>   and today
> Facing this historic land, with its shadows of bridges
>   and thick waterweeds
> I still can present my true self to say farewell.
> We met late, but in the past year
> The tides of revolution in my heart have all
> Surged along your charming banks. . . .
>
>   (from *The Complete Works of Hsü Chih-mo,* 37)

"The tides of revolution" involved more than his decision
to follow a literary career; they also reflected a severe inner
struggle in relation to his family life. He had married at the
age of twenty in China; his wife was from a very prominent
Chang family. She was intelligent and well-educated, but her
temperament was not suited to his. As he came to accept the
free pursuit of happiness as the supreme ideal, he began to
wonder about his loveless marriage. In March 1922, shortly
before his return to China, he wrote his wife that they must
be divorced. He was aware of the severe criticism Chinese
society would direct against a divorce case, but he felt his ac-
tion would bring "unprecedented glory" to the lives of both
parties. He asked his wife to "greet the light of life for both
of us" with the following plea:

> . . . True life must be sought by one's own effort and
> struggle; true happiness also must be sought by one's own
> effort and struggle; true love also must be sought through
> one's own effort and struggle. . . . We both have the will
> to reform society and create happiness for mankind. We
> must set examples ourselves, be brave, and respect each
> other's integrity. . . .[4]

When he returned from Europe, the marriage was dis-
solved, but he never heard the end of criticisms against him.
Even his celebrated teacher, Liang Ch'i-ch'ao, wrote him a

[4] *The Complete Works of Hsü Chih-mo,* 3.

long letter on January 2, 1923, urging him not "to build one's happiness upon others' suffering," and not "to pursue the perfect state of bliss in a dream."[5] Hsü's reply explained his action as an effort to "ease my conscience, maintain my integrity, and save my own soul." He maintained correspondence with and was more considerate than ever toward his former wife. This was very like him, but disconcerting to those who did not know him well.

He joined the faculty of the University of Peking and edited the literary page of the *Peking Morning News*, which soon became an open forum for the budding vernacular literature. His urbane polish and contagious enthusiasm about everything attracted a sizable group of admirers from both the literary circle and the social elite of Peking. All who met him say that he was the life of every party and the spirit of every organization he joined, and that he had a gift for making people work as a team.

Among his admirers, the fair sex was well represented, and a writer named Lin Hui-yin became his close friend. When Tagore visited China in April, 1924, Hsü and Lin were his constant traveling companions, and Hsü acted as his interpreter. His extemporaneous rendition of Tagore's words into Chinese was praised as a work of art.

Hsü Chih-mo was then at the height of his success—his essays and poems were distinguished for their original style, elegant language, and intense feeling, and he was regarded as a rapidly rising star in modern literature. His family was financially secure; the tumultuous social unrest and political upheaval had not yet affected him personally. In the midst of the ideological controversies raging on the literary front, Hsü and Wen I-to launched a *Poetry Journal* in April 1926 to "encourage the development of a suitable form" for the poetic creativity of modern Chinese people. "We recognize that within and outside us there are numerous thoughts that seek embodiment," Hsü wrote in the inaugural issue. "Our duty then is to build suitable bodies for them. . . . We believe that perfect form is the only manifestation of perfect essence."[6]

[5] Hu Shih's preface, *The Complete Works of Hsü Chih-mo*, 4–5.
[6] *Compendium*, II, 332–33.

Clearly the identification of Hsü's ideal with any concrete
course of action was difficult. Hsü was never ready to leave his
smoke-filled studio and his friends for either the battlefield or
the pulpit. When he had to name one thing as the sum-total
of all that he held precious, he could conceive of only love
in perfection, which would also be beauty in perfection, ac-
cording to his romantic view of life. Erotic mysticism, which
he had found in Rossetti, now began to emerge as his central
theme. In love, he found the purification and elevation he
had been seeking:

> Come with me,
> My love!
> The world of man has fallen behind us—
> Look, isn't this an immense ocean, with its
>   unlimited gleaming white?
> An immense ocean with its unlimited gleaming white,
> An immense ocean with its unlimited gleaming white,
>   Let's be in love and forever free!
>
> (from *Selected Works of Hsü Chih-mo*, 100)

The embodiment of these ideals appeared in his life in the
person of Lu Hsiao-man, a talented and vivacious young
woman already married. With her husband, a high-ranking
officer in the army, Lu had nothing in common; her marriage
had been arranged by her parents. When she met Hsü
Chih-mo in the summer of 1924, she realized that she had
been cheating herself all her life and decided that she "must
be true" to herself henceforth.[7] A stormy romance ensued.
Her parents were scandalized. They prevented her from see-
ing or receiving messages from Hsü. Criticism and opposition
made him all the more determined. To win her was a matter
of easing his conscience and saving his own soul, as he had
said on divorcing his first wife, and he was ready to sacrifice
everything to it. Then social pressure mounted, and he found
it necessary to leave the country for a while. He sailed for
Europe on March 10, 1925, traveled in France and Italy and
revisited England where he met Thomas Hardy. Separation
further aggravated the suffering lovers, as he admitted when
stopping on a mountain near Florence:

[7] Lu's diary in *The Complete Works of Hsü Chih-mo*, II, 44.

You cannot forget me, my love, only in your heart can I
Find my life; yes, I'll listen to you, and I'll wait,
Even if it is for the iron tree to bloom, still I'll wait.
(from *Selected Works of Hsü Chih-mo*, 58)

In Peking, Lu Hsiao-man threatened suicide several times
and finally succeeded in divorcing her husband. Upon Hsü's
return to China in 1926, they were married. Their wedding
has been recorded as probably the only one of its kind in
history because their witness, the celebrated Liang Ch'i-ch'ao,
delivered a blistering speech chastising Hsü Chih-mo in front
of all the guests, admonishing him to start all over again with
a clean slate as he had been too "shiftless in his love, which
resulted in the failure of his first marriage."[8]
In 1927 the Kuomintang troops under Chiang Kai-shek be-
gan their campaign against the warlords in the north. Nan-
king was occupied and Peking threatened. Hsü and most of
his friends went to Shanghai where they started the Crescent
Publishing House. The first publication was the *Crescent
Monthly*, a journal that has won an historic position in the
development of modern Chinese literature as the place where
most of the Crescent poets made their debuts under Hsü's
leadership. He wrote in the first issue identifying the new
journal with "creative idealism" and opposing all the prevail-
ing schools of literature in favor of a literature that protects
"the health and dignity of man's soul." He preferred, he
wrote, "reflecting on the eternity of virtue to savoring the
delicious flavor of sin," and to "view the grandeur of life
rather than carve a wine cup inlaid with gems," thus de-
nouncing both the art-for-art's-sake and the *fin-de-siècle*
school.
But even in this statement Hsü appears to have somewhat
modified his view of life and literature. Although he always
admitted that he was an incorrigible "wild horse," the events
since 1922 had a sobering effect on him.
He continued to write, somewhat less in quantity but with
greater mastery of his expressive power. His second marriage
brought him, as he had hoped, more adventures of the soul,
not all of them happy. The "Life" he had sought to live in-

[8] Liang Shih-ch'iu, *About Hsü Chih-mo*, 17.

tensely turned out to be more and more disappointing. An increasing gloom appeared in his lines. Reality was more stubbornly ugly than he had anticipated. "Gold, only gold is man's new darling," he said in "The Cricket," "ruling his day, lording over his dreams." He detested the endless arguments about politics that monopolized the printed page; he hated all that was banal and chaotic; he felt his own creative force ebbing:

> All I have now is a halting, broken breath; like one
> Of the mice trapped between a wall and a rafter,
> I chase after darkness and nothingness.
>
> (from *The Complete Works of Hsü Chih-mo,* 55)

Now and again he freed himself from the engulfing gloom and let his imagination soar once more to a dazzling height. These were the moments when he conceived of his unrestrained "spirit travel," as he described it in "Love's Inspiration":

> Away from this world I soar
> To somewhere unknown; there seems to be
> A cloud shaped like a lotus flower carrying me
> (On her face there is a lotuslike smile)
> To a place extremely distant from here . . .
> Ai, I really have no desire to return
> And that is perhaps what they call nirvana.
>
> (from *Selected Works of Hsü Chih-mo,* 28)

Nineteen twenty-nine and 1930 were his worst years. He was almost totally demoralized, and his friends kept suggesting that he try a change of environment. Early in 1931, Hu Shih returned to the University of Peking to serve as dean of the College of Arts and Letters and invited Hsü to teach there. In making his decision to accept, Hsü had already started on his "journey in the cloud."

He had always wanted to fly; as he had written earlier in an essay:

Everybody wants to fly. It is so tiresome to be crawling on earth all the time, not to mention anything else. Let's fly away from this circle! Fly away from this circle! To the

clouds! To the clouds! Who does not dream of soaring up
in the sky to watch the earth roll like a ball in infinite
space? . . . That alone is the meaning of being man, the
power of being man, and the worthy account of being man.
If this fleshy carcass of ours is too heavy to be dragged
along, throw it away. Wherever possible, fly away from this
circle, fly away from this circle!

(from *The Complete Works of Hsü Chih-mo*, II, 98)

Now his wish became a reality. He often commuted between
Shanghai and Peking by air. Air travel was still a dangerous
and expensive affair, but a good friend in the aviation com-
pany had presented him with a courtesy pass. On November
19, 1931 when he was en route from Shanghai to Peking, the
plane crashed in fog near the famous Mount T'ai in Shan-
tung Province. Hsü died at the age of thirty-six.

He left four collections of poems: *The Poems of Chih-mo*
(1925), *A Night in Florence* (1926), *The Tiger* (1930), and
Roaming in Clouds (1931); three volumes of essays, one
novel, one play, and a volume of his diary and letters.

SERVES YOU RIGHT, BEGGAR

"Kindhearted ladies, charitable sirs,"
> The northwest wind slashes his face like a sharp
> knife.
"Give me a little bit of your leftovers, just a little bit!"
> A patch of dark shadow curls up near the gate.

"Have pity, my wealthy lord, I'm dying of hunger."
> Inside the gate there are jade cups, warm fire and
> laughter.
"Have pity, my lord of good fortunes, I'm dying of cold."
> Outside the gate the northwest wind chuckles,
> "Serves you right, beggar!"

I am but a pile of black shadows, trembling,
Lying like a worm on the frontage road of humanity;
I wish only a bit of the warmth of sympathy
To shelter what's left of me, after repeated carving.

But this heavy gate stays tightly closed: Care who might?
In the street only the wind continues to ridicule,
    "Beggar, serves you right!"

          Before 1925 (?)
          Selected Works of Hsü Chih-mo, 73–74

THIS IS A COWARD'S WORLD

This is a coward's world:
    It tolerates no love, tolerates no love!
Let your hair down, then,
And take off your shoes,
    Follow me, my love,
To abandon this world
And die for our love!
I'll hold your hand,
My love, follow me;
    Let thorns pierce through our feet,
      And hailstones split our heads, if they wish;
Come along with me
While I hold your hand
    To flee this prison, to be free once again.

    Come with me,
      My love!
The world of man has fallen behind us—
Look, isn't this an immense ocean with its unlimited
        gleaming white?
An immense ocean with its unlimited gleaming white,
An immense ocean with its unlimited gleaming white,
    Let's be in love and forever free!

Follow my finger and look
Over there, the blue of a tiny star on the horizon—
    That's an island under a blanket of lush green,

Under an array of flowers, colorful animals and birds;
Hurry and board this swift bark
For that heaven of perfection—

To be in love, happy, and free—leaving this world of
man, forever.

1925 (?)
Selected Works of Hsü Chih-mo, 99–101

A NIGHT IN FLORENCE

You are really going tomorrow? Then I, I . . . well,
You don't have to bother, sooner or later there will be such a
day.
If you wish to remember me, then remember,
Or else forget, while there's still time, that I ever
Existed in this world so you won't be sad in vain when you do
recall.
Treat it as a dream, a fleeting hallucination;
Treat it as the withered blossoms we saw the day before
yesterday
That trembled in the wind, shedding one petal,
Then another. On the ground they lay, trodden by someone
into dust . . .
Ai, trodden by someone into dust—into dust, that'd be at
least clean-cut,
It's really torture to be neither living nor dead, to look
So shabby, unwanted, and to be the object of slighting
glances—
Heavens! Why should you do it, why should you do it. . . .
But I just cannot forget you. That day when you came,
It was like a ray of bright light in darkness.
You are my teacher, my love, and my savior.
You taught me what life is and what love is;
You brought me out of bewilderment back to my innocence;
Without you how could I ever know the sky is high and grass
green?

Feel my heart, see how fast it beats this moment; and
Feel my cheeks, see how hot they burn; fortunately in the
    dark night
Nobody can see them. My love, I cannot even breathe now,
Kiss me no more, this life aflame I cannot bear.
My soul at this moment is a chunk of hot iron on an anvil,
Being struck by the hammer of love, again and again,
Its sparks flying in all directions . . . I feel faint, please hold
    me,
My love, just let me die in your embrace with my eyes closed
In this quiet garden—how beautiful it would be!
The sound of the wind in the birch trees above, rustling,
Rings out a dirge for me; the breeze having come
From an olive grove, brings over the scent of pomegranate
    blossoms,
And takes away my soul. There are also the fireflies,
Sentimental fireflies who light up the way for me
As I halt my steps on the three-arched bridge to listen
To your grief-stricken calls: you hold in your arms my body
That's still warm, hugging it, kissing it, and tightly
        enfolding it . . .
With a smile I follow the breeze on my way again,
Letting it lead me to heaven, or hell, or anywhere,
So long as I leave this loathed human life to realize death
In love. Isn't this death in the embrace of love better
Than five hundred reincarnations? . . . Selfish? Yes, I know,
But I cannot bother now . . . Are you going to die with me?
What? If we are not together, the death cannot be "death in
    love."
To soar to heaven requires two pairs of wings beating in
    unison,
And even in heaven we need each other's care.
I cannot go without you, nor you without me; if it is to hell
That I descend, you would like it less for me to go alone.
You said that Hades is not more civilized than this world
(Though I don't believe it): a fragile flower like me
Surely will face the ravage of winds and rains, and then
Much as I may call you, you cannot hear—
Wouldn't that be plunging into a mire instead of gaining
    salvation,

Letting the unfeeling ghosts together with heartless human
      beings
Ridicule my fate, ridicule your timid carelessness?
This, too, has reason. Well, what shall I do then?
It's so hard to live, and yet unfree even in death, not to say
I do not want you to sacrifice your future for my sake . . .
Ai, you said it's still better to live and wait, wait for that day!
Is there going to be that day?—So long as you live, my faith
      remains;
But you have to go at daybreak, can you really bear
To leave me behind? I cannot detain you, this is fate.
Only we know that when a flower is without sunshine or dew,
Its petals will turn yellow and dry so pitifully!
You cannot forget me, my love, only in your heart can I
Find my life; yes, I'll listen to you, and I'll wait,
Even if it is for the iron tree to bloom, still I'll wait;
My love, you are a star above me shining forever.
If perchance I die I will change myself into a firefly
Hovering low in this garden, near the grass,
From dusk till midnight, and from midnight till dawn.
My only hope is that no cloud will come over the sky
So I may gaze at the sky, at that unchanging star—at you.
My only wish is that you shine more brightly for me through
      the night
And across the sky to link the hearts of love together. . . .

              June 11, 1925
              Selected Works of Hsü Chih-mo, 54–59

BEFORE EXETER CHURCH

This is my own shadow tonight
      Printed here in the courtyard before a church in a
      faraway land.
An imposing shrine so cold and solemn,
      And a shadow so slender and alone.

I ask the statue in front of the church:
      "Who is responsible for the strange course of man's
      life?"

The weathered statue stares at me, looking surprised,
    He seems to wonder: Why this odd question.

I turn to ask the chilly star
    That rises from the back of the building,
But it only responds with a sarcastic blinking of its eyes,
    Leaving me to face my puzzle under its pale light.

At this moment an old tree near me,
    Shelters the guiltless who lie under a tablet recording
    the war dead.
It heaves a long sigh that suggests
    A spell of lonely rain in the lonely courtyard.

It has witnessed the passage of over a hundred years,
    And has seen every vicissitude in the world of man.
It has kept account of the indifference of life:
    The exuberance of spring and summer, and the
    decline in winter.

It recognizes the oldest of the elders here in the village,
    Having watched their baptism when they were still
    fuzzy infants;
And watched their weddings, in the same church—
    And finally their names being inscribed on the
    tombstones.

It has already grown weary of watching the tragicomic farce,
    And it cares less for its own goitered remains.
It shares my feeling this moment, and with a long sigh—
    Ah, a number of fallen leaves have joined my shadow
    on the ground.

                        July 1925
                        Selected Works of Hsü Chih-mo, 44–46

LATE AT NIGHT

Late at night, around the street corner,
A dreamlike bloom of lamplight.

Mist bewitches and shrouds the tree;
No wonder people lose their way.

"What have you done to me—you cruel thing!"
She weeps; he—no answer.

The morning breeze rocks the treetop gently,
Gone is the red blossom in early autumn.

London, September 1925
The Crescent Monthly, Vol. I, No. 11

SECOND FAREWELL TO CAMBRIDGE

Quietly I am leaving
Just as quietly I came;
Quietly I wave a farewell
To the western sky aflame.

The golden willow on the riverbank,
A bride in the setting sun;
Her colorful reflection
Ripples through my heart.

The green plants on the river bed,
So lush and so gracefully swaying
In the gentle current of the Cam
I'd be happy to remain a waterweed.

The pool under an elm's shade
Is not a creek, but a rainbow in the sky
Crushed among the floating green,
Settling into a colorful dream.

In search of a dream? You pole a tiny boat
Toward where the green is even more green
To collect a load of stars, as songs
Rise in the gleaming stellar light.

But tonight my voice fails me;
Silence is the best tune of farewell;
Even crickets are still for me,
And still is Cambridge tonight.

Silently I am going
As silently I came;
I shake my sleeves,
Not to bring away a patch of cloud.

> On the China Sea, November 6, 1925
> *The Crescent Monthly*, Vol. I, No. 10

A SONG OF FALLEN LEAVES

A rustling sound whirled up the steps
(I was on the edge of dreamland;)
This time it must be her footsteps, I thought—
So late at night.

A rapping sound on my window
(I pressed close to the world of slumber;)
This must be her joke—you see, I
Certainly would remain calm!

A breathing sound approached my bed;
I said (half in dream, half in daze;)
"You never can understand me, why then must you
Give me more heartache!"

A sigh fell on my pillow
(I was already only lingering in the dream;)
"I did you wrong," you said—and your hot tears
Burned my cheek!

The sounds disquiet my sleep
(In the courtyard, the fallen leaves dance, again and again;)
The dream is over, ah, the awakening; what torments me
Is but the song of autumn.

> 1925
> *Selected Works of Hsü Chih-mo*, 107–8

"NO. 7, STONE TIGER LANE"

Sometimes in our little garden there ripples infinite
    tenderness.
Giggling vines bare their bosoms for the persimmon leaves to
    caress.
Elms, a hundred feet tall, stoop in the breeze to embrace the
    cherry-apple,
Our yellow dog at the hedge watches over his little friend,
    the sleeping Po-erh.
Little birds create their new mating tunes, singing without
    stop.
Sometimes in our little garden there ripples infinite
    tenderness.

Sometimes in our little garden there spreads a vague dream;
Misty shadows after rain and dark green weave into silent
    shade.
A little frog sits before withered orchids, listening to the
    earthworms next door.
A patch of lingering black cloud rolls and unrolls over the old
    elms,
Skimming along the eaves, whirling in waltz—are they dragon-
    flies or bats?
Sometimes in our little garden there spreads a vague dream.

Sometimes our little garden sighs gently, Ai—
Ai, under a brutal storm, countless blossoms are pounded to
    pulp by the rain.
Ai, in early autumn, leaves still green are already leaving the
    tree with regret.
Ai, in the depth of the night, the moon has already returned
    by a boat of cloud, way beyond the western wall.
Funeral music drifts by in gusts of cold wind from a distant
    alley—
Sometimes our little garden sighs gently, Ai—

Sometimes our little garden is immersed in infinite joy.
At dusk after rain, only pleasant shade, cool breeze and
    refreshing scent in the courtyard.
The heavy drinker, an old cripple, holds a huge cup in his
    hand, his bad foot pointing at the sky,
A pint, two pints, every cup is drained, his chest full of
    elation and his face all flushed.
In the ceaseless peal of laughter floats a godlike old drunkard.
Sometimes our little garden is immersed in infinite joy.

1925
Selected Works of Hsü Chih-mo, 77–78

IN SEARCH OF A BRIGHT STAR

On the back of a limping blind horse I ride,
    Heading toward the dark night;
    Heading toward the dark night,
I ride on the back of a limping blind horse.

I dart into the dark long night,
    To search for a brilliant star—
    And in order to search for a brilliant star,
I dart into the wilderness without a light.

Worn out, worn out is the horse I ride,
    Yet the star remains nowhere to be seen;
    The star remains nowhere to be seen,
While the rider is already tired, dead tired.

Now as a crystalline brilliance appears in the sky,
    A horse has fallen in the wilderness,
    And in the dark night lies a body cold—
Now as a crystalline brilliance appears in the sky.

1925
Selected Works of Hsü Chih-mo, 93–94

GO AWAY

Go away, world of man, go away!
  I alone stand on top of the mountain;
Go away, world of man, go away!
  I face an infinite sky.

Go away, youth, go away!
  To be buried with fragrant herbs in an unvisited vale;
Go away, youth, go away!
  Sorrow has been entrusted to crows in the evening mist.

Go away, dreamland, go away!
  I dash to pieces the jade cup of illusions;
Go away, dreamland, go away!
  I accept with a smile the tribute from the wind and the
    sea.

Go away, all and all, go away!
  Ahead lies a towering peak that pierces the sky!
Go away, all and all, go away!
  Ahead lies infinity of the infinite.

1925
Selected Works of Hsü Chih-mo, 97–98

I COME TO THE SHORE OF THE YANGTZE RIVER TO BUY A HANDFUL OF LOTUS SEEDS

I come to the shore of the Yangtze River to buy a handful of
    lotus seeds.
  I peel the skins of the seeds, layer after layer,
  While watching the gulls fly
  With my tearful eyes—
I think of you and think of you, ah, my Hsiao Lung.[9]

  [9] Hsiao Lung (Little Dragon) is a pet name Chih-mo gave to his
sweetheart, Lu Hsiao-man. He wrote in his diary on August 9, 1924:

I taste a lotus seed, the tenderness I have known once now
    returns:
    The ever-protective screens before the steps,
    Guarding the joy of two hearts beating together,
    And once again your pledge rings in my ear,
"I am yours forever, my body and my soul."

I taste the heart of a seed, my heart is bitterer than the
    seed's:[10]
    All night long I toss in pain,
    Trying to kill the nightmare in vain.
    Who knows my suffering?
It's all because of you, my love—how can I go through a day
    like this?

Yet I can neither blame you as unfaithful nor bear to guess
    you have changed.
    There is only tenderness inside me:
    You are mine, and I am as I used to be
    Embracing you closely, so very closely—
Unless the sky falls down—but who believes that can ever
    be arranged?

1925
Selected Works of Hsü Chih-mo, 52–53

WHAT EXACTLY IS THIS THING CALLED LOVE?

What exactly is this thing called love?
When it came I had not yet been born.
The sun shone for me for over twenty years,
I was only a child, knowing no sorrow at all.

"You are so exquisite, so lively. You truly resemble a little dragon."
The "dragon" image in English is so unbefitting that I leave it un-
translated.—Ed.

  [10] In Chinese, "my heart is bitter" means "I am suffering" and
does not connote "vengeful" or "hateful." The cotyledons of a lotus
seed are bitter in taste, hence the pun.—Ed.

Suddenly came the day—I loved and hated that day—
When in my heart something stirred; something was missing,
And that was the first time I felt this pain.
Some said it was a wound—now, you feel my chest—
When it came I had not yet been born,
What exactly is this thing called love?

From that time on I changed, a wild horse without a rein,
Galloping over the wilderness of humanity. I was
Like the Ch'u man of old who tried to offer his jade,
Who pointed at his heart and said, "There's truth there,
        there is!
Cut me open here, if you don't believe me, and see
If it isn't a jade, this thing dripping blood."[11]
Blood! That merciless cutting, and my soul!
Who is he that forces me to ask this final question?

What a question! This time I'm glad my dream is over.
God, I'm not ill, no longer shall I groan before you.
No longer shall I long for the ethereal; I've no share in
        paradise;
I only want the earth, and to live plainly and honestly.
Never again shall I ask what exactly is this thing called love;
Since when it came I had not yet been born.

                    1925
                Selected Works of Hsü Chih-mo, 63–64

THE JOY OF THE SNOWFLAKE

If I were a snowflake,
Drifting freely in the sky,
        I'd make sure of my direction—
        To fly, and fly, and fly—
There is a direction for me on earth.

[11] Refers to the legend about a man named Ho, of the third
century B.C., who knew that a perfect piece of jade was in a huge
rock. He tried to offer it to the king of the state of Ch'u, south of
the Yangtze River, but was ridiculed and even penalized before the
rock was finally cut open and he was vindicated.—Ed.

I won't go to the lonely sequestered vale,
I won't go to the foothill so quiet and cool,
      Nor shall I loiter sadly in a deserted street—
      I'll just fly, and fly, and fly—
You see, I have my direction.

Gracefully I shall dance in the sky
Until I've spotted that pleasant place,
      Until she comes out to see the garden—
      I'll fly, and fly, and fly—
Ah, there is a subtle scent of the plum blossom on her.

Then I'll count on my body being so light
Gently I'll cling to the lapel of her robe,
      I'll cling close to the soft waves of her bosom—
      To melt away, and melt away, and melt away—
Melt into the soft waves of her bosom.

> 1925
> *Selected Works of Hsü Chih-mo*, 110–11

A P'I-PA TUNE IN AN ALLEY AT MIDNIGHT

Again waking me up from a dream, a tune of p'i-pa in the still
      of the night!
      Whose sorrowful thought,
      And whose fingers,
Like a gust of chilly wind, a spell of depressing rain, and
      a shower of falling petals,
      So late at night,
      In so drowsy a world,
Are strumming the taut chords to send forth these disturbing
      notes
      To blend into the night in the deserted street,
      While a waning moon hangs on top of a willow tree?
Ah, the sliver of a moon, a shattered hope, and he, he . . .
      Wearing a tattered cap,
      With clanking chains on his back,
Laughs and dances on the path of time like a mad soul.

That's all, he says, blow out your lamp,
She is waiting for you beyond her grave,
Waiting for you to kiss her, to kiss her again, and again.
1926
Selected Works of Hsü Chih-mo, 50–51

THE CRICKET

You, cricket, what are you here for? Mankind
No longer knows the old leisure.

Green grass, white dew, a littly silly now,
No use any more, these poet's toys.
Gold, only gold is man's new darling,
Ruling his day, lording his dreams.
Love like daylight—lingering stars
Long ago retired, vanished long ago.
Nor do the stars return at dusk,
Forever the black clouds hang beneath the sky.
Humility, too, has taken leave,
Gone to the desert, there to make her home.
The blossoms may open, but no fruit forms,
Dogma cruelly ravishes thought.

Don't complain that time is crawling:
There's ill-luck behind you right on your heels.
For a good half of this, blame the malice of the soul,
Who likes to get away, to attend to his garden.
"Leave them," says he, "let them wallow deeper,
Let them change to dogs, change to swine or frogs or
            maggots.
When the time comes, when the sun hides in shame,
When the moon has lost the wish to return from the wane,
When that day comes, when the spirit of man is dead,
Then I shall strike—strike the signal for revolt!"

Autumn 1927
The Crescent Monthly, Vol. I, No. 1
(Translated by Cyril Birch)

SPRING ENDING

Yesterday the peach-blossoms arranged here in my vase
Were smile after dimpled smile on the soft cheeks of a girl.
Today their heads are lowered, their whole appearance
    altered,
Pink and white the corpses dangle from each green stem.

Outside the wild weather proclaims that spring is dying
And through the black of night, a clanging like a knell:
"The vase which is your life holds flowers, and these also
Are changed: and who shall dress them, gorgeous corpses, for
    the grave?"

1928
The Crescent Monthly, Vol. I, No. 3
(Translated by Cyril Birch)

THE REBIRTH OF SPRING

Last night
As already the night before
Spring
Took possession of Winter's dead body.

Don't you feel the yielding underfoot?
Don't you feel the mild breath at your temples?
On the branches, a wash of green,
Ripples on the pond, endlessly weaving,
And for both of us, through our limbs,
In our breast, a new kind of beating;

On your cheeks already the peach-blossoms open,
And ever more keenly I gather to me
Your beauty, drink down
The bubbling of your laughter.

Don't you feel these arms of mine
Ever more insistent, demanding to hold you?
My breath homing to strike against your body
As though a myriad of fireflies swarmed to the flame?
All these, and so many more beyond the telling
Join with the eager wheeling of the birds
And hand in hand unite to hymn
The rebirth of Spring.

> February 28, 1929
> *The Crescent Monthly*, Vol. II, No. 10
> (Translated by Cyril Birch)

NIGHT TRAIN

Pressing to its rails through the night the train speeds
Past hills, past streams, past tombs of the ancient dead,

Over bridges, making concrete pillars groan and shake,
Past waste land, past temples with peeling crumbling gates,

Past pools of black water where the frogs beat their drums,
Past the unrelieved darkness of the lockjawed farms,

Past a chilly little station to which no travellers come,
The platform laying open its nakedness, like sin.

By now the train's screeching has woken a little group
Of stars, who find rifts in the clouds to dodge and peep.

'What is this thing up to,' the stars begin to wonder,
'That takes no rest at night, but shouts and snorts in anger?

'This snake-like creature, breathing fiery sparks,
Careless of danger, plunging through the murk,

'All its trust in two narrow lines, some kind of rails,
Mindful of the nightmarish burden it must haul?'

—Burden! These curious, good-hearted folk,
Who have set their minds at ease, and sprawl now asleep,

Pass to the train's keeping their high or humble fates
And care not whether now they climb hills or circle lakes,

Nor whether in the forest monstrous birds curse and scream,
Nor whether the shining planets are marching to their doom;

All they want is peace now, to snore with hanging jaw—
Tomorrow they'll arrive, grab their bags and off once more!

'And that's the way to be! For sorrow is bottomless;
You and I spinning here, no chance to take our ease,

'Our eyes open wide, seeing all things clear and bright,
Yet what hope have we of ordering our fate?

'Light, wisdom, beauty—how can we be so grand?
We like they are prisoners, bound by a single bond.

'No doubt you and I enjoy a greater span of years—
Yet what a silly object, this plaything universe!'

> *The Complete Works of Hsü Chih-mo*, 60–61
> (Translated by Cyril Birch)

TWO MOONS

The moons I gaze on are two,
Like in kind, unlike in form:
One even now displays her cloak
Of feathers as she mounts the sky.
Not grudgingly are her favours given:
Her gold and silver cover the earth.
She remembers the roofs of the empty palace,
The Three Lakes share her limpid light.
She leaps from the screening cloud, leaps to the treetop,
Hides now in the wistaria's fresh green,
So delicate, so lovely is she,
The depths must be filled with tipsy fish!

And yet, she has one little failing,
Always she must dwindle to a shade;
Sometimes the sky is left to the stars,
Gone that round bewitching face,
Although, when the time comes, she will return,
The longing to see her can be hard to bear!

The other moon our eyes do not see
Though her beauty is beyond our praise.
She too has her dazzling smile,
She too her subtly wheeling path;
Nor, in her lavishness, must she yield to the other
—If only you could see the trees in my garden!
How precious, her boundless magic power,
The waves of my spirit drawn by its pull;
I joy in the crashing of silver billows,
The tinkling of bells in the flying spray,
And like horse-tails white flecks of foam
With all the glitter of clear-cut gems.
Full moon of perfect beauty
Whose fullness knows no wane!
I have only to close these eyes of mine
To see her, queen-like, mount the sky!

The Complete Works of Hsü Chih-mo, 67–68
(Translated by Cyril Birch)

MOON-GAZING

Ah, the moon. Through the gauze window curtain in the dark
I watch her freeing herself from the craggy mountain peaks—
A disc of light, still half asleep, still unkempt.
Like a frightened maid guarding her chastity,
Struggling away from the claws and fangs of a brute.

She reminds me of you, my love, and how once
You were gritted between fate's cruel jaws.
Yet now, also like the bright moon in the sky,
You have already risen to the peaks of happiness
To flood with your brilliance the pitfalls of earth.

The Complete Works of Hsü Chih-mo, 24

from LOVE'S INSPIRATION

For a long time I have been gazing at death itself.
Since the day the bond of love was sealed in my heart
I have been gazing at death—
That realm of perpetual beauty; to death
I happily surrendered myself because
It is the birth of the brilliant and the free.
From that moment on I scorned my body
And even less did I care
For the floating glory of this life;
I longed to trust my breath to time
Even more infinite than it.
Then my eyes would turn into the glittering stars,
And my glistening hair, the clouds that are draped
All over the sky. Buffeting winds would
Whirl in front of my chest, before my eyes;
Waves would lap at my ankles, their sacred luster
Surging with each breaker!
My thoughts would be the lightning
That whips up a dance of dragons and snakes on the horizon;
My voice would thunder, suddenly awakening
The Spring and awakening life. Ah!
Beyond imagination, beyond compare
Is love's inspiration, love's power.

1930
The Complete Works of Hsü Chih-mo, 82–92

CHU HSIANG (1904–33)

VERY FEW modern Chinese writers have taken their own lives, but Chu Hsiang was one of them.

At home in Anhwei Province between the ages of six and ten, he had a private tutor who taught him classical Chinese literature; later he went to a village tutor some distance from the Chu house. He was not particularly bright, but he managed to get through the regular curriculum and even to the point of trying to compose essays in the classical style. At the age of eleven, he enrolled in a "modern" school.

His schooling, however, was quite irregular and repeatedly interrupted. Between his elementary school study and a career of college teaching, he spent brief periods in a vocational school studying engineering, and took English courses in a night school. The only interest that he maintained throughout was novel-reading. He started with the historical and picaresque, and was enchanted with Scott, Stevenson, and Henryk Sienkiewicz, the Polish writer. For a time he devoured all the detective stories he could get hold of, but quickly moved on to stories of love and other greater complexities of life. In sharp contrast to Ping Hsin, the woman poet, Chu Hsiang considered *The Dream of the Red Chamber* the greatest of all Chinese novels.

When he turned eighteen, he vowed that he would read nothing but poetry. He abandoned a number of his youthful projects to write stories but concentrated on verse, some of which appeared in literary magazines. Tu Fu, the famous T'ang Dynasty poet, and Shakespeare were his models. He completed his schooling at Tsing Hua University in Peking and the University of Chicago. Upon his return to China he taught English literature at the University of Anhwei. His attempt at a long poem, "Wang Chiao," was well received. Two collections of his verse were published in 1925 and 1927 and a third after his death.

Short lyrics are his specialty—clear, crisp ringing verse in
short lines and short stanzas. He was a purist in handling the
language, and he criticized his fellow poets including Wen
I-to and Hsü Chih-mo for being loose and sloppy. Chu
Hsiang himself experimented with various techniques for de-
veloping a new prosody for the vernacular language; he be-
lieved that his efforts were much more vigorous than those of
his fellow Crescent poets—Wen and Hsü. In his translation
of Shelley's poems, Chu tried to recreate the original Eng-
lish metrical scheme, and his success, while not complete, was
sufficient to impress Professor Cyril Birch, who called Chu
Hsiang an "exquisite craftsman."[1]

He was never quite happy with himself and the world. As
he wrote shortly before his death, "I am really an odd man.
I have succeeded in being neither a bookworm nor a person
adjusted to this world."[2] Teaching at the University of An-
hwei satisfied him only for a time. He left to roam around for
about a year, and then drowned himself in the Huang-p'u
River near Shanghai on December 4, 1933.

BURY ME

Bury me in a lotus pond
So that the eels may swish by my ears,
While on the lanterns—the green lotus leaves,
Fireflies flicker, now dim, now bright.

Bury me under the acacia flowers
So I may have sweet dreams forever;
Or bury me on top of Mount T'ai
Where the wind wails over a lone pine.
Or burn me to ashes and scatter me
In a river where spring tides are surging high,
So I may drift away with fallen petals
To a land that nobody knows.

February 2, 1925
Compendium, 295–96

[1] "English and Chinese Metres in Hsü Chih-mo," *Asia Major*,
New Series, Vol. VIII, Part 2, 1961, 259–60.
[2] *Chung shu chi*, 168.

REMINISCENCE

The pale yellow receding sunset
Disappears in a wink of the eye.
Stilled are all motions,
Hushed all sounds.

A crow, already asleep,
Utters a throaty gurgle in the wind;
The silent, serene evening tide
Has overrun the whole city.

Street lamps aglow—a light blush,
An eagle glides down from the rampart,
Beneath the white blanket of mist at dusk
Rests the purple Chung mountain.

Through deserted alleys and lanes
Shaded by walls of palatial houses,
T'ang, sings the bamboo tube
Of an old dumpling peddler.

> May 15, 1925
> *Compendium*, 298

THERE IS A GRAVE

There is a grave,
In front of it grow wild thickets,
There is a grave,
The grass under the wind crawls like a snake.

There is a dot of firefly,
Encircled by darkness,
There is a dot of firefly,
Blinking its bean-size glow.

There is a strange bird
Hidden in the shade of a gigantic tree,
There is a strange bird
Mourning in a voice unheard in this world.

There is a hook of pale moon,
Peeping from behind dark clouds,
There is a hook of pale moon,
Suddenly sinking beyond the hill.

August 17, 1925
Compendium, 297–98

HOMECOMING

The setting sun shines on the fields in late autumn,
A long shadow moves down the middle of the road;
Leaves, withered and dry, sigh in the wind
And land on the old uniform of a homecoming soldier.

With a caw a crow flies over the man's head,
As its fledglings call it from the tree above,
They are saying that the nest is warm, and food plenty,
Why does their father stay away, not coming home?

Golden sparks and white smoke rise from the chimney,
Pots and pans ring from behind the walls,
The sweet scent of rice drifts outside the gate,
The womenfolk at home are awaiting those who are to
    return.

From down the road comes a buffalo herder
Walking, leading his animal behind.
The boy sees him and stares at him
With eyes half curious and half afraid.

The old soldier recalls how in his youth
He proudly rode on horseback together with his young
    friends,
They joined the army, together they went beyond the Great
    Wall,
And all, except him, have become bleached bones on the
    frontier.

A farmer passes by, with a smile on his face,
But his expression changes the moment he sees the soldier;
His eyebrows now knotted in a deep frown, he stares
And stares at the soldier with eyes of enmity.

He cannot blame the farmer, for twenty years before,
Wouldn't he, himself, have clenched his teeth when
    encountering a soldier?
Fortunately, by tomorrow evening he will have removed
His uniform to pick up again his plowshare.

The sun sinks in the midst of distant blue hills,
Only a thread of afterglow still hangs on the tree;
Evening haze fills the valley and covers the fields,
The chirping of the insects tugs at the traveler's heart.

Look, a birch tree is looming up in front of him,
And below that tree, there is a ring of adobe walls.
Although the gate is tightly closed to him,
Joy has already filled his heart to the brim.

He thinks of his mother who must be staring at a lonely
    lamp,
Gazing at the burned wick while thinking of someone far
    away.
And father must be studying the stems of tea leaves,
Predicting the arrival of an important visitor today.[3]

[3] It is a Chinese folk belief that the shape of the burned wick in
an oil lamp reveals things about to come, and that the position of
tea leaves in a bowl also can serve the same purpose.—Ed.

The old soldier recalls how his wife cried
When he left—they had been married only a half month:
Possibly she is at this moment wondering
Why her eyelids have been twitching all day.[4]

As he thinks of these things his heart skips a beat,
Joy and sorrow surge in his heart at the same time.
No longer can he see the road before him clearly:
Tears, restrained for twenty years, now come streaming
    down.

Daylight outside the gate grows dim, yet
People inside do not hasten to open the door.
He taps and taps, no matter how loudly he pounds,
The sound of his knocking falls on a deep silence.

A dog responds from inside with its loud barking,
And louder barking follows more persistent pounding.
When the man outside stops knocking on the door,
The dog inside also ceases making noise.

"Who is it?" A feeble voice is heard calling from within
    It moves out of the hall and halts on the steps.
"Who is it? Is there someone looking for shelter overnight?
    Or a good neighbor stopping in for a visit?"

"Mother, it's me, not anybody looking for a room;
    We have been so poor, when did we ever have close
        neighbors?
    (Ah, mother must be getting old, let me say it louder.)
Mother, I'm your very own boy!"

"Son? You disappeared over twenty years ago,
    How can you still be alive in this world?
    Ah, I know, but your mother is so very poor,
    How can I afford to burn more paper money for you?[5]

[4] The Chinese people say that the involuntary twitching of eyelids
foretells unusual events.—Ed.
[5] Traditionally burned for the benefit of the dead.—Ed.

"Son, after you became a soldier and died far away,
  Your father and wife followed you to the other world.
  Ah, son, how cruelly you three left me all alone,
  Alone to cry my heart out among the living."

"Mother, I'm not dead, I'm still here!
  You must have just heard the dog's barking.
  The more I pounded on the door the louder it barked,
  If a ghost approached, it would only whimper slowly."

"Son, I did not expect you to return alive;
  What a pity your wife should have poisoned herself.
  Ah, son, although I have waited till your return,
  My eyes, ah, my eyes can see no more.

"Let me, then, touch you with my hands—
  Why have your cheeks become so thin?
  Son, you hear the night wind howl over the grass,
  Why don't you come in to rest your tired feet?"

The sky has turned dark and gloomy outside the gate,
  The moon and the stars have disappeared from the sky.
  In the blurred twilight one can only see
  Two neglected graves covered by tall weeds.

April 11, 1926
Compendium, 304–7

WINTER

Bare branches curl up in the icy air,
A few lingering leaves sway on the twigs,
The singing birds fly south leaving their empty nests behind—
      The tree is silent
      As it dreams
Of midsummer tonight.

Only thick hoary frost spreads all over the world,
Only a disc of chilly moon hangs in the sky,
Where the fair lunar goddess sleeps alone in her sequestered
     palace—
     The moon becomes dim
     As it dreams
Of the fragrant laurels.

July 1933
Literature, Vol. I, No. 1, 177

THE PAWNSHOP

Beauty runs a pawnshop,
Accepting only the hearts of men.
When the time comes for them to redeem their belongings,
She has already closed the door.

Wen, *Complete Works, Hsin,* 655

A RAINY SCENE

Many a rainy scene I love:
The trickle in front of the window that taps on my dream in
     spring;
The spattering sound on banana leaves—that crisp ring;
The fine sprinkle that caresses my cheeks like fog;
And the cloudburst that pours down from the lightning—
I love them all, but above all, the moments just before the
     rain comes.
They are the moments, gray but pristine, translucent,
And pregnant with silent expectation,
While from the clouds, from somewhere unknown
Comes the clear call of a bird.

Wen, *Complete Works, Hsin,* 655

JAO MENG-K'AN (1901?–   )

A. E. HOUSMAN's influence on the Crescent school is most clearly seen in Jao Meng-k'an who gained acceptance among the Crescent poets in the early 1920s by translating that poet's simple, gemlike short stanzas. Jao's translation of Housman's "Culprit"[1] is a technically perfect reproduction of the original in its clear rhythm and ringing rhyme. The first stanza of this poem

> The night my father got me
> > His mind was not on me;
> He did not plague his fancy
> > To muse if I should be
> > The son you see.

was rendered by Jao as follows:

> Na wan-shang fu-ch'in ch'u te-che wo,
> > T'a ch'üeh ling yu pieh-te hsin ch'ing;
> Na shih-hou t'a chen mei-yu hsiang-tao
> > Tzu-chi-te erh-tzu tao ju chin
> > Hui che-yang pu-chang-chin.[2]

Even the lengths of the translated lines parallel the original. The total effect of the poem comes through remarkably well and does justice to Housman. It is a tour de force of translation and must have been a painstaking piece of work. Such discipline prepared Jao Meng-k'an to write his own poems with the same crystal quality. It is a pity that this poet of Kiangsi Province turned away from poetry too soon.

[1] *Last Poems,* XIV.
[2] *The Crescent Monthly,* Vol. I, No. 5.

MARCH 18[3]
ON THE BLOOD SHED AT THE IRON LION LANE

"Son, you come here." "Yes, Mother."
"Why do you walk with your robe rolled up?"
"I made it a bit dirty on the way home.
 It isn't much though, I'll just change it."
"Where is your brother, why hasn't he come home with you?"
"He, well, he probably wasn't running as fast as I . . .
 It's nothing, Mother, nothing, he—he—
 He knows his way home by himself, doesn't he?"
"No; last night I dreamed of your brother . . .
 And when I woke up I heard the crows caw . . ."
"I'd say, Mother, you mustn't be superstitious.
 How could the crows affect the affairs of man?"
"Why are your eyes so swollen and all red?"
"Ah, the sand in them is hurting me badly."
"O! Is that blood on your robe, is it?"
"A moment ago, eh, I ran into someone butchering a lamb."
"Son, you, you are telling a lie, you are!
 Tell me what happened to him, what exactly . . ."

> 1926
> Wen, *Complete Works, Hsin,* 653–54

UNTITLED

Even if the world never knows our true identity,
We shall not pass a single day in vain.
Ask those fleeing from the islands to the valleys,
Has any one of them escaped from this prison?
        Why then do you still sigh with sorrow?

[3] On March 18, 1926, Peking police clashed with students and other demonstrators who protested against government policies yielding to the demands of foreign powers. Over forty died and about 200 were injured.—Ed.

Since the world cannot tolerate our true identity,
We might as well go on with spirit and gusto.
You be a songstress, carrying a little drum,
And I dress myself like a traveling musician—
     At the sound of the strings you'll start to sing.

                         April 9, 1926
                         Wen, *Complete Works, Hsin,* 653

THERE IS AN OLD HORSE

There is an old horse, there is an old horse;
It cannot count the battles it has won
This old horse, this old horse,
So pitifully—look—falls in the wind and snow

With nobody feeling sorry. Nobody feels sorry.
Only a "sympathetic" hungry buzzard circles above.
Speak not of pity, speak not of pity,
For once, it too had flaunted its elegant harness in the
     spring wind.

Like a falling star, like a falling star,
In the dark of the night it had stormed hundreds of miles of
     enemy camps.
Like a falling star, and like a falling star
Its heroic soul has now lost its luster.

It issues a long neigh, with only a long neigh
It disappears forever at this precise moment.
It issues a long neigh, and it's this very long neigh
That has recalled its majesty on the battlefield of old:

Like collapsing pillars, like collapsing beams,
Look, those numerous warriors fall at the sound of its
     approach.
Like collapsing pillars, like collapsing beams,
And you see this time Fate rides on its back, and together they
     tumble.

There is an old horse, there is an old horse;
It cannot count the battles it has won
This old horse, this old horse,
So pitifully—look—dies in the wind and snow.

April 10, 1928
The Crescent Monthly, Vol. I, No. 2

HELLO!

Once in the depth of a birch grove
I heard a "Hello" that sounded familiar.
The moon was shining on a stone statue,
And the statue was staring at me.

I waited to hear that "Hello" again, but in vain,
Startled, I searched all around.
There was only the statue staring at the moon,
And the moon grinning coldly at me.

July 27, 1928
The Crescent Monthly, Vol. I, No. 6

PILGRIMAGE

I've heard of the sacred mountain for a long time
Today I went there with a group of pilgrims:
Holding high the boxes of incense, we found
Our way up the mountain step by step.

The mountain wind blew and I shivered;
Strangely the incense smoke was undisturbed.
It rose quietly toward the sky as we walked
In single file one after another.

This prodded me to feel still more pious,
To conquer another series of craggy hills.
Lo, a peal of temple bells started suddenly
From somewhere beyond this world.

At a distance I made out clearly the top of the hill,
And I knew the ancient temple lay not far ahead.
I followed everyone entering the gate and did
As they all did—making a wish.

Nothing out of the ordinary happened to me,
I have offered incense to the gods in vain;
Everyone came home in glee but I
Returned with infinite dejection.

> 1929
> *The Crescent Monthly*, Vol. II, No. 12

SUMMONING THE SOUL
In Memory of My Friend Yang Tzu-hui

Come, don't hesitate,
While the roosters have not yet crowed.
Look at the lamplight in the distance
Flickering like a fisherman's torch, now dim, now bright—
Under that light I'm waiting for you.
Come, then, don't hesitate.

Come, why do you pace the ground over there?
I have made for you a pot of light tea.
Look at these storks, one by one
Winging their way over the surface of the pot—
Doesn't all this look like the old days?
Come, why do you pace the ground over there?

Come, you don't have to wonder any more;
While I'm lost in thought, unsuspecting,
You need only drift over gently
Like a leaf falling beneath the steps outside
To give me an unexpected pleasant surprise.
Come, you don't have to wonder any more.

> Wen, *Complete Works, Hsin*, 652–53

CH'EN MENG-CHIA (1911–   )

A FAVORITE student of Hsü Chih-mo and Wen I-to, Ch'en Meng-chia completed his apprenticeship in poetry in the Crescent school. He had started preparing himself for a career in law but stopped his law studies upon his graduation from the Central University of Nanking in 1930. The influence of his father, a Protestant clergyman in Shang-yü (in Chekiang Province), led him toward theology for a brief period in Yenching University, but the approach of war brought him to Shanghai in 1932. This began his most productive period in poetry.

His poems are clear and crisp, and their simplicity reflects his excellent craftsmanship. He takes hold of simple images and, without any pretension to profundity, turns them into thought-provoking lines that invite repeated reading and are easily remembered. He seems to have succeeded as well as that penetrating essayist, Chou Tso-jen, in seeing the significant in the insignificant, and he says it in infinitely better verse than Chou's. Hu Shih, upon reading Ch'en Meng-chia's works in 1931, admitted that modern Chinese poetry had gone much farther in the thirteen years since he had first started to promote it than he had dared to hope.[1] Hu admired the elevated tone and originality of the younger writer's poems.

If Ch'en had stayed with poetry, he undoubtedly would have been among the foremost later Crescent poets. Instead, in the late 1930s he turned to historical research, through Wen I-to's influence, and never again wrote poetry. In addition to a long poem entitled "At the Beginning" (1934), he published two collections, *The Poems of Meng-chia* (1931) and *The Wind Chimes* (1933).

[1] Hu Shih, "On the Poems of Meng-chia," *The Crescent Monthly*, Vol. III, Nos. 5–6.

A WILD FLOWER

A wild flower blooms and falls in the wilderness,
Its life so tiny you cannot see it, yet it smiles to the sun.
The wisdom given it by God, it knows,
As its joy and its poetry sway gently in the wind.

A wild flower blooms and falls in the wilderness,
It sees the blue sky but not its own humility.
It is accustomed to hearing the wind's tenderness and the
        wind's angry roar.
Even its own dreams, it is prone to forget.

January 1929
Wen, *Complete Works, Hsin,* 659

HESITATION

In darkness you held my hand,
You hesitated, nor did I move.
I said nothing, as words remained in my throat,
And a breeze made me shiver slightly.

A soft breath issued from your mouth; I felt
It pass through my body and my heart;
I yearned to keep that moment forever,
But it fled without a pause.

1929
The Crescent Monthly, Vol. II, No. 9

ON A DEWY MORNING

Quietly I wound my way along that narrow path,
Not daring to knock down a single pearl of dew.
O, that? That was a soft breeze passing by,
        Not I, not I!

Secretly I hid the spell of a quickened heart-beat,
Not daring to let fly a bird of hope.
O, that? That was a soft breeze passing by,
     Not I, not I!

I shouldn't have paced here all alone; last night
Who put up those decorations on the flower vines?
     They must have been arranged for someone else.

I went through the evergreen trees and left quietly,
Burying myself in the midst of the willow twigs.
     They must have been arranged for someone else.

     April 1930
     The Crescent Monthly, Vol. II, No. 12

THE WILD GEESE

I love the wild geese in autumn,
That know no weariness all night long,
(They seem to be reminding you, seem to be answering you)
As they call, as they fly afar.

Never do they ask on which patch of cloud
Their songs have been left behind.
They only sing along and fly along—
Dark is the sky, and light their wings.

I'd rather be a wild goose
To forget all and all—
And whenever I mention it, whenever I think of it,
It is neither laughter nor tears.

     October 1930
     Wen, *Complete Works*, Hsin, 659–60

I SEE YOU AGAIN

I see you again. A falling star of November
Disappeared; someone points to the sky and sighs.
The star itself only awaits the decree of its destiny,
Without thinking what next, without wondering about
The reason of that unpredictable delightful flash.
It lets light rush through the sky proudly for the last moment
Without asking when it will end
In destruction never to reappear. It retains
Its faith to dream of that moment of indulgence in
     liberation.
Glory glitters only within its heart and it bothers not
About turning into a gray rock—this death
Reveals the beginning of change in life.
Who says that one flash is not eternity?
     I saw the falling star, and I look at you again:
Like a flashing light you dart across my heart and again I see
Those days of mine that will never return.
In those days since I first saw you, I repeated
Your name, morning and night, and a flow of warmth
Like spring spread over my heart. In those days
I saw you—I only gazed at you,
Watching you in front of me, without saying a word.
Many a night I spent pacing the street while
Gazing at the wall of your house and that light,
Thinking you must be there. My sighs
You did not hear; only the lamp before the door
Feebly awaited and expected the dawning
That would not occur. Sadder still
Was the call of a swan flying low
Through the darkened sky, as I stood
Below the bridge. In those days I also
Sauntered along the seashore, unable
To restrain my tears, as God would bear me witness.
Before me the sea flaunted its strength
Of which I had none, absolutely none: I only

Dared not see the sea again, or the sky again,
As my shadow trailed me all the way home.
            I've forgotten none of these, none
At all: I remember all clearly as if it were right before my
            eyes—
In those days I wished I were
A humble blade of grass with the dewdrops spelling out
My heaven. But you left only a blurred
And confusing track which I wanted to trace;
I have no grudge against heaven. I waited
And waited for you to return, just once more,
Even if it were only your tears and your hate.
Yet it was not until autumn when I saw
A light leap back on my barren branches.
You were gleaming white, unchanged was your purity.
I heard the fallen leaves and you together
Approach me, knocking on my door;
You asked to stay once more.
I had already decided to await the arrival of winter
To freeze me in my love to form a perpetual silence.
This time I could not think it over again
As I heard the tiny buds of blue sky
Push through the solid earth, groping their way,
And their tiny voices softly calling
"I'm seeing you again, seeing you again."

                    November 25, 1930
                    The Crescent Monthly, Vol. III, No. 4

AN ABANDONED ROAD TO THE CHI-MING TEMPLE

This is a road leading to heaven;
Flanking it, two rows of ancient trees shoring up the sky.
            Crows flying high like dark smoke;
                The sound of meditative temple bells pursues
                    northern winds.
I want to go to the midst of the white clouds,
To the blue void, not solid ground.

Ah, ocean, I can gaze at your shore;
And mountain, I climb to your top to shout . . .
> The wind of karma levels cities thousands of years old,
> Where can one find again the sages and heroes?
I want to go to the midst of the white clouds,
To the blue void, not solid ground.

> January 1932
> Wen, *Complete Works*, Hsin, 661

SHADOW

It is the shadow of a tree,
Step by step it shifts.
Perhaps there is something on its mind,
Perhaps it is unwilling to see
> The moon move from east to west.

At first it lay on the dirt,
Then it seemed to be rising up,
And slowly it embraced the branches of the tree.
At last it fell under the tree again
> When the moon had already sunk in the west.

> December 1932
> Wen, *Complete Works*, Hsin, 662–63

THE WESTERN HILL

How many white pines are there, rustling in the wind?
How many strands of cloud, like gauze, hanging on the pine
> branches?
How many mountain creeks whispering secretly to one
> another?
And how many camel bells passing beyond the hill, how
> many?

Who believes that the clouds accompany the sheep
Descending the hill, treading on pine needles, who believes
    it?
Tonight, do the distant camel bells ring out as many stars,
Under a moon of the seventeenth of the month?

1932 (?)
Wen, *Complete Works, Hsin,* 662

SPRING COMES TO A LITTLE TEMPLE

I want the sun to shine
On the few blades of grass over my roof,
And the rain and wind to come in season
Throughout the year.

Let that flagpole
Fall asleep on the crumbling wall,
And the ivy crawl on its back
String upon string . . .
I want to sun myself and catch lice
On my much mended robe;
A Buddha once I was but in this incarnation
I pass as a monk.

February 1935
Wen, *Complete Works, Hsin,* 663–64

SUN YÜ-T'ANG (1905?–   )

A MEMBER of the Crescent school, Sun Yü-t'ang did not stay
long with poetry but turned to literary and historical research
and, as an avocation, to drama. His verse has, however, a
distinguished quality that captured what the Crescent poets
set out to find—a new prosodic scheme to accommodate new
images in a different linguistic medium. His long poem,
"The Precious Horse," published in 1939, is a valiant effort
to create an epic based on the historical story of the quest
for Bactrian horses by the Han Dynasty emperors in the sec-
ond century B.C.

THE BAT

An ancient pagoda hidden in mountains.
Around it at dusk bats fly in circles,
Whirling back and forth, like filaments of a midnight dream
That finds no place to return.

Why do you whirl and whirl ceaselessly,
Can't this old pagoda be your home?
You bats, why don't you stop wondering;
The sun has already set beyond the mountain.

The Precious Horse, 125

WHAT DID I LOSE?

I lost it—what did I lose
In this forest? At midnight I bring a lantern
To stroll in the woods to search;
I recognize the route paved with wild flowers,

Every tree, and every blade of grass. Ah, how did I
Lose it in a place so familiar!
What I lost must be right here, for
Next to this I know no other world.

With a lantern in hand I trace my way step by step.
The dewdrops, glistening, are weeping on the bough.
The stars wink above the trees,
All so quiet, so very quiet, all around.

Really, I did lose it in this place,
With a lantern I have been searching here every night,
But I could not find what I have lost,
Only I know that time hastens me along the path of age.

The Precious Horse, 132–33

COMPLAINT

Yes, you loved me, just for that wink of an eye—
Like a swallow's wing-tip touching the water,
A whiff of gentle breeze, leaving no shadow to be caught,
No light to be traced—like the flash of a falling star—

It was gone. You did not mind at all,
But unthinking, untied my anchor chain.
Thus on white sails, swollen with warm dreams,
I flew out of a river, across the sea, and soared over the hills,

Through blue clouds I darted into the depth of night,
Losing myself, and missing my road;
All because I took that instant to be eternity,
Thinking that the silver stars were your eyes.

Then you laughed, and that awakened me,
Awakened me to my earlier hasty belief.
But, ah, what do you want me to do now?
Now that you have slammed shut forever the door of my
        paradise.

The Precious Horse, 176–77

PURGATORY

No life in this patch of sky, as dry as a sheet of blue-black
      steel,
I've long known that this land is wilderness paved with
      parched, parched sand.
For seven days, seven full days, I walked on the barren sand,
      bags on my back.
Barren sand I crossed, yet still more barren sand—it appears
      to have bound my limbs.
I cannot find a trickle of water, not even any kind of puddle;
Glancing up at the sky, and down at earth, I dream of a
      withered ghost
That dances in rainbow-colored sunlight, with round, popped-
      out eyes and a shriveled tongue;
It points at earth, gestures toward the sky, and seems to ask
      who is the master, heaven or earth?
The sun burns savagely, like a sensuous woman in May,
Under my feet is hot burning sand. During these seven days,
      these many hours.
During these many hours, these seven days, with
      dry rations but no water,
I can feel the circulation throughout my body, that
      is my crimson blood.
How I wish to hang my head on the sky, making it a star,
So that it may greet a thread of cloud, a drop of dew, or mimic
      the sound of gurgling water,
Or learn a line or two of rain-making songs from the village
      lass, so that the desire of my heart may be quieted.
Ah, the sky is an inverted bronze cauldron, choking me on the
      barren sand!
These seven days, seven high noons, from seven early mornings
      to seven evenings.
How I wish I could die, and through the baked sand locate a
      door to hell;
How I yearn to smash the cauldron—yet my outstretched arms
      cannot touch heaven;

Look, all around me the sky passionately kisses the earth, and I
   seem to feel the tips of the tongues of heaven and
   earth;
Perhaps heaven and earth are in love with me, passionately,
   too intimately.
Have mercy on me, O God, I cannot bear any love.

       The Precious Horse, 107–9

OLD HORSE

Carrying two baskets of iron, one sack of sand, I trudge on
   the dust of the ancient road,
Cross a valley, and circle a mountain, with stars shining
   above.
The depth of the night, the silence of old pines, where
   dewdrops mourn the fallen petals;
This long, long road—when will it lead me home?

As I circle a hill and again edge across a vale, the starlight
   leads the road into the distance;
Like sorrow, like regret, the wings of the bats flutter before
   my eyes.
Slowly, ever so slowly I walk; dusk rises from the ancient road
   under my hoofs.
Heavy is my load, heavy my age, and my tired, tired heart.

Tired am I of the sun, of the moon, and of the stars revolving
   in the sky;
This aged world, this aged evening, no longer deserve my
   lingering.
With tears in my eyes, I long for home; this must be time to
   go home,
With two baskets of iron and a sack of sand on my back, and a
   bosom full of despair and grief.

I cross a valley and edge over a mountain, with the stars
   shining on my lonely self.
The depth of this night, and the silence of old pines, where
   sobbing dewdrops cling to the branches.

This long, long road—when will it lead me home?
To a perpetual quiet, a perpetual rest, a mound of earth
  beyond the horizon.

       The Precious Horse, 69–70

DEAD SEA

Let me be a dead sea with barren mountains all around;
They may not be pretty, but I hope they will be tall
Enough to block the winds from all directions.

Let the barren mountains be tall enough to shield the sun,
And let darkness forever shroud the sea's face.
Here I need no starlight, nor moonbeam,
Nor any sharks, nor sea swallows to build their nests.

And all I ask is an eternal peace.
Let the passing clouds take away all lingering affection.
No waves to roll out laughter of silvery light;
No sea gulls to herald any approaching spring.

Decidedly I prefer to be a dead sea;
With nothing to cause me any sorrow.
Nor do I beg happiness of anyone;
Sympathy, comfort—I reject them all.

This way I may find my joy
In my perpetual youth and perpetual old age.
Peace is a volume of infinite pages,
Helping my soul to pray to heaven and earth.

When the call finally summons me to the last judgment,
The world then will no longer be a world
God may nod his head and smile: Only this
Pitiful, dead sea has no sin to its name.

       The Precious Horse, 72–74

SHAO HSÜN-MEI (1903?–   )

LIKE HSÜ CHIH-MO, Shao Hsün-mei was born of a wealthy family in Chekiang Province and educated in England. Also like Hsü Chih-mo, he sought to rid his work of the moralistic bondage of traditional Chinese poetry and to treat what is sensuously beautiful. He admired Swinburne and openly imitated his style, even its rhythm and alliteration.

Yet Shao's praise of the sensuous is not without vestiges of moralistic awareness, as his change of title for his collection of poems indicates. It first appeared in 1927 as *Heaven and May* and was reissued the next year as *The Flowerlike Sin*. In his poems he seems to be on the one hand asserting that outside of the reality of senses nothing exists, and on the other admitting, with a wry smile, that flesh is temptation and motion, sin.[1]

For a few years (1928–32) he operated the small publishing house in Shanghai that printed the famous literary journal, *The Crescent Monthly*. Later he turned to writing short and witty essays.

SPRING

When Spring extracts new buds from barren branches,
And fresh flowers, the color of a virgin's lips, bloom all
      over the wilderness;
She whose tears have melted white snow stays in the midst
Of a long night, a long night, a long night.

[1] The attitude of the Taoist toward motion is such that, if speaking of "sin" is relevant to Taoism at all, he would regard motion as sinful.—Ed.

Ah, look, how the oriole hidden behind the willow screen
Alone with trembling wings pours out the colorful sunset;
Boredom, envy, pain, and hope accompany her
Through a long night, a long night, a long night.

Ah, because of spring barren branches burst out in new buds,
And fresh flowers bloom all over the wilderness, because of
    spring;
But why, ah, why must she linger
In a long night, a long night, a long night?

The Flowerlike Sin, 29–30

A DREAM

The lovely, the terrible, and the proud
The tip of a virgin's tongue, the tip of a lizard's tail
I cannot understand; can you tell me,
Is there true happiness among four lips?

Ah, the rose-colored, the ivory-colored, a bed full,
This sweet dream keeps my soul on errand:
I am a loyal disciple of sin,
I want to see a worldly nun disrobe.

The Flowerlike Sin, 37

MAY

Ah, lusty May is again burning,
A sin is born of a virgin's kiss;
Sweet tears tempt me, always tempt me
To feel between her breasts with my lips.

Here life is as eternal as death,
As the trembling happiness on a wedding night;
If she is not a rose, a rose all white,
Then she must be redder than the red of blood.

Ah, this firelike, and fleshlike
Darkness of light and tears of laughter
Are the soul of my love's soul
And the enemy to the enemy of my hate.

Heaven has just opened two large gates,
O God, I am not one to enter.
I have already found comfort in hell,
Already have I dreamed of an awakening in the short night.

The Flowerlike Sin, 6–7

PREFACE

I, too, have learned: There is an end to everything in the
    universe;
And in the end, even the yawning of the leaves breaks the
    solitude of the woods.
Formerly asleep with death, but isn't this instantaneous
    awakening
Due to the temptation of flesh, the prompting of sounds, and
    the sin of motions?

These half-spent lives, soiled and degraded souls,
Strewn on earth at random like abandoned corpses;
Let them sink in the ocean for the fish and vermin to nibble,
Ah, better for them to be charcoal to kindle life, dreary and
    cold.

The Flowerlike Sin, i

THE SOUL OF SHANGHAI

I stand on top of a seven-storied building,
Above, there is the inaccessible sky;
Below, the cars, telephone wires, and the horse race track.

The front door of a theater, the back view of a prostitute;
Ah, these are the soul of a metropolis:
Ah, these are the soul of Shanghai.

Here one need not fear the rain or the sun:
Or the autumn and winter of death, or the spring of life:
How can any fiery summer be warmer than the lips!

Here there are true illusions, false sentiments;
Here there are unsleeping evenings, smiling lights;
Come, then, here is your burial ground.

The Flowerlike Sin, 47–48

TO SWINBURNE

You are Sappho's brother, so am I
Our parents are the gods who made Venus—
The sunset, the rainbow, the tail of the peacock and the
        feather of the phoenix,
The birth of all beauties are their—our parents'—genius.

You like her, so do I, and I like you too;
We all yearn for love, for love's secret;
We like the pure union of blood and flesh;
And we like the poison of sacred nectar, and the bittersweet.

Ah, we are like three wild flowers blooming on a deserted
        mountain,
We let nobody plant us in a pot or put us in a ewer;
We've come from dust, and to dust we shall return,
Our hope is to remain in dust forever.

The Flowerlike Sin, 23–24

CHU TA-NAN

ONE OF THE early contributors to the *Poetry Journal* founded in Peking in 1926, Chu Ta-nan of Szechwan Province, did not live to become a principal member of the Crescent group. His poems, however, helped Wen I-to and Hsü Chih-mo to test their theories about the new poetry. He took meticulous care to balance meters and unify the end rhymes.

A curious blending of the old and the new is found in Chu's work. His "Fueling" presents a fantasy that occurs after man is freed from his inhibitions by wine. In places this fantasy parallels T'ao Ch'ien's (365–427) "Drinking Songs" which describe in similar terms of ecstasy a liberation of man's soul and imagination. Compare Chu's:

> I'm thinking for your sake, poor fellows:
> How many ounces can your dry bones weigh?
> When you empty your pockets for a drink,
> What matters if your bones become still lighter?

with T'ao Ch'ien's:

> We treasure these bodies of ours
> Isn't it because we have a life:
> Yet how long does life last,
> Since it flees like frightening lightning?

When T'ao had a cup in his hand, he could be "happy day and night." Chu too would "be happy in that imaginary paradise" after drinking his wine. The contrast with T'ao becomes sharp only when Chu uses the image of a rushing locomotive to depict man in total freedom. T'ao prefers the chrysanthemum blooming serenely near the eastern hedge and a bird returning to its nest after a tiring day.

FUELING

When you drink with gusto, emptying the pot,
Black coal is added in the locomotive
To bring life to the stagnant, and
To let feeling take your thought on a wild flight.

I'm thinking for your sake, poor fellows:
How many ounces can your dry bones weigh?
When you empty your pockets for a drink,
What matters if your bones become still lighter?

While there is no stinking money in your pocket,
While your minds harbor no seed of hesitation,
Just like that lightweight locomotive
You can speed ahead, full-throttle.

Linger not in the graveyard of reminiscence
To bemoan and mourn the piles of rotten bodies;
Enter not the empty hollow of hope
To dream of a substance supposed to be there.

Drive, then, to the land of imagination,
Soaring beyond the sorry world of reality.
By order of your own will, complete and total,
You begin to build a pavilion of ivory.

At the wink of an eye cobwebs turn into jeweled pendants,
Hung all over the glittering walls of a gold room.
Jade latticework replaces broken windowpanes,
And gilt pillars stand where dank walls used to be.

The green clay cup looks inlaid with gems;
The bean-size light seems to shine like a pearl.
The shadows sway to the rhythm of a dancing goddess,
The crickets are playing music divine.

Let prosperity cover desolation,
And let sorrow melt away in infinite joy.
You may, if you choose, indulge and flaunt,
And be happy in that imaginary paradise.

You'll fear no violent force that robs others,
No weak ones to eye others with jealousy.
Immerse yourself in pleasure in the fairyland of fantasy,
Without the slightest suspicion.

. . . .

You'll laugh at the goddess who prepares a stone to mend
        heaven
As sillier than the bird trying to fill the ocean with
        pebbles.[1]
Look, we only pour down cups of cold wine,
And it evens out the unequal destinies.

Let the stagnant come to life, and
Let feeling take your thought on a wild flight;
When you drink with gusto, emptying the pot,
Black coal is added in the locomotive.

                    October 1923 (?)
                    Compendium, 339–41

DREAM IN A STORM

Cold, dreary rain sobs at the corner of the house;
The random footsteps of the wind on windowpanes greet my
        eyes:
The rustling papers echo the flipping pages in my heart:
Word by word the storm reads aloud all my inner secrets.

[1] The stories about the Goddess Nü Kua mending the sky and the
black bird trying to fill the ocean with pebbles both belong to ancient
Chinese legend.—Ed.

In dream I see immense ocean waves,
But my heart is only a dried sea, or its forgotten remains.
The dried sea sinks to the bottom of an unending night,
Where there is no surging wave, nor buffeting storm.

In dream I see a stretch of deserted sands,
The gray shadows of camels, and green buds of wild grass.
But my heart is only a clod of frozen earth—home of ice and
    frost,
Where there is no trace of budding green, no sighing bells.

Loneliness weighs on my heart, so heavy, like lead;
I groan in a nightmare, though the sun is shining brightly
    above.
Who says the sound of a storm can wake a man from his
    empty dream?
The dream in the sound of a storm is the emptiest of all.

                                   1928
                                   Compendium, 341–42

WAKING UP FROM A DREAM

A strange crystalline light filled a clear quiet dream;
Beyond the veranda shaded with green, someone's robe
    fluttered.
Quickly I seized the corner of that robe to talk to you:
In the deep courtyard fallen petals scattered like scented
    snow.

Suddenly I woke up to face the pale white empty walls;
There seemed to be someone gently biting my eyelids, in jest.
Ah, that's not you, not your face that has lost its pink.
I saw you leap through the window, walking farther away,
Only to pause, lost in thought, showing a bit of your gleaming
    teeth.
But why did you come and go, uninvited, invading my dream?

                                   Compendium, 342

SMILE

A flame of a smile dances behind a gauze curtain red as
      evening clouds.
So soft is the flame of a red candle.
Some smiles can comfort you through quiet and lonely long
      nights.

A blossom of a smile sways in the lake, green as the
      kingfisher's feathers.
So clean and lean is that fresh bud of white lotus.
Some smiles can wake you up from a dizzy early morning.

A blade of a smile prances in a brass sheath.
So flashing white is the sword.
Some smiles can end the carefree rambling of your thought.

Compendium, 338

TIME SPEAKS

Of old, people said life was a roadside inn,
And death, your home where you ultimately returned.
      Blame me not for hastening you along,
      Do pity me for nowhere yet do *I* belong,
Ah, this ceaseless mad rush for thousands of years!
Whom did I fail to accompany to the door of his grave,
As I never accompanied another before the first had settled?
      Now all of you are resting quietly in the graveyard,
      Only I, over the growing weeds, keep my lonely watch,
Ah, the good earth I have no hope to reach!

Compendium, 339

EVICTION

Since you moved in to live in my heart,
Disquietude is the rent you have been paying me.
I long for the day when there will be serenity:
Without your song and dance, my heart will be free.

When did I ever put up a "For Rent" notice?
All my life I have loved only void and quiet.
Get out, unwelcome intruder,
You sing and dance without stop, day and night.

My heart cannot bear this disturbance,
Your dance's rumble and your noisy shout.
Get away, don't pretend to be silly;
One day I will serve notice and chase you out.

Compendium, 341

FANG WEI-TEH (–1935)

FANG WEI-TEH's great-grandfather was Fang Pao (1668–1749), the staunch standard bearer of the T'ung-ch'eng school which made one of the last efforts to uphold the classical Chinese literary tradition and to defend an orthodoxy of literary style. Wei-teh's aunt, Fang Ling-ju, was also well regarded in Chinese literary circles around the beginning of the century.

In 1927 Wei-teh studied at the Fourth Chung-shan University (predecessor of the National Central University) where he met Wen I-to. But Fang did not attract Wen's attention as a young poet until 1930 when in collaboration with Ch'en Meng-chia he wrote a long poem, entitled "Regret and Return," and it was submitted to Wen I-to for comment. Wen praised the poem as "the most memorable event of the year."[1] The poem was a bold attempt at a new style (blank verse without punctuation), making use of a new poetic vocabulary against the prevailing literary taboo. It impressed Wen I-to so much that he immediately sought out Fang's aunt to ask for a photograph of the young poet to grace his desk.

Fang's short lyrics prove him a worthy disciple of Hsü Chih-mo and Wen I-to. Some people have found a resemblance to Masefield in his style, but a closer scrutiny might reveal a larger debt to the techniques of Emily Dickinson and Sara Teasdale. Dying early, he left only one book of poems.

[1] Wen I-to, "On 'Regret and Return,'" *The Crescent Monthly*, Vol. III, Nos. 5–6.

I HAVE

I have a thought
As I walk past you;
Like a mountain stream,
It's neither love nor attachment.

I have a thought
As I walk home;
Like a touch of afterglow
It's neither sorrow nor dejection.

1931
The Crescent Monthly, Vol. III, No. 7

THE QUIET ONE

Every night when I lie in bed,
A heavenly river flows through my dream.
In the river there are boats, and lights on the boats,
        I call aloud to the boatmen,
        "Hurry to bring over The Quiet One."

The day breaks and I open my eyes,
The sun has already risen above the tree.
Old Ti pushes the door open to get me up,
        I laugh at myself,
        "It's just as well The Quiet One didn't come."
                    Wen, *Complete Works, Hsin*, 667

THE VOICE ON THE SEA

The other day I walked with her along the seashore,
She gave me a lock and a set of keys.
She said: "Open the door in your heart;
Let me deposit a heart there; and
        Please keep it,
        Please keep it."

Today she asked me to open that door again;
But I long ago lost the keys on the seashore.
All day long I have been searching here,
And a voice from the cloud cries,
    "Give me back my heart,
    Give me back my heart!"

Wen, *Complete Works, Hsin,* 666

SOFT VOICE

I count the stars in the sky,
And I ask: "Which one is it,
That now shines over her home?"
The stars are silent,
Tonight
Dewdrops fall on my cheeks.

I cross a river,
And I ask: "What time was it
When you passed by her home?"
The water gives me no answer,
Tonight
Silence falls on my heart.

Wen, *Complete Works, Hsin,* 667–68

STORM

A storm surges over the sky;
Lightning flashes through the wood:
This is not the sound of the wind, but someone calling.
A face presses against my ear,
(A burning passion, a flaming torch.)
"My love, don't be afraid, it's I!"

A storm surges in my heart.
In the darkness I cannot tell the earth from the sky.
Yet clearly this is in broad daylight,
Without thunder, or a whisper of wind.
A shadow darts ahead,
"Ah, good heavens, who is that?"

Wen, *Complete Works, Hsin,* 667

A BUDDHIST HYMN

One early morning I arose,
The sun was at my window asking about my dream:
"I still display yesterday's light
Without any change, what I love is the ordinary."

That night I went to bed,
The moon greeted me at the window:
"The sun shines during the day, but at night
I neither show off nor do I hide."

1931
The Crescent Monthly, Vol. III, No. 2

FENG CHIH (1905–   )

THE APPEARANCE of the professor teaching courses on Goethe and Rilke at the National Southwest Associate University in Kunming in the early 1940s was not one to impress his students. His rather rotund figure, round and ruddy face, and his ever-present loose gown of faded blue, seemed to belong more to the proprietor of a small grocery store than to a poet. Even his silver-rimmed glasses could not add a poetic or scholarly touch. Yet this was a seasoned poet whose works had won quite a following since the 1920s.

Feng Chih studied literature in Germany. He began writing for the literary magazines early and edited one himself in Peking in 1925, which he called *The Sunken Bell*, after Hauptmann's play. His journal had a fitful existence, a fate common to most Chinese literary journals in those days; finally it ceased publication in 1932. During those years he completed two volumes of poems and essays, *The Songs of Yesterday* (1927), and *Northern Travels and Others* (1929), both of which were very well received.

Feng Chih earned a name as the only true story poet of his time in the early stages of his career. He developed and retold some of the old legends in his verse. His "The Silk Cocoon," for example, is taken from an ancient legend about a young maiden who was transformed into a silkworm. He also wrote short lyrical poems, and those published in 1923 and 1924 already demonstrated a poetic mastery of the vernacular that few of his contemporaries had achieved. His clear and effortless sense of rhythm has stayed with him. Thirty years separate his "Windy Night" (1924) from his "I Sing of the Anshan Steel" (1954), yet both have the same ring. And his narrative skill in poetry has survived the years. His "Han Po Chops Wood" of 1952 has the same gripping power as "The Silk Cocoon" of 1925.

The sustained quality of his poetry is surprising in view of the frequent interruptions in his creative activity. Between 1931 and 1939 he wrote hardly anything. His continued study of Rilke, however, encouraged him to turn to the metaphysical. One winter afternoon he contemplated the universe as he walked in the countryside near Kunming. The appearance of several silver-colored airplanes in the bright blue sky carried his thought back to the legend about somebody dreaming of the gigantic bird called the "roc." The lines that took shape in his mind during that solitary stroll became a variation of the sonnet form. As he put it, "The beginning was accidental, and yet I felt within me a sense of growing responsibility: There are experiences of our minds that return to our consciousness again and again, never stopping." And to everything that offered something to his experience he wished to record his gratitude in verse. This wish resulted in his twenty-seven sonnets written in 1941. He pondered on man's position in the universe, and wondered about the relation between life and the impressions one gathers in the course of one's life:

> So many faces, so many voices
> All so vivid and intimate in our dreams.
> Be they close to us or totally strange,
> They are all splinters split from my own life.
>
> (from Sonnet XX)

Feng Chih himself explained that he had not intended to transplant the sonnet form to China, but he agreed with Li Kuang-t'ien who considered the form perfectly suited to Feng's materials. Li had commented on the structure of Feng's twenty-seven sonnets, saying that they show layer upon layer of ascent and descent, "they gather together the divergent strands and then let them loose again." In rhythm, Li said, the sonnets show variety in uniformity, allowing a rapid and free movement within. Feng Chih did not believe that the rather rigid structure in any way interfered with his thought; on the contrary he found it helpful in organizing his ideas.

The carefully worked out prosodic scheme in these sonnets

certainly demonstrates the possibility of applying a metrical scale to vernacular Chinese, something the Crescent poets advocated in the 1920s. Feng Chih, however, did not choose to go farther in this direction. The year 1941 had been a relatively peaceful one in his life. His years of trudging about in China, always living with a grave uncertainty about the next day, had just been brought to a temporary halt as he resumed teaching at the National Southwest Associate University. During this brief respite he could look back and screen his impressions. But soon after 1941 the Japanese began to bomb Kunming. Feng abandoned his search for perfect texture and structure for his poetry and let his words follow his feeling with less restraint.

He did not become involved in the political upheaval shortly before and after the 1949 change of government, but his post-1949 writings make it clear that he no longer values his 1941 sonnets. As he looked back in 1955, he considered the things he wrote prior to 1939 rather trivial, and his poems written in 1941 too affected and difficult to understand. He preferred to re-examine his world view and avoid creating poetry that could eventually become meaningless. He wanted to learn more, work harder, and do things more beneficial to people.

His readers outside of mainland China are likely to disagree with the Feng Chih of 1955 and to consider his 1941 sonnets a high point in his poetic career.

RAINY NIGHT

In the woods are gathered
Many many shadowy spirits,
They sing and dance
To the tune of the storm.

Crickets sing in the weeds,
They never, never stop:
Is there a traveler who has
Lost his way in the woods?

Lightning flashes through the trees
To light a trail for him.
The cicada suddenly calls on a branch
And birds respond in the valley.

Thunder strikes at the trees;
The shadowy spirits scatter,
Toward places more sequestered
To sing songs sad and lonely:

The withered tendrils of the acacia flower
And the dwarf fig trees weeping all over the hills,
All ride on the cold rain and chilly wind
To enter the pretty dreams of man.

1924
Selected Works of Feng Chih, 6–7

WINDY NIGHT

"It was a windy night like this,
And in a similar autumn.
I brewed fine wine with my life,
And offered it to your lips,
One cup, two cups, three cups . . ."

I counted on my fingers silently,
It has been exactly one year.
I have been lost in this murky, dusty city,
Like the boards of a ship wrecked in the sea,
One piece, two pieces, three pieces . . .

Tonight I rest quietly under autumn stars,
The boards of the ship have drifted to a bay.
No longer can they stand the waves in the ocean,
And I fear to look at the starry sparks in the wind,
One blink, two blinks, three blinks. . . .

1924
Compendium, 162

A DRAPE
A Folk Legend

Who has ever gazed at that lush mountain side,
At that section of red wall half hidden behind the green,
Without seeing the ethereal beauty of quietude
And letting his thought carry him away?

Those who live there, man or woman
Have all severed their many ties and concerns.
Yet in their hearts, those deep pools and ancient wells,
Lingers still the feeling of medieval romance.

It is the western end of the T'ai-hang range
Where two unnamed peaks stand facing one another.
One a monastery, and the other a convent—two temples
Nestle in the bosom of these two hills.

Two hundred years ago, a youthful nun in the convent
Embroidered a rare, precious drape.
At every spring festival when the villagers come to offer
    incense,
The drape is displayed, strangely, in the monastery on the
    other side.

The rather puzzling and mysterious reason for this custom
Was explained in the simple words of the villagers:
They said that when the young nun was seventeen,
She knelt before the shrine and shaved off her hair.

Her parents belonged to a rich, ancient family,
And she acted so not because of hunger or cold.
Though she had been frequently ill, she never had
Pledged herself in front of the Buddha.

One moonlit night when plums were barely blooming
She quietly stole out of her house.
Quietly she hid her suffering and unused talents,
As she heard an oriole singing its sorrows in behalf of man.

No one knows how many times she lost her way,
She walked until the full moon sank in the west.
The song of the larks led her to the door of the convent,
Where a pool of water gleamed under gentle ripples.

It seemed that she could not be happy in the world of man,
As she recognized her own pretty face on the water.
Resolutely she walked into the convent, ready
To exchange the bloom of her youth for bare branches.

The old nun said to her, with a smile,
"Since you've made up your mind, I cannot stop you.
From now on you must rid yourself of all untamed thoughts,
This is not an ordinary game for children!

"You feel that the sea of your suffering is without shores,
But exactly who was he who woke you up, my child?
Even if you are unwilling to let me know,
You must explain it when you confess before the Buddha!"

"Teacher, nobody really enlightened me,
Only that I heard, by accident, someone say
The one with whom I was to spend my whole life,
Was a man with neither good looks, nor a good mind.

"Yet the marriage contract had long been signed by my
          parents,
And the wedding banquet was being arranged by relatives.
As they cheerfully chatted, forgetting about me,
The only thing I could do was to flee to this mountain.

"Teacher, what I've said is all very true,
And I trust you as much as I trust the Buddha.
I'm willing to banish all my tender sentiments
To stifle the cries of my soul, to freeze my heart."

Tears followed her clear voice, word by word,
And drop after drop, drenching her clothes.
The old nun said, "You've cut off your 'attachment to
    sorrow,'
Now you must also let your tears go with it."

Soon after the spring breeze had spread green on the
    mountain,
Chilly autumn rains bent the fragile willows under the eaves.
Much trouble had arisen in the world of man,
Yet the convent remained untouched, its quietude unbroken.

Evening drums, morning bells, and the chanting of sutras
    and the Buddha's name continued:
Who could tell if they were awakening man or lulling him
    to sleep?
Her heart declined together with her flesh and blood,
And her tearless eyes lost their luster day by day.

To her, a day passed as slowly as a year;
It would soon be a full year, yet it seemed only a day
As she looked back. Ice already formed on the water,
And loneliness and desolation came from the distant hills.

The sunshine at noon, warm as in early spring:
Playful white pigeons soared in the sky.
Their fluttering wings brought in two youths, a brother and
    his sister
Who came to worship the Buddha, by their mother's decree.

She saw that behind the eyebrows of that handsome young
    man
There was hidden an inexpressible sorrow.
His vivacious sister whispered in her ear,
And what she said pricked her heart, each word a needle.

"Beautiful sister, let me tell you!
  Now, you are intelligent, won't you say he's really foolish?
  Just because a fiancée has left him,
  My brother pledged that he would never marry."

She felt dizzy, sitting alone at the gate.
The setting sun seemed spiritless, and the northern wind
        chilly.
She stared at them, the brother and sister going down the
        mountain,
Until they disappeared, without leaving a single trace.

The shivering crows cawed, perching on barren branches,
Only the evening twilight remained, blurry with mist.
Her hot tears melted the ice on the frozen pool.
She seemed to hear nothing of the repeated strokes of the
        bell.

Though the old nun had long smothered her soft
        sentiments,
Still she could not help pitying her, being so young.
So young indeed, yet she had
Such a strange, unfortunate destiny.

She pitied her, a lovely girl from a good family,
And told her to rest quietly in a small chamber in the back.
She was ill, nobody knew exactly how long,
Till once again cuckoos were heard in the forest so freshly
        green.

Snow on mountain tops was melting in the warm winds,
And golden mantled beetles flew about in the spring light.
Her head was always bent, a girl long given up
For lost, with no hope to reach paradise or Buddhahood.

She only looked forward to her own withering, day by day,
And to her burial under a grave mound three feet tall.
Ah, nothing at all in this world, nothing at all
Could yield, for her, the least bit of joy.

A whiff of smoke from the incense burner lulled man to
    sleep;
The herald of spring entered the window, riding on the wind.
A shepherd, playing a flute clear and loud,
Herding his sheep, passed by beneath her window.

The farther went the notes of the flute, the more melodious
    they became,
Two blossoms of red cloud rose to her pale cheeks.
She took out a length of silk, crimson in color,
Stared at it for a long time, and then laid it aside.

The sunshine of the second day and the same music of the
    flute,
Mixed in her heart a song more overpowering than wine.
From her heart bloomed a white water lily,
And she embroidered it in the center of the drape.

From that time on every day in the sound of the flute
There was always a tune, refreshingly sweet.
She followed her heart's direction, and with her colored silk
    threads
She embroidered inseparable pairs of fish in water, and birds
    in the sky.

Every moment every day she was seen at her needlework,
Creating a happy paradise on the drape with her embroidery,
Where the leaves interwove, and the creeks seemed to
    chatter,
Only the left corner was left totally blank.

She had thought that she would fill that corner
With her sorrow sewn stitch by stitch.
But time passed, and the dewdrops had again turned to hoar
    frost.
And again there returned the lone swan calling at midnight.

The leaves of the *wu-t'ung* tree fell off sadly,
And maple leaves turned red in tears of blood.
The wind whistled and the rain battered, as she opened her
    window
To await the shepherd who played a flute.

"This is a drape which I embroidered in the past half year.
I thank you for the music of your flute which inspired me.
I am a nun of eighteen and in my life
There have been only endless tears.

"And yet we are forever separated
In two different worlds . . ."
She dropped the drape wrapped in a bundle,
And in a hurry she closed her window.

Next day the sky was covered with black clouds,
The universe was half ill and half in grief:
A shepherd was initiated in the monastery on the other side,
And in the convent the young nun was consumed on a
    funeral pyre,

Now, over two hundred years have passed,
The drape is still carefully locked up in the monastery.
Only the corner of its left side,
Remains blank to this day, and nobody can fill it.

> Early autumn 1924
> *Compendium,* 167–72

SONNET II

Whatever can be shed from our bodies,
We'll let it be reduced to dust;
We arrange ourselves in this epoch
Like autumn trees, one by one

Handing over to autumn winds their leaves
And belated flowers, so they may stretch their limbs
Into the severe winter; we arrange ourselves
In nature, like cicadas emerging from earth

To abandon their shells in the dirt;
We arrange ourselves for the death
That lies ahead, like a song and

As the sounds fall from the body of the music,
There remains only the music's essence
Transformed into a chain of silent blue hills.

The Sonnets, 5–6

SONNET III

You, a tree rustling in autumn winds
Are a movement of music that builds
A solemn temple near my ears
To let me enter with care;

You are also a tower piercing the sunny sky,
Rising majestically in front of me,
The body of a saint
Sublimating the noises of the whole city.

You never cease shedding your physical shell,
And in your withering one sees only your growth;
On the fields crisscrossed by narrow paths

I regard you as my guide.
Wishing you a life eternal: I'd like, little by little,
To change myself into the soil beneath your roots.

1941
The Sonnets, 7–8

SONNET IV

Often as I ponder on the life of man,
I feel compelled to pray to you.
You, a cluster of pale-white weeds,
Never failed to deserve a name;

And yet you elude all possible names
To lead a life, insignificant and humble,
Never failing in your purity and nobility, but
Completing your life cycle in silence.

Of all the forms and all the sounds,
Some fade away, as they approach you,
And some become part of your quietude:

This is your great glory, though
Accomplished only in your self-denial.
I pray to you, for the life of man.

1941
The Sonnets, 9–10

SONNET XI
To Lu Hsün[1]

One evening many years ago
You felt "an awakening" because of several young men.[2]
No one knows how many times you were disillusioned,
But that "awakening" remains forever.

Forever I retain this feeling of gratitude
To gaze at you, for the sake of our time:
It has been ruined by stupid people,
Yet its guardian has been, through his life,

[1] Lu Hsün, who died in 1936, is probably the best remembered modern Chinese essayist and literary critic.—Ed.
[2] Author's note: There is one section entitled "An Awakening" in Lu Hsün's *Wild Grass.*

Exiled from this world—
Several times your searching eyes discovered a ray of light,
Only to be hidden by dark clouds, as you turned your head.

You have completed your difficult journey, and
Amidst the hardships only the little roadside grass
Has ever drawn from you a smile of hope.

1941
The Sonnets, 23–24

SONNET XIII
To Goethe

You were born in an ordinary bourgeois family:
You've shed tears for many humble maidens;
Before the powerful ruler of the time you also bowed.
The eighty years of your life were peaceful—

Like the universe quietly revolving, it
Never stops for even a minute or a second,
Evolving new seeds of life any time anywhere,
Despite the weather, stormy or clear.

From severe illness you derived new health;
From lost love you derived fresh sustenance;
You knew why the moth plunged toward the flame,

And why the snake grew only when it shed its old skin.
Myriads of things are profiting from your famous words,
That reveal all the meaning of life: "Death and Change."

1941
The Sonnets, 27–28

SONNET XV

Look at those pack horses, one train after another,
Bringing in loads of goods from afar.
Water could also carry over some dirt and sand
From faraway places with unknown names.

From thousands of miles away the wind would
Sweep over the sighs of a distant country:
We have traveled over numerous rivers and hills,
Staying with them for a moment, but leaving them all the
        time.

We are like birds that soar in the sky,
And control the space any time and all the time,
And yet all the time feel totally dispossessed.

What is this thing called our reality?
Nothing can be brought over from afar, and
Nothing can be taken away from here, either.

                                1941
                                The Sonnets, 31–32

SONNET XVI

We stand together on top of a towering mountain
Transforming ourselves into the immense sweep of view,
Into the unlimited plain in front of us,
And into the footpaths crisscrossing the plain.

Which road, which river is unconnected, and
Which wind, which cloud is without its response?
The waters and hills we've traversed
Have all been merged in our lives.

Our births, our growth, and our sorrows
Are the lone pine standing on a mountain,
Are the dense fog blanketing a city.

We follow the blowing wind and the flowing water
To become the crisscrossing paths on the plain,
To become the lives of the travelers on the paths.

1941
The Sonnets, 33–34

SONNET XVIII

We often pass an intimate night
In a strange room. How it looks during
The day, we have no way of knowing,
Not to speak of its past or future. The plain

Stretches from beyond our window to as far as we can see,
We can only vaguely remember the road whence we came
In the evening, and that's all we know of the plain,
And after our departure tomorrow, we'll not return.

Close your eyes! Let those intimate nights
And strange places be woven in our hearts:
Our life resembles the plain beyond the window.

On the dusk-shrouded plain we discern
A tree and the glimmer of a lake. The infinite wilderness
Hides a forgotten past, and a dim future.

1941
The Sonnets, 37–38

SONNET XXII

In the depth of the night, and in the depth of the mountains,
Listening to the weary rain.
The village ten miles away, and
The town twenty miles away,

Are they still there?
The mountains and rivers of ten years ago
And the dreams twenty years old
Are all drowned in the rain.

It's so narrow all around that it feels
As though one has returned to the womb.
God, I pray in the depth of the night

As an ancient man once did:
"Please give my limited heart
An unlimited world!"[3]

1941
The Sonnets, 45–46

SONNET XXVI

We travel on a familiar road every day
To return to the place we live,
But in this forest, there are hidden
Many narrow paths, secluded and strange.

When we walk on one of these strange paths we panic,
Afraid of getting farther and farther, getting lost;
Yet, without knowing, through a clearing in the woods
Suddenly we see the place where we live,

Displayed on the horizon, like a new island.
So many things around us demand that we
Make new discoveries.

Think not that everything is already familiar.
When you lie dying and touch your own hair and skin,
You will wonder: Whose body is this?

1941
The Sonnets, 53–54

[3] Author's note: I recall such a saying somewhere in the *Koran*.

SONNET XXVII

From a pool of freely flowing, formless water,
The water carrier brings back a bottleful, ellipsoid in shape,
Thus this much water has acquired a definite form.
Look, the wind vane fluttering in the autumn breeze

Takes hold of certain things that cannot be held.
Let distant lights and distant nights,
And the growth and decay of plants in distant places,
And a thought that darts towards infinity,

All leave something on this banner.
In vain we have listened to the sound of the wind all night
    long,
In vain we watched the whole day the grass turning yellow
    and the leaves red.

Where shall we settle our thoughts, where?
Let's hope that these verses will, like a wind cone,
Embody certain things that cannot be held.

    1941
    The Sonnets, 55–56

HAN PO CHOPS WOOD
A Dialogue between a Mother and Her Son

The nineteenth of the first lunar month,
It had been raining several days and nights.
Suddenly it stopped after midnight,
Leaving a waning moon in the sky.

Moonlight filled the whole room
The old woman was startled from her dream,
She woke up her son and said
"There is a man's shadow outside."

The son said, "So late at night,
How could there be anybody?"
"You young people don't know," said she,
"This is the spirit of Han Po.

"Han Po was a woodcutter
All day long he chopped wood in the mountain,
He owed his landlord more usurious debt
Than he could expect ever to pay back.

"He chopped wood all his life
So that his landlord might cook and eat;
He chopped wood all his life
So that his landlord could keep warm with a fire.

"But he himself never
Ate or wore enough;
No matter how bad the weather was,
He never ceased chopping for a day.

"As it is now, it was that year,
The rain had lasted several days and nights,
By the nineteenth of the first lunar month,
The rain had turned into heavy snow.

"He was frozen to death
For many days afterwards nobody bothered,
Later even the tatters on his body
Were rotten in the storm.

"But his spirit after death
Still had to continue working;
Since he was stark naked he could
Come out only late at night.

"Every year on the day of his death
There was always moonlight after midnight,
To shine on the deep valleys,
Turning them as bright as day.

"Our spring rain here
 Falls one whole month in a stretch;
 Only on this special occasion
 It would stop for half a night."

She told this story, sending
 Chills down others' spines;
 Outside, in the moonlight, there
 Seemed really to be a man's shadow.

Her son said, "Mother,
 Han Po's death was really sad,
 But this was a story of the old days,
 It is not our present time.

"In the past in our village
 Everyone was a Han Po
 But now among all of us
 There is not a single one like him.

"So many Han Po's in the past
 Died in cold and hunger;
 And we expressed our sympathy
 Only through a half night's moonlight.

"In the moonlight now perhaps
 There is still the spirit of Han Po;
 But he is coming out not to chop wood
 Rather, to avenge his old grievance.

"Tomorrow we'll struggle against the landlords,
 He will also clear his account with them;
 No longer will he be timid,
 He will appear in broad daylight."

1952
Selected Poems of 1953.9–1955.12, 240–43

I SING OF ANSHAN STEEL

I sing of Anshan steel.
Because of many wishes, I sing of Anshan steel.
When the train reaches the riverside, we wish for a bridge;
When the survey team arrives in wild mountains, it seeks
        deeper ore deposits;
For all these wishes, I sing of Anshan steel.

For much happiness, I sing of Anshan steel;
The farmers can have the proper tools they need;
And better looms weave more clothes;
For much happiness, I sing of Anshan steel.

For one famous saying, I sing of Anshan steel.
"What we don't understand we must learn."
The insight of this suggestion is proven here.
For one famous saying, I sing of Anshan steel.

For the many exemplars of man, I sing of Anshan steel.
Man tempers steel, and steel tempers man:
Heroes of a new order emerge without stop.
For the many exemplars of man I sing of Anshan steel.

For the many marvelous sights, I sing of Anshan steel.
Molten iron flows from the furnaces, thick smoke surges
        towards the sky,
All day long ceaselessly, and every night the sky is red.
For the many marvelous sights, I sing of Anshan steel.

For a lasting peace, I sing of Anshan steel.
As the harvest of steel increases, so grows the strength of
        peace;
Let the brave white dove soar ever higher and farther.
For a lasting peace, I sing of Anshan steel.

                    Between 1953 and 1955
                    Selected Poems of 1953.9–1955.12, 93–94

PIEN CHIH-LIN (1910–   )

In 1949, the poet Tsou Ti-fan observed in a long apostrophe to Peking, and especially to its blue sky:

"Yours is not the blue sky of which Pien Chih-lin has sung."

(from *All-out Attack*, 1)

There is indeed a Peking that belongs to Pien Chih-lin, or rather, to his poetry. He has created an image, all his own, of that monument of Chinese culture. The image is composed of the sounds and smells and colors of Peking against a crystal blue sky. When Pien Chih-lin gazes at this image, the image of himself is also strangely reflected on that infinite stretch of blue sky.

He loves the ancient city. He meditates on the shadows of the trees lining a deserted street, on the old man strolling down an alley, on the street peddler's calls, and on the pigeons that forever circle above the city wall. His heart throbs in unison with "The Heart of An Ancient City," and he dreams together with "The Dream of An Ancient City."

Yet his verses are not choked in dust. Some passages are obscure points in his lines, but most of his poems breathe a clear, pure air. They represent life through a series of impressions, often quiet but never as trivial as they may seem to be at first reading.

Or should we cast the above remarks in the past tense, since Pien Chih-lin seems to have undergone a dramatic change during World War II?

The contrast between his home country in coastal China not far from Shanghai, and the northland around Peking must have inspired him to contemplation in 1929 when he enrolled in the University of Peking. He started publishing his verses in literary magazines almost immediately but he did not collect them into his first book, *Leaves of Three Autumns*, until shortly before his graduation in 1933. By diligently translating from the French he acquired insights into the art of such writers as Mallarmé, Verlaine, Valéry, Eluard, and Fort. He gained enough from these experiences to enable him to teach a course in the art of translation very successfully at the National Southwest Associate University in Kunming during the first years of World War II. Speaking with a heavy eastern Chinese accent and with no flair for eloquence, he made his lectures as difficult at times, as some of his most chewy poems. His extra-thick eyeglasses and frequently unshaven thin cheeks accentuated his reticence.

Soon after the Japanese, in 1937, spoiled Pien Chih-lin's quiet and peaceful Peking he left his academic life to travel in northwestern China and work with the youth groups then agitating for action against the national enemy. It was a number of months before he returned to his teaching, and when he did his interest shifted toward Yeats, Auden, and Eliot, in verses that were more simple and unadorned.

One of the most promising modern Chinese poets, Pien Chih-lin has been writing very little since the end of the war.

AH!
A Dialogue at Dusk

"I saw you blindly turn many an empty millstone,
   And even saw you once on a Bodhisattva statue on a
      dust-clad pedestal,
   You had a bed to support half of your body
   For a long time already; now what do you want to do?"
     "Yes, what do I want to do?"

"Perhaps you know, at first I was on the roadside,
   Somehow I returned to a courtyard even more desolate,
   And then into a room, then close to the corner of a wall.
   Think for me, will you? Where should I go?"
     "Yes, where should you go?"

1930
The Han Garden, 118–19

A MONK

Striking his bell day after day
A monk remains in his pale-gray deep dream.
The traces and shadows of so many past years
Appear in memory like a patch of incense smoke
That spreads everywhere in the old temple.
The remains of sorrow stay in the censer
Together with the grief of devout men and women.
Boredom meanders perpetually round and round in the sutras.

Sleepy words trickle from his mouth, a man talking in his
        dream,
His head nods along with his knocking of the wooden fish,[1]

Both so empty yet so heavy.
Stroke after stroke, the hills and rivers are lulled to sleep.
The hills and rivers sleep lazily in the afterglow,
As he finishes tolling the funeral bell of another day.

                    1931
                    The Han Garden, 124–25

LONG JOURNEY

If riding on camels in a line of swells
We surge on a huge slumbering desert,
And if, as a peal of faint bells
Pierces the solitude of the twilight,

[1] Wooden fish, the hollowed wooden box which a monk strikes
with a stick while chanting sutras, owes its name to an old legend
about some precious, original Buddhist sutras being swallowed by a
marine monster on their way to China. Striking the wooden fish,
therefore, becomes a gesture demanding the monster to disgorge the
Word.—Ed.

We set up our tents wherever we happen to be.
Let us brew fatigue into a sound sleep,
Sour and sweet, a huge urn-ful of strong liquid
To soak us in thoroughly.

Let us not bother about whether we could dream of an oasis,
We have, anyway, already become dead drunk.
Should a stormy wind carry sands and stones quietly
To bury us, that also would be quite all right.

> 1931
> *The Han Garden,* 120–21

WESTERN CH'ANG-AN STREET

Long are the shadows of bare trees, slanted
And faint, and of the old man walking under the trees
And of the cane on which he leans—
All on the wall, on the wall painted red by sunset.
The red wall is also long, and the blue sky beyond the wall,
The blue sky of the north is also long, very long.
Ah, old man, you must feel that the road
Is long, and so is this winter day?
Yes, I believe so.
Look, I am coming closer; no harm
To chat a bit as we walk along, just a little bit?
Yes, we say nothing, not even making a sound,
Only following our own shadows,
Walking . . .
        For how many years have they been walking,
These shadows, these long shadows?
Forward again and again, still farther,
Into the deserted open country, are they marching beyond the
        Great Wall?
There seems to be a cavalry bugle, it must be a large troop
Of mounted soldiers marching forward, facing the huge disc
        of a rising sun.

The rising sun is the red face of everyone, and the hoofs of
   the horses
Kick up the golden dust, ten feet, twenty feet high—
There is nothing around, I am still on the sidewalk,
The old man of the old days nowhere in sight. Two or three
Yellow-garbed soldiers stand in front of a gate.
(Is this a headquarters? Formerly a mansion?)
They stand erect, two or three tombstones,
Saying nothing, making no noise, perhaps still thinking of
   their homeland,
Of their homeland under the northeastern sky? Certainly!
But it's so futile to think of it now,
Even if they thought of the enemy's battle horses this moment
Going to drink water at the wells
In the old homestead,
Or of the hens this moment
Wandering over to the cornfields, or also
Of temporary homes—where could they be? *Pai, pai!*
What? Gunshots, from where?
They are from locally made guns, belonging to our own people,
   Don't be scared, don't!
But the sound of the crickets has already invaded
The green curtains of the corn, and the curtains have faded!
Are you still thinking? But it's utterly useless now.
Think about it tomorrow, at this moment you'd better
Make no sounds, say nothing, just bend your heads.
Watch the car rolling over the tar pavement in the long road,
So "modern" and so comfortable! However stylish it may be,
How could it compare with the huge banner of the bygone
   days,
And those smiles spreading over the faces under a red sun?
If you don't believe me, just ask the three crimson gates
Ahead that sadly stare
At the autumn sun now.
   Ah, under the setting sun there is
A good friend of mine in a city
Still older. How is he at this moment?
Perhaps he is passing through a deserted street there,
Accompanying a long shadow, slanted and faint.

Please tell me your first impression of Ch'ang-an
(There seems to be your shadow at my side)
Ai, let's not be like the old man,
Let's talk a little. . . .

September 11, 1932
The Han Garden, 162–67

SEVERAL INDIVIDUALS

The hawker calls, "Candied apples!"[2]
He seems not to mind at all swallowing a mouthful of dust.
The man with a bird cage in hand gazes at the white pigeons
in the sky,
And strolls casually over the sandy creek.
As a young man meditates in the deserted street:
A carrot peddler idly toys with his little knife, whetted
gleaming sharp.
A load of carrots smile their silly smiles in the setting sun.
As a young man meditates in the deserted street:
Some hold a bowl of rice in hand and sigh,
Some listen to other people talking in a dream at midnight,
Some pin a red flower in their white hair,
Like a setting sun supported on the horizon of a snowy
land . . .

October 10, 1932
The Han Garden, 170–71

THE TRAIN[3]

Pulling a cartload of the gold of the setting sun,
The mule wobbles along in its unsteady steps
As it moves through a desolate forest, sparsely wooded but
immense,
Silently stirring up a huge cloud of dust.

[2] Crabapples, usually.—Ed.
[3] Possibly a misprint in the original. A slight change would make
the title "Mule Cart."—Ed.

Let those sitting idly in faraway places dream
Of the heroes in ancient fairy tales
Who rode on clouds to soar to unknown distances.
A long sigh of the wind emerges from the old trees.

October 19, 1932
The Han Garden, 174–75

GRASS ON THE WALL

A patch of dying sun at five o'clock,
Half a ring of lamplight at six.
Just think, there are people who spend all their days
Dreaming a little and watching the wall a little,
While the grass on the wall grows tall and then yellow.

October 19, 1932
The Han Garden, 176

REED-LEAF BOAT

Cool breeze from an ancient land
Blows a palm fan from a man's hand,
He who soaks himself in the sea
Should get out now
To remove his bathing suit,

Leaving one or two rows of footsteps
On the beach
For shells to occupy.

He has already said there is no conch shell,
But the naughty child still dreams
Of listening to the roar of the surf
In the pocket that has returned from the sea.

You ought to be ashamed!
Now you should only look at the yellow leaves
Floating on water;
Think no more
About the reed-leaf boat
—Where did it go?

Is the traveler from beyond the sea
Also tired of watching the distant sails?

August 17, 1933
The Han Garden, 186–88

THE HEART OF THE ANCIENT CITY

You can hear your own footsteps
In the market, at 7:30 P.M.
(This is still said to be the heart of the ancient city.)

No wonder the shopkeeper is sleepy,
Look, even the electric lights are drowsy.

The shopworn merchandise on the shelves,
Some having come from Tokyo, some from Shanghai,
Must be mourning their own degradation—

So thinks a traveler passing by, perhaps.

Teleteletele . . . there is a musician's drum.
The drum echoes the feeble tremor of the market.

Pao-ting, October 27, 1933
The Han Garden, 192–93

AUTUMN WINDOW

Like a middle-aged man
Looking back at his footprints—
Every step a desert—
Awakening from confused dreams
He listens to the half sky full of evening crows.

Seeing the setting sun on a gray wall,
He thinks of a tubercular victim, still at an early stage,
Who dreams of the pink of his youth
In front of an ancient mirror covered with evening haze.

October 26, 1933
The Han Garden, 194–95

THE AQUEOUS ROCK[4]

The man near the water wishes to carve a few words on the
    rocks:

[4] Pien Chih-lin's own translation of this poem appears in *Contemporary Chinese Poetry,* ed. Robert Payne (London: Routledge, 1947), pp. 85–86, but his seems to be more of a rewriting of the original into English. It follows:

Pondering on leaving some inscription
on the rock beside the stream, the traveller
pours his feeling into a quiet flow of words:

The boy who admires the charms of the baby
asks his own mother: "Was I like this too?"

The mother, reminded of her own photographs
which have turned yellow in a dust-sealed drawer,

and of the profusion of splendours outside the window
garnered in a frameful of shrivelled pods,

exclaims: "What a seed of sorrow!"

"O water, O water!" sighs the traveller,
startled at the sudden realisation
that wave over wave of ancient emotion
has flowed like the running stream,
leaving behind layer after layer of sorrow.

The big lad finds the little child lovely,
Thus he asks his mother, "Was I like this before?"

The mother recalls her yellowed photographs
Piled in the drawer of a dust-clad old desk;

She recalls a trellis full of rosy color
Hidden in dried beanstalks before the window,

And sighs, "These seeds of sorrow!"

"Ah, water, water!" the meditating man suddenly sighs:
 The feelings of ancient people, like flowing water,
 Have accumulated sorrows layer upon layer.

> 1934
> *The Han Garden,* 204–5

CONTRAST

Assuming myself a philosopher, I
Find comfort in a rotten apple on the wayside;
Only after the earth has rotted, mankind emerges as parasites,
Learn then from the distant pagoda; you stand alone on the
        mountain gazing at the sunset.

Today I tasted newly ripened grapes.
Sour? Bitter? I question myself.
The flavor of early autumn plus a reminiscence of three years.
You have slept a spell in the creek.

> 1934
> *The Han Garden,* 202–3

A PIECE OF BROKEN SHIP

The tide came in, the surf offered her
A piece of broken ship.
      Wordless,
She again sat, motionless, on the rock,
And let the setting sun sketch her hair
On the piece of broken ship.
      After a long pause she
Again gazed at the horizon beyond the sea
Where the white sail had disappeared.
The tide receded; she could only return
That piece of broken ship
      To be washed away by the sea.

              The Han Garden, 168–69

TO THE YOUNG PIONEERS OF THE NORTHWEST

You have arranged a rendezvous with the rising sun:
Let's meet on the hilltop three miles from here.
A troop of hoes cuts through the lingering night,
Racing to be the first to greet the dawn.

Squeezing fat out of a deserted and barren land,
You demand that the yellow earth produce grains.
With their winter clothes of blackened grass torn open
One thousand mountains all change their color.

You arrange the individual colors and lines of each crop
Into the over-all design of the fields.
You observe nature's ways to enrich nature
With the fullest force man can muster.

To let you taste a bit of sweetness in the midst of hardships
The earth yields flavorful grassroots, splendid!
All hands, once so tender, have grown callous,
When they shake hands with a girl, she might scream.

No need to worry that the hoe is too primitive,
Step by step it will open up a tomorrow.
You face the real and the present, and
"Hope" thus acquires many smiling faces.

November 27, 1939
Selected Modern Chinese Poems, 111–12

LI CHIN-FA (1900?–   )

LI CHIN-FA came from the southern Chinese province of Kwang-tung. His travel in Europe and study of the French poets led him to spearhead a symbolist movement in modern Chinese poetry. Although his own works drew much unfavorable criticism for being difficult and odd, he must be given credit for indicating a new direction to the new poets in China in the 1920s. Unlike most of his bohemian fellow writers, Li was not prone to reveal his experience in autobiographical accounts and little is known of his life. Three volumes established his position in modern Chinese poetry: *Light Rain* (1925), *I Sing for Happiness* (1926), and *The Long-Term Visitor and Hard Times* (1927). Later he was associated with Lin Yutang in publishing ventures. After the 1920s Li wrote more essays than poems.

A THOUGHT

Like fallen leaves
Splashing blood
On our feet,

Life is but
A smile on the lips
Of death.

Under a half-dead moon,
You drink and sing,
The sound splitting your throat
Disappears in the northern wind.
Ah!
Go and caress your beloved.

Open your doors and windows,
Make her timid, and
Let the dust of the road cover
Her lovely eyes.
Is this the timidity
And anger
Of life?
Like fallen leaves
Splashing blood
On our feet.

Life is but
A smile on the lips
Of death.

Compendium, 213–14

EXPRESSION OF TIME

1

Wind and rain on the ocean,
Dead deer in my heart.
Look, autumn dream has left on spread wings
Only this dejected soul remains.

2

I pursue abandoned desires,
I mourn discolored lips.
Ah, on the shadowy grassland
The moon gathers our silence.

3

In the ancient palace of love,
Our honeymoon took ill and fell;
Take a half-burned candle, hurry,
Dusk is spreading over fields and hills.

4

What do I want at this moment?
I seem to fear being scorched to death in the sun.
Go away, the garden gate is open,
And bees have entered on filmy slippers.

5

I await the wakening from a dream,
I await the sleep of a wakeful day:
With your tears in my eyes,
I cannot look back into the past.

6

You lean on a snowbank, thinking of spring,
I listen to the cicadas in withering grass;
Our lives are barren and laid waste,
Like a rice field in the wake of a stampede.

7

I sing folk tunes unrhymed.
With my heart keeping the beat,
Trust your sorrow, then, to my bosom
Where it will find its cure.

8

A lotus in the shade,
Cannot understand the brilliance of the sun and the moon,
Row your boat into the secluded pond,
To let the blossom learn a bit of the love of man.

9

Our memories
Are searching for their way home from the wilderness.

Compendium, 211–12

NEVER TO RETURN

Go with me, child,
To an old city built in the Middle Ages—
It has lain asleep through the nights of the centuries;
There the creeks eternally sing songs of monotone—
Sighs of the poets from the East.
The cavernous hearts of the city
Are filled with lichens.

Still farther
Stands a dilapidated wall all alone,
Keeping vigil over a garden abandoned long ago,
Against a silence of black and dark blue.
These things befriend severe winters
And have no knowledge of the prime of summer.
In the thin layer of sand you may
Find chips of a wooden frame,
(But hardly an appropriate gift for anyone).
Snails are chuckling in a shady nook.

There the birds are tired
And bees linger in their dreams,
And departing yellow leaves
Fly in the sky,
Nodding to the old pines,
To the flowing water.

You can only smell
The epilogue of the season—the odor of the rotting things.
Pale shades of the trees
Sometimes lull you to sleep,
With a little light from over the horizon
You may better discern their forms.
But their hearts are bleeding, rueful and cold.
If you want to hear our laughter,
Bring your lute
To play a "Never to Return."

Compendium, 208–9

TENDERNESS

My fingers rude and crude
Touch the warmth of your skin;
The little fawn lost its way in the forest,
There is only the sound of dead leaves.

Your low whisper
Resounds in my barren heart.
A conqueror of all, I
Have broken my spear and shield.

Your eyes cast a glance,
Cast a butcher's warning;
Your lips? No need to mention them,
I'd rather trust your arms.

I believe in the fantasy of fairy tales,
But not in a woman's sentiment.
(Ah, making comparisons is not my habit.)
But you really resemble the shepherdess in a story.

I played all the tunes,
But nothing pleased your ear;
All colors have been exhausted,
Yet nothing can describe your beauty.

> Berlin, 1922
> *Compendium,* 206

A NOCTURNAL SONG

We stroll on dead grass,
Sorrow and anger entangle our legs.

Pink memories
Rotten animals on the roadside, emitting stench

And spreading it all over the little city
To disturb the sound sleep of many.

The wheel of my heart, already broken,
Turns and churns forever in the mud.

Tracks and ruts invisible
Crisscrossed by the slender shadows of the tender and
    affectionate.

Ah, the moonlight still fresh as thousands of years ago,
Will finally understand my dream.

No matter where I may be, you
Always print my shadow on ordinary sands and rocks.

But the unchanging reflection, accentuates the intense black
    behind the house,
—A bit too stiff and too funny.

O Great God, weigh your anchor,
I'm tired of smelling the sweat of all forms of life.

Quickened footsteps
Interrupt the rhythm of my heart.

Mysterious years,
I shall end them by swallowing the sweet herbs in the garden.

He has lost his heart,
It is mixed in the bag of a traveling salesman going far away.

We all wrong each other,
Leaving behind only silent hatred.

However we may pledge faithfulness eternal,
By whispering on the bridge over a murmuring creek,

You always cover the frightful cavern
With your soul,

Or we may die of old age together,
Like defeated heroes, in a roadside ditch.

Yet our bodies have
Already been covered with gunpowder.

Can one find a place of rest
In the dried old pond?

Dijon, 1922
Compendium,   202–4

WOMAN ABANDONED

Long hair hang down before my eyes,
Cutting off all glances of contempt and shame
And the rapid flow of fresh blood, the sound sleep of bleached
bones.
Insects and the dark night arrive hand in hand,
Over the corner of this low wall
To howl behind my ears that never have been soiled.
They howl like winds in the wilderness,
Frightening many shepherds and their charges.

By way of a blade of grass I communciate with God
in the deserted vale.
Only the memory of the roaming bees has recorded my
sorrow.
Or I may pour my sorrow along with the cascades tumbling
over the cliff,
And drift away among the red leaves.

At each of her motions she feels the weight of her sorrow
     increasing;
No fire of a setting sun can burn the ennui of time
Into ashes to float away through the chimneys and attach
     themselves
To the wings of itinerant crows,
And with them perch on the rocks of a roaring sea,
To listen to the boatmen's songs.
Sighs of her timeworn skirts,
As she saunters in a graveyard.
Never will she again drop a hot tear
On the lawn
To adorn this world.

Compendium, 200

TAI WANG-SHU (1905–50)

WHEN THE symbolist poet Li Chin-fa shocked the reader of modern Chinese poetry in the 1920s and 1930s with his baffling verse, Tai Wang-shu, also a symbolist, won a good following with his simpler and more lyrical lines.

His home was in the beautiful eastern city, Hangchow. Like Li Chin-fa, Tai received his early training in France where he absorbed the works of the French symbolists. One of his very early poems, "The Alley in the Rain," fully represents the lyrical quality of his poetry and has won him the nickname of "the poet of the rainy alley."

The finesse of his thought and sentiment was such that even a prison experience could not harden it into something sharp and biting. His tone remained subdued and his grief quiet when he was writing, of all places, on a prison wall after being jailed by the Japanese (in Shanghai?) in 1942. As Wen I-to aptly put it, it was no longer an age for the refined notes of chamber music. Tai was fated to be silent, as the war became intense and most Chinese writers turned to the battlefield. He wrote very little during the war years.

He is at his best when he contemplates life and its mystery in the gleaming reflection of a white butterfly's wing, or in the lingering music of a tiny finch. And he is particularly moving as he mourns the loss of those elements that made poetry what it was for him:

> Such lazy shadows under the sun
> Such warm quietude,
> The aroma of lunch being prepared—
> So familiar, so familiar.

This terrace, this window
And happiness peeping from behind.
And those shelves of books, those two beds,
And that vase of flowers . . . a paradise

I haven't forgotten, this is home,

. . . .

March 10, 1944
(from *The Troubled Years*, 64–65)

He once confessed to his wife:

I'd rather spend my life quietly
Shrouded in the light you radiate.
If some day someone must talk about me,
Let him say I was the happiest one that ever lived.
(from *The Troubled Years*, 82–83)

Immediately after the war, he went to Hong Kong where
he stayed until 1949. Then he returned to the mainland,
where he died shortly afterwards.

THE ALLEY IN THE RAIN

Carrying an oilpaper umbrella, I alone
Paced the long, long
Lonely alley in the rain,
Hoping to encounter
The lady who carried her melancholy
Like a clove flower.

She had
The color of clove blossoms
And the fragrance of clove blossoms
And the melancholy of clove blossoms
She carried her sorrow in the rain,
And in the rain she sauntered.

She seemed to be, in this rainy alley,
Carrying an oilpaper umbrella
Like me,
And like me she silently
Paced, her steps moving slowly
In loneliness and quiet sorrow.

Silently she came close;
She walked close to me and cast
A glance, like a sigh,
She drifted away—
A dream,
Such a soft and blurred dream.

Like a spray of clove flowers
Drifting by in a dream,
The lady passed by me,
Receding into the distance,
To the toppled hedges and walls,
To the end of the alley under rain.

Her colors
And her fragrance
Vanished in the sorrowful tune of the rain,
And vanished also
Her sighing glance,
And her clove-like melancholy.

Carrying an oilpaper umbrella, I alone
Paced the long, long
Lonely alley in the rain,
Hoping to see drifting by
A lady who carried her melancholy
Like a clove flower.

1925 (?)
Compendium, 220–21

A SONNET

Light rain fell on your unkempt hair:
So many little pearls sprinkled in black kelp,
So many dead fish tossed about on the waves,
With a mysterious, sad gleam

Luring and bringing my cheerless soul
To retire to the dreamland of love and death
Where purple sunshine lights up the golden air,
And pitiful creatures, unrestrained, weep happy tears.

Like a black cat, so old and thin,
I shall wither away and yawn in that soft twilight,
Pouring forth all my pride, both false and true;
Then I shall follow that mysterious gleam to stumble
In the hazy twilight, like a bubble of rosy wine floating in
      an amber glass,
Letting my sentimental eyes hide in the dark, murky memory.

            1927 (?)
            Compendium, 219–20

SUNSET

Evening clouds spread a brocade in the sky,
Molten gold fills the creek under a setting sun;
My shadow, tall and lean, skates along the road,
Like the lonely ghost of an ancient tree on the hill.

Distant mountains turn purple, having mourned
So much the death of a day; but
Fallen leaves dance in joy to greet
The flowing robe of the night—that cool breeze.

The scent of antiquity seeps from the graves,
Binding the bats in a spell above an old tree;
They chatter privately, softly, without end,
While circling low in the evening mist.

Night quietly returns from the end of the world;
I, alone, continue my lingering steps.
From my heart of solitude have vanished
All sorrows and all joys I have ever known.

1927 (?)
Compendium, 217

A LITTLE TUNE

The bird, weary of singing, hides its beak in colorful feathers;
Where is it hovering—the little soul of music?
Withered blossoms retire to dust, petal by petal;
What does it cling to—the little soul of fragrance?

They cannot be in hell, they cannot;
Such beautiful, beautiful little souls!
Are they then, in heaven, in paradise?
But St. Peter shakes his head.

Nobody knows where they are, nobody;
The poet only smiles in silence.
There is something which blends the clouds
In the unchanging universe of his heart.

May 14, 1936
The Troubled Years, 20–21

I THINK

I think, therefore I am a butterfly—[1]

The little flowers' gentle call, after endless years,
Comes to vibrate my multicolored wings
Through the cloud of dreamless perpetual sleep.

March 14, 1937
The Troubled Years, 37

WHITE BUTTERFLY

What wisdom do you offer me,
Little white butterfly?
You open your wordless pages, and
Close again your wordless pages.

In your opened pages:
Solitude;
In your closed pages:
Solitude.

May 3, 1940
The Troubled Years, 40

WRITTEN ON A PRISON WALL

If I die here,
My friends, don't be sad.
I shall live forever
In your hearts.

Dead is only one of you
In a prison under Japanese occupation.
He nursed a deep, deep hatred,
That you must always remember.

[1] The reference is to the famous Taoist legend attributed to
Chuang Chou (fourth century B.C.?) who supposedly dreamed of his
own transformation into a butterfly.—Ed.

When you return and dig up
From the earth his mutilated body,
Please let your victory cheers
Bear his soul to soar in the sky,

And please place his bleached bones,
On a mountain top to bathe in the sun and wind:
This, my friends, was the only dream he had
In that dark and dank dungeon.

April 27, 1942
The Troubled Years, 46–48

WITH MY MAIMED HAND

With my maimed hand I touch
This immense land:
This corner has been reduced to charred debris,
And over there, only blood-soaked mud remains:
This lake must be my home country
(Where spring brings a belt of brocade to the dike,
And that rare scent, from a broken willow twig.)
I feel the weeds and the refreshing cool of the water,
And the biting cold of the snow-capped Ch'ang-pai Mountain.
The silt-rich water of the Yellow River seeps from between
                my fingers:
Rice paddies of the south, your young rice sprouts
Used to be so soft, so downy . . . but now only weeds;
The lichee blossoms south of the Five Ranges wilt in
                loneliness.
Over there I dip my finger in the bitter waves of the South
        Sea—
        No fishing boats in sight.
My shapeless hand glides over the boundless land,
My fingers are covered with blood and cinders, and my palm
        with dark shadow.
Only that distant corner remains intact, unspoiled,
Still warm, bright, sturdy, and growing strong.

There I touch with my maimed hand, gently, lovingly,
As I would the hair of my sweetheart, or an infant his
		mother's breast.
I place all my strength in my hand, together with
All my love and all my hope, to press on that corner.
Only there I find the sun and the spring
That dispel darkness and bring an awakening;
Only there we live not like beasts, nor die
Like ants . . . there we find, forever China!

> July 3, 1942
> *The Troubled Years,* 49–52

MU MU-T'IEN (1900–   )

Mu Mu-t'ien was among those who advocated the development of "pure poetry." He regarded poetry as "a rhythmic movement through time and space, unified and continuing," and he attempted to integrate the sounds and cadence of the language with the images it carries.

He wanted poetry to be suggestive rather than informative —preferring light sketches to bold lines—and found the French symbolists very much to his liking. Together with Wang Tu-ch'ing, he made a serious effort to adopt the French techniques.

A native of I-t'ung (in Kirin, Manchuria), he studied at the Imperial University in Tokyo and followed a career of college teaching. A member of the Creation Society, he was one of the most active poets during the 1920s. *The Traveler's Heart,* his one book of verse, was published in 1927.

VILLAGE AT DUSK

Misty haze
Gently
Surrounds a floating village
Straw-thatched huts
Whitewashed adobe walls
And waving columns of smoke above the houses
Small clusters of birch trees sway lightly
On the path before
Behind
And on the side of the village
Spreads an unnamed dreamy and soothing scent
That supports the wings shuttling through the air
And overflows the winding path—a line drawn in space
Gates woven with willow twigs

Protect resting cattle and sheep
A shepherd boy sits on a rick singing low
A dog lies against the door
An old woman with a child-like expression puffs on her pipe
She smiles at the children while
Listening to the pecking sound of the chickens feeding in the
       yard
The ripples in the air stirred up by a swooping bat
And the waves of chirping that rise little by little as the
       insects begin to sing
At a distance
On the border of a field
The villagers are leaning
To gaze at the undulating line of mountains on the horizon
And ponder on the white sails gliding slowly over the thin
       white line afar
From the beach behind the village
Often comes the sound of rowing
On the trail in the thick willow grove
Those coming home are singing
The quiet whisper of the water in a ditch
Circles round between the sky and the plain
My peaceful home village
Under immense gauzy clouds

July 24, 1925
Compendium, 235

THE PALE TEMPLE BELL

Pale   bell sounds   decadent   and blurred
Diffuse   in the exquisite   but desolate   misty
       vale
—Dried weeds   thousands   of layers—
Listen   the perpetually   fantastic   ancient bell
       sounds
Listen   the thousands   of strokes

Ancient bell sounds   drift away   on gleaming waves
Ancient bell sounds   drift away   to the gray and green
                                    birch treetops
Ancient bell sounds   drift away   in the rustling winds
—The moon's reflection   floating   floating—
Ancient bell sounds   drift away   on sailing clouds

A tangy scent   whiff after whiff
Withered grass   in the marsh   near   the deserted
                                    road
—An old grief   a perpetual   vision   a new wine
                                    cup—
Listen   that desolation   stroke after stroke
From the ancient bells   drifting out   drifting out
                                    to an unknown   blurred land
Ancient bell sounds   vanish   in the wafting
                                    floating haze

Ancient bell sounds   sink quietly   in the murmuring
                                    gentle waves   of a sleepy stream
Ancient bell sounds   sink quietly   in the   faint
                                    distant   cloud-clad hills
Ancient bell sounds   flow   into   the universe
                                    immense
—Half-forgotten   bygones   eternal joy   and sorrow

Soft   ancient bell sounds   soar along   the
                                    moonbeam
Soft   ancient bell sounds   continue   to enter
                                    the long Milky Way
—Ah   distant   ancient bell sounds   echo   the
                                    songs of an ancient land—
Fitful   ancient bell sounds   reflect   the songs of my
                                    fatherland

Listen   broken   ancient bell sounds   in the vale
                                    yellow and gray
They enter   the unlimited space   with their free
                                    and refined tone

Withered leaves   dead grass   follow   the severe
                northern wind
Listen   the thousands   of strokes—misty and blurred—
The fantastic   unlimited   decaying   yet perpetual
                bell sounds   of my fatherland
Listen to them   in a deserted vale   at dusk

> January 2, 1926
> *Compendium,* 236–37

WANG TU-CH'ING (1898–1940)

"I USED TO write poetry with Byron and Hugo in mind; now I want to apply myself to the art of poetry by developing the color and music in my language," wrote Wang Tu-ch'ing to a fellow poet, Mu Mu-t'ien, on February 4, 1926, after his return to China from Europe. He had become an ardent admirer of Lamartine for his feeling, of Verlaine for his music, of Rimbaud for his color, and of Laforgue for his force.

The Byronic quality of Wang's poems had much to do with his early background and training. He was born in the ancient Chinese capital of Changan in Shensi Province. The historic pageantry and scent of antiquity of that city nurtured his early yearning for the grand drama of humanity. When he visited Rome in 1925, it was a realization of his dream, and he inevitably compared it with his native city, Changan. He reread the ancient Chinese anthology, *The Songs of the South*, reviewed Goethe's lines on Rome, and wrote a long poem himself.

> Springtime, but a sky full of dreary rain,
> I come to visit the Changan on the Mediterranean Sea.
>
> (from *Selected Works of Wang*, 50)

He had come a long way before reaching this point. At the age of thirteen he was already trying to write and even receiving some pay for the essays on current topics he wrote for a newspaper in his hometown. A small measure of success was assured him when he took over the editorship of the same daily paper at the age of sixteen. His radical expressions quickly acquired barbs, the paper was suspended by the government, and he, at least partly because of pressure, left China for Japan.

Like many of his fellow students who had the good fortune to go abroad in those days, he chose to study science and applied himself to biology. But his interest in literature drew him away from his studies. For a while he wanted to do research in classical Chinese literature and actually worked on the T'ang dynasty poet, Li Shang-yin (813–58). The May Fourth incident in 1919 brought him back to Shanghai where he again worked in the editorial office of a newspaper while taking part in the labor union movement. Leading a busy life, he had little time then for creative thinking and writing.

When he went to Europe to study, he found in Paris all that a young man full of wild dreams could desire. There were museums, cafés, and nude models for his youthful senses; the brilliant talks of Anatole France on Montmartre, the heated debates between Henri Barbusse and Romain Rolland in magazines, and the book stalls on the Seine for his mind. Wang took in all of them, but first started a wild romance with a young Chinese girl.

The complications that followed the birth of a child to the girl tossed him into an abyss of self-pity and disillusion. For many months he led a life of dissipation, during which time he wrote most of the poems of his that are drenched in melancholy and decadence.

His familiarity with the political and intellectual tides in China and his association with the active Chinese student groups in Europe kept him in touch with developments at home. Time and again, his earlier political ambitions returned to plague him. By publishing his poems in Shanghai magazines, he established an acquaintance with Kuo Mo-jo, then in Japan. This soon grew into a friendship that was to lead Wang into the small circle that founded the Creation Society in 1922.

Wang admitted that he began his literary career seriously in France when he traded his biology books for Kant, Nietzsche, and Spinoza on the banks of the Seine. He locked himself in a tiny room in the Latin Quarter, reading philosophy for months, and later through an unknown Marxist café frequenter named Robert Bollier, met Pierre Loti and Anatole France.

The tumultuous events in China were casually reported in French papers with distortions which upset Wang badly. He decided to return to where he believed he was wanted. Although the China he found upon his return in 1925 was a

bitter disappointment, he plunged into the literary contro-
versies and pledged himself to support a revolutionary litera-
ture. He wrote a number of short stories and plays, none of
them too successful. As his friend, Mu Mu-t'ien, observed,
Wang Tu-ch'ing reflected the atmosphere of a China with her
revolutionary energy all spent.

Wang's poems are collected in five volumes: *Before the Im-
age of the Holy Lady* (1926), *Venice* (1927), *Discipline*
(1927?), *Before Death* (1927), and *Miscellaneous Poems.*

A FADED ROSE

Under a pale green lamp I gaze at her,
I gaze at her light golden hair,
Her rougeless cheeks, her eyes blue and clear,
Ah, under a lamp of pale green color.

She gathered in her hands a pile of rose petals,
Bending her head, she kissed them again and again,
She offered them to me and told me
To hold them close to my lips as did she.

Ah, roses—I thanked them secretly:
You brought so close to me the scent of her hair,
You mingled our breaths in your own sweet remains
And your sweet remains sealed a kiss of ours.

Because in you our breaths are forever entombed,
Ah, roses, I wish to hold your sweet remains forever.
—I wish to keep this pale green lamp always,
And always sit this way, always next to her.

Selected Works of Wang, 70–71

I CAME OUT OF A CAFÉ

I came out of a café,
Carrying a load of fatigue
Aggravated
By wine,
I don't know
Where shall I go to find
My temporary lodging . . .
Ah, deserted streets,
At dusk, under rain.

I come out of a café,
Carrying in me a load of wine,
Silently
Walking alone,
Feeling inside
The sorrow of a homeless man
About to lose his country . . .
Ah, the quiet and chilly streets
At dusk, under rain.

Selected Works of Wang, 68–69

from THE LAST SUNDAY

Ah, I seem to see "death" slowly go by,
I really seem to see "death" slowly go by . . .
This weather, the sudden wind and sudden rain!
The wind comes to ravage the trees, wantonly,
And keeps throwing down the withered branches that are
          leaving the trees . . .
Ah, the rain with its somber and heavy malicious élan
Comes to drench the buildings in the market, the factory
          chimneys, and park benches, all and all.
Ah, wind; ah, rain.

The year is again about over, again about over.

My homesickness, my melancholy, and my ennui,

The exotic festivities, bright and gay, have all fled,

Even the last Sunday is spoiled by the sky full of black clouds.

I'm startled by the colors, scents, and tunes, all faded without
a trace.

The sad looking woods on the river, flowers in the fields, and
the birds on the wing.

Ah, pity me—despair has wrought in me a fatigue never to be
cured,

I fear the last Sunday of the year is also my own last day.

Well, I wish this last Sunday were my own last day

So that my useless remains could fade away like the colors,
scents, and tunes.

Ah, this last Sunday of the year, the year is about over, about
over. . . .

Selected Works of Wang, 62–63

from VENICE

1

Who is that singing there gently and low,

That strikes the chord of my heart, already ill?

Wordless, I walk past this bridge, as though

Half frail, half fainting, from unlimited sorrow . . .

The water under the bridge moves in a calm flow,

Ah, that bewitching voice, who is that singing there gently
and low?

Who is that playing a violin, sending off a refrain,

On a day like this displaying neither sunshine nor rain?

The air seems to vibrate with that soft strain,

And time, pale and wan, appears almost to remain

Still as I, wordless, lean on the bridge's railing;

Ah, those depressing notes, who is that playing a violin,
sending off a refrain?

10

I will let the evening breeze
Blow, as it wishes, on my cheeks red with wine.
My heart beats
And a disquieting shiver rocks this body of mine.
Ah, I wish I could lie down right here, and instantly die,
Let the soft moonlight cover the corpse that was I.

I turned my wine-warmed temples
To greet the night breeze so fresh and clean;
My body still trembles
And my heart still throbs in pain . . .
Ah, I wish I could lie down right here, and instantly die
Let the soft moonlight cover the corpse that was I.

1926
Selected Works of Wang, 6–18

from ABOUT TO SAIL FOR HOME

I am a Chinese!
From a land where an ancient civilization grew with pride,
Where heroes and great men shed blood and gave their lives,
Where there have been poets and men of stature who sang
          and sighed . . .

Ah, I am a Chinese, I mustn't seek any happiness, any peace:
I should return right away
To give what I can give, my tears and my sacrifice.

The strong aroma of alcohol in the bars
Can help people forget all their troubles.
Every time when grief gripped me,
Near that aroma I wanted to be . . .
Ah, it did cure the paining heart
And hastened sorrows to depart
—But, thank you so much, thank you,
No more shall I enter these bars, from now on, no more.

Whatever peace and quiet to my soul you may restore,
Here I shall forever remain a man from an alien shore.

Farewell, Latin Quarter, chestnut trees, bookstalls on the
    Seine . . .

Ah, chestnut trees,
On warm spring days,
Often I came under your broad foliage to stay,
I loved your broad leaves
That spread their intense green against a soft blue sky.

Ah, chestnut trees,
When the season turned autumnal and cool,
I often stood listening to your falling leaves, all alone,
I loved the sound of your falling leaves,
That sad and tired tune.
Enough, enough, nothing here is mine. No matter how I
    pine and
Linger, no meaning can come out of it. I must leave stoically!
It's better to leave stoically!

I know time has come, the end to my decadence must now
    begin,
I know besides loving my fatherland, I cannot atone for my
    sin.

Yes, my fatherland, there a great nation is falling apart,
    dying,
I must hurry home, hurry, this is not a place for me to
    remain.
Here a man is tempted to seek pleasure, but for pleasure I
    have no more inclination,
Here it is the center of modernity, but I have grown sick of
    this civilization.
I say good-by to my sins, to my youthful ecstasies that shall
    never return,
From now on only for my fatherland my blood shall swell
    and boil and burn!

Ah, all my fatigue, dissipation, and decadence that has been
    and is to be,
You all stay right here by yourselves, and don't come along
    with me.

          December 1925
          Selected Works of Wang, 29–39

from THE SORROW OF SHANGHAI

1

Do you believe it?
A startling miracle is about to occur here?
On this side the stream of cars are sounding their ceaseless
    horns,
And the towering buildings, all lighted, make you dizzy when
    you look up at them.
Over there, there is only a row of shacks—look carefully—only
    one-story structures,
Sketched out under almost lightless oil lamps,
Men's shadows huddle on the ground in front of the doors
—Ah, men? Are they human beings? It's but a cluster—
Squirming a little, and faintly groaning a little . . .
Ah, miracle, miracle, do you believe it?
On this side lie Paris and London,
But on the other side shiver Egypt and Jerusalem!
The metropolis of Shanghai exists only for this miracle.

          Selected Works of Wang, 23–28

from I'VE RETURNED TO MY FATHERLAND

Ai, a pallor blankets the whole of Shanghai, all of Shanghai
—Except the red turbans of Indian gendarmes who club the
    factory hands.

. . . .

Ai, ai, they say this is the fatherland for which I longed over
    ten years.
They say this is the Shanghai which I've always wanted to see!
But now I have only painful silence, very painful silence,
I regret that I did not die a homeless exile beyond the sea.
I kiss this land, the land of sad pallor,
My heart burns in a fire that leaps up in the air.
What does a fatherland like this mean to me
When it sends me nothing but unlimited sorrow and despair?
I pray for the factory workers clubbed by the Indian
    gendarmes,
I pray for the coolies who in clouds of dust continue to suffer,
I pray for them, pray for them with piety and fervor,
Pray for them to shed this pallor for a new color!
Ah, arise, arise, and arise in a gale
To destroy this fatherland, sad and pale.

> June 1925
> *Selected Works of Wang,* 46–47

LI KUANG-T'IEN (1907–   )

HIS FATHER recited the poetry of the fourth century idyllic poet T'ao Ch'ien (372–427) when he had a cup of wine in hand—and he almost always had a cup in hand. His uncle on his mother's side tilled the land, diligently and honestly, always working hard but never becoming rich. His father had infinite stories and anecdotes to tell; his uncle's mouth seemed to have been made only for terse comments on practical daily matters. His uncle stubbornly clung to his farmer's tradition and old ideas; and it was his uncle who reared Li Kuang-t'ien, although the poet-essayist never ceased to admire his poetry-reciting father.

This explains much about the "pastoral" (or should it be the agricultural or rice-paddy?) element in Li Kuang-t'ien's poems. He likes the plain, humble peasants in his native village in Shantung Province; he likes the plain, pleasant life of the farmers when they can have it, and when they cannot have it, he suffers with them. He likes the plants, the birds, and the insects that surrounded his childhood. And, grown up, he still likes Gilbert White (*The Natural History and Antiquities of Selborne*) and W. H. Hudson (*Green Mansions*). It was in this frame of mind that he wrote his poetry up to 1936.

He felt, however, that he was by temperament more suited to prose and turned to the essay. Two collections of essays, published in 1936, established him as a prose stylist in the tradition of Chou Tso-jen, Lu Hsün's brother, from whom Li Kuang-t'ien learned much about Chinese literature.

Like almost all of his friends, in 1937 he had to flee Peking, where he had completed his study of Western literature at the University. He walked from Hankow in Central China (Hupeh Province) to northwestern China (Shensi Province), then southward to Chengtu (Szechwan Province). The poverty and ignorance he saw in what he called the "outside the

circle" places pained him. As he noted in 1941, many peas-
ants did not know that Shantung was in China, or that Li
Kuang-t'ien and his traveling companions were Chinese, in
spite of their common language.

He told himself, "Please don't blame the mirror, if your
face is really ugly," and proceeded to note his observations in
a collection of essays called *The Trip to the West* (1942).
Always an admirer of the Stoic school of philosophy, he was
stoic about his experiences. But he also admitted that, being
"outside the circle" it would no longer be possible for him to
find meaning in such lines as this one of Ch'in Shao-yu
(1049–1100):

> A dreamless sleep is awakened in the sun

or this one of Wang Wei (699–759):

> Cold sunlight on the cool pine branches

because life would no longer permit him to experience that
kind of world. He had to live in the present, not in the past.
With this as his belief, he stopped writing poetry.

THE SCENT OF AUTUMN

Who has smelled the scent of autumn
While looking at a garden from a window with tattered
        curtains?
From distant lakes
The scent of rotten leaves fallen on the marshes,
And from the depth of a forest
The smell of ripe berries on withered branches
Are brought here by a cool breeze—
The scent of autumn?
The scent
Wakes me up from an old dream,
So faint
Like the autumn clouds this moment

Being blown along by the western wind,
And again blown away,
As I gaze at them from the window.

September 1931
The Han Garden, 70–71

A JOURNEY

Whose house is it behind this high wall,
White, reflecting an autumn sun already low in the western
     sky?
On the wall are hung melons red and green,
And swaying yellow leaves, the size of fans.

Like good news brought from good friends far away,
But why only these two or three words?
The voices and the faces are still familiar,
Yet the people, yes, where are they?
The two black lacquered doors are ajar.

Quietly I peep inside, and again
I'm on my way, dragging heavy steps.
The sun is down, the insects are flying, and the crows are
     also in flight.

October 20, 1933
The Han Garden, 58–59

THE WINDOW

Is that your face of nine years ago
Cast, by accident, on my window this moment?
The green curtain has faded into pale white,
But nine years ago remains nine years ago.

Is that your autumnal sadness of nine years ago
Returning together with the breeze and the chirping of
     fallen leaves?
Ancient sadness buried deep in earth
Seeded today's grass of grief, so very green.

You were a migrant bird on its journey,
And only by accident you visited my autumn woods,
(Now, I myself have changed into an autumn forest,)
And you went on, far away, without lingering a moment.

Far, far away, to the edge of a sky unknowable,
You went to search—for a forest of spring?
Here I sit alone before my pale window curtain, in silence,
Gazing beyond, at that patch of white cloud on the blue.

> 1933
> *The Han Garden*, 58–59

SYMPHONY

Wind, wind everywhere toward noon;
Riding on the wind, a pigeon's whistle.
On a stove in the tiny room
Mutters an old man's voice—a pot of boiling water.

Syu, syu, syu . . .
He snores with eyes closed,
Dreaming a ripe, old
Eighty-year-old drunken dream.

The symphony at a wedding banquet,
The symphony at a funeral banquet,
Marches on in cadence
With life's forced march.

Syu . . .
A fruit falls into perpetual silence.
Time is like an immense ocean
With its symphony never still.

> 1933
> *The Han Garden*, 62–63

A FALLING STAR

A falling star, falling,
And falling with it
Are tears.

Thinking of a summer night with croaking frogs
In an ancient village,
While the falling stars are flying, who would

Tie a knot for you with the black silk from her hair,
And say she wishes to string the pearls that light up a
    ship's channel
As a gift of perpetual friendship?

Thinking of certain distant dates,
Certain distant footsteps on the sand . . .

Tears fall in the night,
Like dying stars that drop
To the bottom of an ancient pool in the woods.

> January 19, 1934
> *The Han Garden*, 64–65

GOING TO THE HEAVENLY BRIDGE[1]

"Going to the Heavenly Bridge?" The child thought.
"Going to the Heavenly Bridge?" The father said.
Well, then, let's go to the Heavenly Bridge, let's go—
Let the trolley, that swimming dragon
In the sea of humanity
In the sea whipped by the southwest wind,
Ting-tang, ting-tang . . .
Dragging a body full of ants,
Move toward the Heavenly Bridge—the Heavenly Bridge is
    over there!

[1] The Heavenly Bridge (T'ien-ch'iao) in Peking is a historic playground where temples, bazaars, and vaudeville are available to poor and rich alike.—Ed.

March,
The time for flying kites,
Aren't the swallows from the south
Surprised at these companions in the sky?
So blue is the sky.
Looking at it who would not indulge in daydreams.
But what does one dream about, and how would he tell it?
"Where are you going, where do you want to go?"
Ah, blue sky, blue sky, are you calling people
To go beyond the heavens?

The child knows what heaven is,
And what a bridge looks like,
Only he has never seen a Heavenly Bridge.
"The colorful arc on a rainy day is a road to heaven,"
(So he has heard people say).
Isn't the Heavenly Bridge a rainbow on a sunny day?
Let's go to the Heavenly Bridge, let's go
Don't laugh at the child, you, blue sky outside the car
          window.
The child is smiling at you now.

Pigeons draw circles in the blue sky,
A butterfly sweeps across the window.
A yellow blossom in the wind.
The roadside yellow blossoms are in full bloom.
"A butterfly wants to fly into the sky . . ."
Ai, the butterfly has brought home a story:
A butterfly wants to fly into the sky
To ask the rainbow,
Whose colors are prettier?
Rain falls and then stops,
A rainbow hangs in the sky,
A butterfly wants to fly into the sky,
Up to the sky and falls, down and down.
Its wings wet in the rain,
The butterfly falls crying in a muddy puddle.

Not a drop of rain,
Ting-tang, ting-tang,
Let's go to the Heavenly Bridge—it's over there!
The pushing and the crowding.
Why does daddy keep on smoking?
The talking and the chatting.
Why does daddy keep on smoking?
"The weather is too good, too good.
There really must be some rain, some rain."
"It'd be nice to have some rain, to stay home
To watch the rain patter on apricot blossoms."
(Yes, it'd be nice to have even a spell of heavy rain,
Let a sky full of dark cloud cover the blue,
Let an oilpaper umbrella cover the gazing eyes,
Let a row of rain water dripping from the eaves serve as a
          pearl screen
To cut off the courtyard full of spring.
No one would have to say,
"Such good weather, such good weather,
Where are we going, where shall we go?")

Ting-tang, ting-tang,
Red walls, green trees, and again green trees, red walls.
Good-by, good-by,
Big stores, small shops, and again small shops, big stores . . .
"We are about there."
The heart of the child throbs, throbs,
Isn't this a dream?
Wedged in the crowd,
Daddy says, "Look, son,
This is the Heavenly Bridge."

Yes, this is the Heavenly Bridge.
Here everyone carries a smile.
(A forced smile? Who knows?)
Somewhere someone pretends to laugh, then pretends to cry,
Begging for a meal from the old and the young.
He yells, his voice hoarse, and his waist bent like a bow.
Lying on the ground? Who cares about the black dirt on the
          ground.

A pair of feet presses upon another pair,
The child is losing his torn shoes.
Yellow faces, dirty faces, bubbles on a dead sea,
Surging and surging, even a strong wind cannot blow them
        out of the Heavenly Bridge.
Let's go to the Heavenly Bridge, but where is it?
The child wants to ask, but look,
Daddy is again gazing at the blue sky, lost in thought.
Let's go to the Heavenly Bridge, let's go.
Where is it?
Where? Where is the Heavenly Bridge?

There isn't any, there isn't any heavenly bridge.
Here there is no kite flying,
No pigeon's whistle to be heard.
Only an eagle circles round and round in the sky,
Circling up, circling up
Higher and higher,
The eagle is almost beyond the sky.

"Isn't the Heavenly Bridge in heaven?
Isn't it there?"
Such a blue sky, why
Are you making rain in the child's eyes?

1934
The Han Garden, 103–12

A DEAD TURK

Was he English, or French?
Some said he was a Turk.
Anyway, he was a foreigner
Ending his journey
In this village.
Here
No one hears any chanting from a church,
Or any prayer;
Only several calls of a rooster at noon,
Those several sad reports,
Announced the departure of this man.

Was it cholera, or scarlet fever?
Who knows?
Some said his was homesickness.
But people here don't understand
What homesickness is.
They proceed from homes to the fields,
And from fields
To their homes,
Walking back and forth
For ten generations, a hundred generations,
While the roadside weeds turn yellow and green again.

Migrant birds come and go.
They are familiar with all these
And they know
Whose dog it is that barks like a wail,
Or the old man of which family
Has lost several teeth . . .
They never paid attention
To why there are people leaving their hometown
To travel here and there
Like tumbleweeds in autumn wind
Like homeless souls,
Like this Turk.
Now, the Turk
Is lying down on an earthen *kang* in a small inn,
His face covered
By perpetual peace.
In peace perhaps
He is listening to people talk—
They don't know how
To dispose of this strange person:
"Throw him into a mountain creek?"
Someone asked.
Another wanted to drop him in the river,
Letting him follow the water away
And leave nothing behind, not even a trace.
Yet a third one said, "He too is a man,
He too has a soul,
Only when the dead are in peace
Can the living live on undisturbed."

They are, then, to bury the Turk in earth,
In a pauper's graveyard where
There are graves of orphans and widows,
That have been reduced to handfuls of dirt,
Where the bleached bones of beggars and night prowlers
Are gleaming under the weeds dark green,
Where those having sold all they had
And having been drunkards and gamblers over half of their
        lives
Also go to stay.
To this home for all homeless souls
They now are sending that Turk.
He,
A lonely traveler
From the shores of the Black Sea,
Had once dreamed of strange lands
And their beautiful sights.
He also had heard fairy tales of the Orient,
About someone summoning the wind and the rain,
About an old fox explaining sutras and parables at midnight.
There were also in the Orient women with bound feet,
Their shoes resembling tiny bridges,
And people said of them, each step a water lily.
There were the blue sky and yellow sea of the Heavenly
        Kingdom,
Limitless huge plains,
And golden dust . . .
But did he ever dream
Of occupying a plot of the Oriental earth,
Together with these lost Oriental souls,
Lying down,
And of letting the warm East wind blow
And cold rains drench
The mound of weedy dirt that covers pleasant dreams?
Perhaps
Perhaps he still thinks of Istanbul,
Of the Turkish prairie,
And of the cattle and sheep over there.

Now only the hard-working farmers here
Will walk from their homes to the fields
And again from the fields
Back to their homes.
Smoking their long pipes
And cloaked in the morning sun and the afterglow,
They'll pass by
Time and time again.
Perhaps by chance they'll mention:
On a certain day in a certain month of a certain year,
There was such and such a human being. . . .

1934
The Han Garden, 94–102

THAT CITY

That city—
Do you still remember that city?
I'm afraid you will only say, "No."
Like a night breeze
Gently blowing a torn window curtain,
Perhaps you have really forgotten it,
Like forgetting an old acquaintance who is far away,
Or things bygone.
But I'm a historian
Always fond of turning
The old leaves of thick volumes
To search
And to point out some old traces.
So again I found,
When the trees are bare and the leaves
Are drifting in the wind,
I found again
That city:
Several patches of smoke hover over the city
Like clouds in a dream.
About the stone walls tinted with lichen,
Someone has said,
"A rain on Ts'ang-chou turns all green."

The city is old,
Old and small.
The watchtower on the city wall, out of repair, fallen,
Yields to the owls
To make their nests,
And highlights the late autumn setting sun.
The streets are crooked and broken,
With few pedestrians
Very little noise,
And almost no carts or horses.
On a street, so desolate,
O, no, it was somewhere in this old city,
We met, by accident,
And we became acquainted.
Without any design,
We parted.
It was long, long ago,
And far, far away.
Where did you go?
In which city did you land?
You said "I'm going to sail the high seas."
I too have sailed the high seas.
There, for directions,
I had to rely on the waves.
Yes, you also said,
"I wish you'd go to the end of the world,"
But where is the end of the world?
Even riding on the gusty wind of late autumn
It would still be, I'm afraid,
Difficult to find a trace of you.
Yet, my thoughts always return
To that city
And the sunny sky
And rainy sky over that city,
And the oilpaper umbrella
We shared
Over the muddy road in the rain.
There were also the pine forest beyond the city wall,
The chatter and laughter under the foliage,
The creek and the grass near it,
And the startled chirping insects in the grass . . .

In autumn
On a cloudy day
Or in the evening
Suddenly I would think of all these.
Yes, every thing is an accident,
What is not accidental?
You watch a frozen cicada
Fall to the ground,
Or a yellow leaf
Leave the branch,
Or a stranger happening to be on the same road,
Walk away and disappear
In an unknown strange land.
A small plot of land, and over it a patch of grass
Make a secluded abode for someone.
All these must be accidental.
Thus, quite without any design
Everything ends
And falls into silence.
Only I am still thinking:
When shall I again return to that city?
When shall I again return to that city?

1934
The Han Garden, 86–93

HO CH'I-FANG (1911–   )

A VERY THOROUGH traditional training prepared Ho Ch'i-fang in the Chinese classics, volume after volume of which he could recite. By the age of fifteen he had completed that stage of his education and enrolled in one of the modern schools in Chengtu, Szechwan Province. During the next five years he witnessed the dramatic disintegration of the old Chinese family under the impact of foreign ideas that generated an upsurge of disrupting social forces. The students read in the budding new publications about Darwin, Kropotkin, American democracy, and Marx. They responded to the call to action issued by their fellow students in Peking and Shanghai. Chengtu saw some of the dark days when local warlords resorted to drastic measures to get rid of the leftists. A wave of suppression, including murder, forced many young men to flee. Ho Ch'i-fang was not among the threatened, but he saw enough to plant in him a seed of rebellion and a skepticism about the value of the old heritage, including the literary heritage of which he had had an ample feast.

In 1931 he left Chengtu to study philosophy at the University of Peking. By that time he had already started writing poetry. His excellent literary discipline gave him a superb control of the language. But it was his youthful longing for lasting love and beauty that permeated his verses. They are exquisite, if a bit thin, as he himself later admitted. "Prophecy," one of his earliest poems, gives full evidence of a thorough blending of his sensitive appreciation of nature and his baptism in nineteenth century Western romanticism. He became a close friend of Pien Chih-lin and Li Kuang-t'ien with whom he published a joint anthology in 1936 entitled *The Han Garden*—the name of the street where the University of Peking was located. At the time the three of them had much in common in their styles of writing. In the same year Ho also published *Sketches of Dreams*, a collection of prose which won him a literary prize. Poetic prose was then in fashion.

Shortly afterwards the war drove him back to Szechwan, but soon he left again to go to Yenan, then used by the Communists as their headquarters. There he taught literature in the Lu Hsün Institute of Arts and became part of the inner circle of the leftist literary movement. He studied Marxist theories about society and literature and decided that he must cease writing about his personal dreams and fancies that he felt were of no value to anyone. He admitted in 1937:

> I loved those clouds, those fleeting clouds . . .
> I considered myself the stranger from a faraway
> place
> Who, in Baudelaire's prose poem,
> Cocks his head and sadly gazes at the sky.

But as he traveled and saw the endless tragedy that engulfed the cities as well as the countryside, he made up his mind:

> From now on I shall talk noisily.
> I'd rather have only a straw-thatched roof.
> No longer shall I love the clouds, the moon,
> Or the innumerable stars.

He resolutely parted with poetry and went to the battlefield to experience life. He hoped to report on the drama of life and blood. He expected to view resounding victories and the shining smile of the war victim who opened his arms to greet the liberating army of his own country. But he was disillusioned. The night marches were endless, for weeks at a stretch; yet, he never actually saw the enemy. He heard the enemy, certainly, as whistling bullets drove him to take cover. His untrained body soon gave out. In nine months he managed to write only one report. The poet was heading toward a painful awakening to the ugly realities of life, and he confessed: "It is not easy to write reportorial pieces. It requires the writer to penetrate deeply the life of his objects. This [experience of mine] also proves that it is not easy to penetrate the collective life of the workers, peasants, and soldiers, on the front line and in the countryside."

He went back to teaching in Szechwan. In the evenings after work, he would jot down the impressions he had gathered in his northern trip and war experience. He returned to poetry, writing more freely than before. He tried to let the characters he had encountered on the front line and in the villages do their own talking and tell their own stories. He justified his return to poetry by the thought that his own conflict between a lingering feeling for the old and a realization that new things and ideas must be grasped, was worth recording. His *Nocturnal Songs* (first published in 1945) was completed in these years.

Yet even before he presented *Nocturnal Songs* to the reader he had begun to feel a sense of guilt. And he himself criticized the collection: "At a time like this, in a country like this, how little indeed of the things that have happened, the suffering, awakening, and struggling of the people and the heroic deeds they accomplished, has been preserved in my poetry. This is a world of tumultuous action, yet in it my songs appear so feeble, so out of tune." He felt guilty because in his *Nocturnal Songs* he had written at least once:

> Life is so banal
> And so full of cruelty.

In 1942 he had once again left poetry and tried to be an integral part of the events and characters he wished to portray. He had also begun to reappraise his style and language, which he now believed were too "Europeanized" and remote from the reading masses. He went north to study and to collect folk songs. One collection of Northern Shensi folk songs that he edited appeared in 1951.

But when he returned to poetry again in the mid-1950s, Ho Ch'i-fang still retained his refined literary language. His study of the folk songs left no marked effect on his style.

PROPHECY

It has finally arrived—that heart-throbbing day.
The sound of your footsteps, like the sighs of the night,
I can hear clearly. They are not leaves whispering in the winds
Nor the fawns darting across a lichened pass.
Tell me, tell me in your singing voice of a silver bell,
Are you not the youthful god I heard about in a prophecy?

You must have come from the warm and exuberant south,
Tell me about the sun there, and the moonlight,
Tell me how the spring air blows open the hundreds of
        flowers,
And how the swallow lovingly clings to the willow twigs.
I shall close my eyes to sleep in your dreamy songs—
Such comfort I seem to remember, and yet seem to have
        forgotten.

Stop please, pause in the middle of your long journey
To come in. Here is a tiger-skin rug for you to sit on.
Let me light up every leaf I have gathered in autumn,
Listen to me singing my own song.
Like the flame, my song will dip and rise in turn, again
Like the flame, will tell the story of the fallen leaves.

Don't go forward, the forest ahead is boundless,
The trunks of old trees show stripes and spots of the animals.
The serpentine vines intertwine, half dead and half living,
Not a single star can fall through the dense foliage above.
You won't dare to put your foot down a second time, when
        you
Have heard the empty and lonely echo of your first step.

Must you go? Then, let me go with you.
My feet know every safe trail there is.
I shall sing my songs without stop,
And offer you the comfort of my hand.
When the thick darkness of the night separates us,
You may fix your eyes on mine.

You pay no heed to my excited songs,
Your footsteps halt not for a moment at my trembling self.
Like a breeze, soft and serene, passing through the dusk . . .
It vanishes, and vanished are your proud footsteps.
Ah, have you really silently come, as in the prophecy,
And silently gone, my youthful god?

> Autumn 1931
> *The Han Garden*, 4–7

THINKING OF A FRIEND AT YEAR'S END

When a dried pine cone falls,
And the wings of low-flying birds rustle by
You pause in your solitary stroll in the woods;
When fish go hiding and the water is chilly
And your lonely fishing line floats in the pond,
When winter's white frost seals your window,
Hiding yourself in a long spell of illness
Do you still think of your house in the north?

In the old rattan chair in the corner,
In the shadow of the wall,
Stayed much of my unhappiness;
Often I had much unhappiness, but
Often yours was a congenial silence.
Often in the folds of the old cold cotton window curtain
There were lizards jerking their gray legs.
In the courtyard outside
The sound of a woodpecker, hollow and tremulous
Dripped from among the fine leaves of the elm tree.
You asked me if I liked that sound.
If then were now, I would surely say I like it.

In the west wind a train of camels in their new coats
Lift their heavy hoofs
And let them down again, gently.
There is already a thin layer of ice in the street.

> December 7, 1931
> *The Han Garden*, 29–31

AUTUMN

Shaking down the pearls of dew that cloak an early morning,
The sound of a woodsman's ax drifts from a sequestered vale.
As sickles, saturated with the scent of new rice, are laid aside,
And bamboo baskets marched off to carry home fat pumpkins
      from the vine,
Autumn rests on the farm.

Casting a round net in the chilly fog over the river,
To bring in the shadows of black leaves like blue flounders,
While the mat canopy of the boat bears a layer of hoarfrost,
The boatman gently paddles his small oar, homeward-bound.
Autumn plays on a fishing vessel.

The grassy wilderness gets more desolate and broader with
      the crickets' chirping.
The water in the creek becomes more crystalline as it stoops to
      bare the rocks.
Where did they go, the notes of a flute that used to ride on a
      buffalo's back,
And the flute's holes whence the fragrance and warmth of a
      summer night used to flow?
Autumn dozes in the eyes of a shepherdess.

> Peking, between 1931 and 1933
> *The Prophecy,* 19–20

A WREATH
Laid on a Little Grave

Most fragrant is the blossom that blooms and fades in an
      unvisited valley.
Most glittering are the morning dewdrops that no one
      remembers.
I say, you are fortunate, my little Ling-ling,
Because clearest is the tiny creek that has never reflected
      anyone's shadow.

You have dreamed of green vines crawling in your window,
As small golden flowers fell on your hair.
You have been touched by the tales told by the rain on the
      eaves,
And you loved solitude, and the solitary light of the stars.

Yours were a young girl's tears, those shining pearls,
Which often let flow an unnamed sorrow.
You had your days so beautiful that they made you sad,
Yours was an untimely departure that is even more beautiful.

Peking, between 1931 and 1933
The Prophecy, 21–22

UNDER THE MOON

Tonight there will surely be a silvery dream,
Like a white dove spreading its bathed wings,
Like a white lotus petal fallen from its watery shadow,
Like the sound of autumn flowing from glassy *wu-t'ung*
      leaves
To frost-coated tiles on the roof.
But, Mei-mei, are there also silvery ripples of moonlight
      over your place?
Even if there are, perhaps they have jelled into a
      transparent cold.
Can a dream, a boat with winds astern,
Sail into a frozen night?

Peking, between 1931 and 1933
The Prophecy, 28

WRITTEN IN SICKNESS

The water in the lake this moment
Must be churning black waves,
As the wind sweeps over the gray
And yellow tiles on roofs,
And the sand and dust whirl in the street

Like wheels. Faraway in the country
A mule cart halts en route
No houses in sight . . .
The four walls make me feel lonely.
Today the walls are even thicker
In the waves of wind, and the waves of sand.
Tonight the northern wind roaring like ocean surf
Shakes my little
Boatlike hut. My companion in solitude,
Are you tired of this long, long journey?
We are going to the tropics
Where we shall all turn into plants.
You'll be a vine, evergreen,
And I'll stand, a huge linden tree.

At dusk I gently turn on
My light, open my book,
And open that jeweled box, my memory.

Peking, between 1933 and 1935
The Prophecy, 53–55

THE NIGHT SCENE (I)

The town roar subsides,
Like the tide retreating from a sandy shore.
Under every gray roof
There are souls peacefully asleep.

The last old horse cart passes by.

Beyond the palace gate, some laborers
Sleep with their heads pillowed on cool stone slabs.
One wakes at midnight to kick his companion,
Saying that he heard someone cry
Fitfully, now far, now near,
In the abandoned palace behind many locked doors,
And on the sentry box above the city wall where crows are
        perching.

The companion's reply is even more weird:
One evening
Someone saw tears in the eyes of the stone lion . . .

Receding afar with soft sighs
The night breeze sways the withered weeds on the city wall.

Peking, between 1933 and 1935
The Prophecy, 56–57

GET DRUNK
To Those Who Sing Ever So Gently

Get drunk, get drunk,
Those truly drunk are lucky
For paradise belongs to them.

If alcohol, books,
And lips that drip honey . . .
If none of these can cover up man's suffering,
If you proceed from being dead drunk to half sober
To fully awake finally,
Wouldn't you keep your hat cocked and
Your eyes half closed,
To act slightly intoxicated throughout your life?

The flies shivering in the cold wind
Flutter their wings before the paper window pane,
Dreaming of dead bodies,
Of watermelon rinds in high summer,
And of a dreamless void.

In the epilogue of my ridicule
I hear my own shame:
"You too are only buzzing and buzzing
Like a fly."

If I were a fly,
I'd await the sound of a fly swatter
Smashing on my head.

Lai-yang, Shantung Province, 1936–37
The Prophecy, 85–87

NOCTURNAL SONG (IV)

I must get up, to go among the children,
I must live with them.
I'll teach them to read
And tell them simple but touching stories.
I'll also tell them how important it is to be clean
And frequently wash their hands for them.

I must play with them, together,
"Are you ready?"
"Ready."
Because of my loud reply
They will easily find me behind the door
Or behind the curtain.
And since I'm squatting
They can easily, laughing,
Throw their arms around my neck.

I'll talk to them about this and that,
Letting them dig to the bottom
Of everything.
I'll tell them all I know.
If I can't answer,
I'll say honestly, "I don't know either."

I must succeed in not getting angry with them,
When they are too naughty,
When they get into a little mischief,
Or take advantage of weaker little friends,
Or kill a small bird,
I must kindly and patiently explain to them what's right.

I must get up to go among the workers;
I must live with them.
I'll want them to tell me the stories of their lives.

If he is a child laborer
He will tell me that he went to work in a factory when very
    little.
Because he worked too long every day
He often dozed off near the machines.
He once saw a child, smaller than he was,
Dragged away by a belt on the machine during his sleep,
And the machine, madly turning,
Swallowed him all of a sudden;
Even his bones were chewed to bits.

If she is a woman laborer,
She will tell me that the first day of her work in a factory
The long hours of standing made her legs sore, her back
    ache, and the soles of her feet swollen.
She could steal only a short rest in the washroom.
And in that small, bad-smelling room with only one tiny
    window
Already were crowded many women workers like her, sitting
    or asleep.
Someone would say, "Let's hurry back,
The foreman is coming to check on us in a moment."

She will tell me:
One pregnant woman
One night suddenly stopped in the midst of her work
And slumping on the floor she cried.
They arranged a leave to let her go home.
On the way she could not walk any farther and she lay
    down.
The night was quiet, only the frogs were croaking.
She sat up and her child was born.

Other workers will tell me other stories.
I'll say, "Comrades, I've never taken part in any struggle,
I'm ashamed."

I must go down to the river alone.
I'll sit on a rock
To listen to the waterfowl sing so happily,
And to reflect on myself.
I'm already a man,
I have many duties.
And yet I'm still like a boy of nineteen
So in need of affection.

I give so little
And I receive even less.

I know that when I put it this way
And calculate this way,
It's shameful,
But I eventually said it aloud to myself.
It helps.

I must get up,
But I'm not going anywhere.

I must get up to light my lamp,
To sit before the table
To read the papers of my comrades
And reply to their letters,
And read,
Or plan tomorrow's work.
In all,
I must do all I should do.

June 20, 1940
Nocturnal Songs, 50–58

I SEEM TO HEAR THE ROAR OF THE WAVES
To the Flood Fighter of Hankow

I seem to hear the roar of the waves,
Hear their heads, long and disheveled hair streaming,
Smash against the dike, again and again,
Letting out angry howls of unhappy wild brutes.

I seem to hear violent storms
Thundering above, but your running,
Your hearty singing while battling the flood,
Rings louder and more sonorous than thunder claps.

I seem to be standing in the river with you,
Completely forgetting cold and danger,
I hook my arm with yours
Bracing the dike with our bodies.

The flood beyond the dike intends to destroy all.
Behind the dike the rice plants grow so green.
They rise and rise, so full of confidence,
Smiling a smile that forecasts a bumper crop.

The flood water beyond the dike measures above the roof,
Behind the dike wild roses bloom on the roadside.
Blue smoke drifts from the chimneys of the factories
That have exceeded the planned production quota.

The flood beyond the dike rises higher every day.
But "The Ox-herd and the Weaving Maid" goes on in the
       theater.
In the hospital babies are born, joyfully
Greeting the bright sunshine with their lusty cries.

Every day we spread out the newspaper
To breathe in excitement together with you,
And then to sweat with you, side by side,
To cheer in unison our daily victory.

What miracle is there that we cannot create?
Which enemy is there whom we cannot defeat?
Ah, flood, don't dream of rising
Higher and faster than the dike we build.

Now that the flood bows before us,
Like some of those stubborn people who,
Having received a heavy blow from us,
Just begin to rub their eyes with their hands.

Look, what a great change
Has already occurred on our Chinese soil;
Look, how we six hundred million people
So closely share our hardships and our fortune!

September 3, 1954
Selected Poems of 1953.9–1955.12, 309–11

CHENG MIN (1924?–   )

BESPECTACLED AND with her hair in two long pigtails, Cheng Min quietly walked about the campus of the National Southwest Associate University in Kunming in 1942. It was a time and place for the leading poets to gather and keep alive the spark of literary creativity under wartime pressures. Feng Chih, Pien Chih-lin, Wen I-to, and Li Kuang-t'ien all were there; they sponsored gatherings and discussions and were the inspiration and sustaining force of many young writers. But Cheng Min seldom took part in these activities. She had a beautiful voice. She liked to sing, but she liked even more to read books in her field—philosophy.

She wrote quietly and published very little in those days, but every poem that appeared in print brought a breath of fresh air to the reader. In her verses the reader can see the sensitive and often troubled heart that lies beneath her calm and gentle exterior.

Her style is elegant and polished. It combines something of Feng Chih and something of Pien Chih-lin, particularly their poems of the late 1930s.

She has not published much since her 1949 volume which collected about sixty of her poems written between 1942 and 1947. In the early 1950s she studied English literature at Brown University in Providence, Rhode Island, and returned to mainland China in 1959.

LONELINESS

Is this small palm tree
Standing, all year round,
Here, in front of my door?
It seems that I have just returned from a noisy party
As the twilight at dusk

Reveals the tree standing alone
In the green of the moss.
Suddenly I fall back into the world
Into the innermost heart of the tree.
Here I feel it
Quietly encircling me, all round,
Like a pond sinking down, down . . .
My eyes, it seems,
Are opened in a youthful night
To see all things
In their most secret conditions.
My ears
Are awakened
To all in the closing of the day,
All saying their say.
I, alone, face the world,
All alone.
When darkness is about to swallow the day,
I sit at the door.
In the sky outside
Hovers
That vanishing laughter.
At a distance
There is someone strolling on the riverside
And I see
The swallow pecking at the bosom of the water,
And the trees in early spring
Spreading their canopy over the river.

Think of the two rocks in the sea,
Some say, they are not lonely;
They bask together in the sun,
Together they splash the white sprays,
And together they stand vigil over the silence of the sea.
To me they are only
Two immobile trees
Planted in the garden.
Their arms seize one another,
And their hair intertwines,
But they are no more than two panes

In a window
Forever keeping their separate posts.
Ah, with what thirst do men
Yearn for life in perfect union.
If only within this body there is the body of another,
And within this soul there is another soul.

Where in this world is there a dream
That someone shares with us?
We climb together the snow-capped mountains,
We walk together by the slow-flowing river.
But can man embody in himself,
Others, his friends, even his sweetheart,
Even the one whom a pledge has bound to him,
To remain with him
To listen to the words that life speaks to him, alone,
To see the picture that life shows to him, alone,
To feel the fear, the pain, the hope, and the joy
That his own heart feels, alone?
Many are the starlights, and shadows
In my heart;
No one can see them.
When I take a walk with my love,
I see many demons and angels,
I smell the smell of the first breath of spring,
I see a flying patch of rainy cloud.
Now I hear the delight of the oriole
And now the cuckoo reporting weather.
But, because man always
Separately lives his own life,
They always remind me
Of the rocks one by one
And of the trees, one by one,
And of the dream that can never be shared.

Why do I often long
To cling to a huge tree trunk, like a vine?
Why do I often feel
I am being pushed into a crowd of strangers?
And often I pray:

Come, stay together with me,
Not just to play,
Nor just to work,
But didn't you say you have also seen
That storm rapidly gathering in my heart?
When loneliness edges close to me
And the world so rudely, coldly,
Walks straight into my bosom,
I can only watch that full cypress tree, in silence,
Wondering if it would open up its round body,
Open up that perfect world,
And let me hide myself there?
One day, just as I feel
Loneliness gnawing my heart like a snake
Suddenly I realize:
I am together
With a most loyal companion
When the entire world turns its face away
And the whole of mankind heeds not my greeting,
It perpetually clings to my heart
To let me watch every part of the world
From under a ray of quiet light.

It lets me have a pair of eyes in the air
To see myself sitting in the room:
To see his (my) feelings, and his (my) thoughts.
When I was a child playing with toys,
When I was young and in love,
I was perpetually lonely.
We have walked many miles together
Until finally we see
"Death" in evening twilight
Draped in its long, long, robe.
Ah, please remove your strange, longing gaze
From the trees and the rocks.
They are all deaf, mute, and senseless.
I think of people seeking a "pious" last rest
From the ordeal of fire,
From the gnawing of loneliness.
I, too, shall seek the most solemn meaning of life.

For it men struggle, ceaselessly,
Whether in the violence of a winter storm
Or on angry waves, they struggle.
Come, my tears
And my pained heart,
I like to know that my loneliness is here
Tearing and pressing my heart.
Into its infinity I throw
All feelings—petty, laughable, and ignoble—
Of mankind,
And then I see
Life is but a river rolling on and on.

> Kunming, 1944
> *The Poems,* 44–55

THE RICKSHA PULLER

In motion, perpetually in motion, are his legs
Running in this world of suffering, like the everflowing water.
He strikes a stance beyond suffering, his sense of pain has
    long fallen asleep.
Despite the passage of time, he still can hold himself erect
As a perfect embodiment of the patience of this ancient land.

Who is racing with him?
Death, death wants to embrace
This Marathon runner racing with life.
If he loses, death will seize him;
If he wins, no triumphal march will be heard.
A breeze stirs on the sea, saying
This is a shameful strange sight;
It must be erased by the ingenuity of man.
Thus, the strength of man's body, an ancient glory,
Has been turned into a modern disgrace.

The storms in the sky, the rugged roads on earth,
The direction of departure in the morning, the route of return
    at night.
All lie beyond his prediction, his design.

His answer is only an unbreakable silence.
The wishes of the people on the road drive him,
His own wishes are tossed on the roadside.
An aimless man lives to fulfill the wishes of others.

Every time he stops,
Still panting, he stretches out his dirty hands.
(Please reflect, reflect, I beg of you:
Beneath this dirty skin flows clean blood
While in those clean fingers flows dirty blood.
Which is our shame:
The dirty blood, or the dirty hands?)
With his worn feet he opens up for you
The roads leading to innumerable different destinations.
(After having your innumerable purposes fulfilled, would you
        also
Think of a way out for his purpose that has lain long
        smothered?)

It's not that there is no way, there is a way,
And it has become the prayer of all men;
It is waiting in the dim distance
For all our hands, all our feet
Both the hungry and the well-fed, to remove
The spreading weeds, and to tread out a smooth road.
In motion, forever in motion are his legs
Running along a road that begins and ends with life.
In the wind of winter, the rain of hunger, and the thunder
        and lightning of death,
Moving, forever moving are his legs.

The Poems, 142–46

THE HORSE

What a magnificent form, standing still
In the wilderness of wind and tall grass.
It packs the force of a running charge
That defies the height and distance of the firmament above.

Once it was determined like an arrow,
Its mane trailing, its front hoofs thrown skyward,
It darted forward like water from a broken dike.
But in this rugged world

Heroes are still only shining dreams,
Heroes are still ideals, too glaring to behold.
Now the road, endless, stretches out from under its feet.
During the day it treads the mountain trails, feeding on
    desolation,
And at night it is driven into the narrowness of the city streets.

Perhaps it knows that the man holding a whip behind
Is bearing even more merciless whippings in his life.
So it stiffens its neck muscles, without a groan,
Moving ahead in silence, bearing its heavy load.

The form gradually loses its former magnificence.
Its elegance is worn away day by day.
Perhaps one morning it will collapse on the roadside
Abandoning its burden and its pathetic companion.

In that remaining frame
Never again will be found a trace of the heroic.
The hero of the past has already turned into a saint
Upon the completion of its journey over the rugged roads of
    the world.

The Poems, 149–51

A GLANCE
Rembrandt's "Young Girl at an Open Half Door"

Exquisite are the shoulders receding into the shadow,
And the bosom, locked up, rich as a fruit-laden orchard.
The shining face, like the flush of dream,
Echoes the hands resting on the half door, so slender.

The river of time carries away another leaf from the tree of
      calendar,
Her half-closed eyes, like a riddle, speak of a blurred silence.
In the limited life the unchanging hurried pace is still too
      hurried,
She casts, in a casual evening, a lasting glance at the ever
      changing world.

The Poems, 154–55

I SING OF LIENTA[1]

You were born in the depth of suffering, but that time
We nursed a hope. Righteousness filled your bosom
As you departed in the midst of wild cheers, but
From that moment began more unhappiness and disaster.

Ah, the eucalyptus trees are your youthful arms, as
They stretch toward the cloudless blue sky.
Promising us, they seem to be, the same cloudless bright sky
In which we all like to join, and for which we all are willing
      to die.

All passed, time has washed away all dreams.
Life is a greedy drunkard, anxious to drain youthful joy:
There is never too much patience when days seem to stretch
      themselves into years.
We have only a tried courage to offer to the cruel jaws of
      history.

Finally, like seeds bound to part with their mother plant upon
      maturity,
We were gently flung to the earth in all directions.
When every tender bud struggles to grow in the darkness,
You, Lienta, are the only sun radiating in our memory.

The Poems, 156–57

[1] The Chinese name for the National Southwest Associate University, the "refugee" university in wartime Kunming.—Ed.

LIFE

We are cast into the long river of time
Perhaps only because of a moment of pleasure.
The Creator touches his pen lightly on the map of life;
To the traveler it is already a dangerous journey over countless
    rivers and hills.

Beginning from their childhood when they are pushed around,
    men
Make progress every minute but every progress a difficult knot.
From the solution found each time with their tears and pain,
They bit by bit discover the awakening of their self-
    consciousness.

Smile, as the beating received by the organs and the flesh
Melts into blood; and in blood everyday is nurtured
    submission.
And one day, man wakes up to sweep submission aside, like a
    huge wave washing away the traces on sand.
Like the elm in early summer, ah, youth, he reaches out
    his happy arms to greet life ("Let submission
    become my special characteristic").

Who is that perpetually silent sufferer that never blooms?
When life explodes its hidden crises at every step,
And hidden whirlpools moan under every body of water,
The timid have already gone down, and the brave eventually
    become tired.

Burning hopes in early life, through the unending suspense
Grows the moss of doubt, and convictions
Are shaken. The four limbs suddenly lose their strength.
Ah, look at those indecisive ones, they are sinking below the
    waves of life.

Who are they? Heroes? This torch-like light burns brightly

Once to turn the timid night into day on the battlefield, with
     cheering battle drums.
The saintly are only a lighthouse fighting darkness every night
     all year long
With light that hurts nobody's eyes, but bears everybody's
     forgetfulness in a storm.

Let us talk about it:
Let us tell the story: When gentle musical accompaniment
     rises
At a distance, this is a journey that has started casually but
     permits no desertion,
A journey that man—having dug from pain
     his love for the Creator—has completed.
Still he prefers to go on, for the sake of his present
     and future companions.

                The Poems, 164–67

THE DROUGHT

Hot wind sweeps over the vegetable patches
"Death, death . . ." a whisper everywhere.
A farmer passes by, on his shoulder,
A beautiful new water wheel.
Ah, but it's only an infant
That cannot be born.
All the creeks and ditches are bare
Bare to their dry, cracked, mud beds.
Like the white bones of sailors lying
On the bottom of a dried sea
The barren branches stick out on trees.
A calf stands forlorn on the edge of a pond
Gazing at the people, inquiringly.
The creek passes under an arch of interwoven branches,
Passes under a low bridge, and wears the look
Of an old man living in sweet reminiscence,
But brings no sound of rippling laughter.
It passes, like a rude transient carrying no gifts.
All in the field is quiet as death.

On the abandoned land, men
Have nothing more to say to each other.
All sounds, all hopes
Have been entrusted to Heaven where
Only ceaseless hot winds race on treetops
Like so many fleeing feet.
In the hearts of men there is the fear
Of a mother, and her pain
When she hears the silent weeping of the land.

The Poems, 20–22

THE LOTUS FLOWER
On Viewing a Painting by Chang Ta-ch'ien

The one, with its apparently unfailing cup,
Holds the joy of blooming and stands
Like a towering mountain bearing an eternity
For which man has no words.

The young leaf, in no hurry to unfold itself,
Retains a hope in its untainted heart to loom up
Through the haze on water, gazing at the world
That wears, with reluctance, an old and faded costume.

But what is the real theme
Of this performance of pain? This bent
Lotus stem drooping its blossom

Toward its roots, it says nothing
Of the ravage of storms, but of the multiple life—
The solemn burden—it has received from the Creator.

The Poems, 134–35

WILD BEASTS
A Painting

Behind them, the forest desolate and immense,
Nurtures its inhabitants in its own way.
Piercing its gloom is the breathing of the winds.
No light rends the night there. They

Bear a life, far more chilling and fearful,
That circulates in their salty and tangy blood
Through their tough veins until their sad eyes
Mirror the loneliness of the entire wilderness.

You are ashamed of being petty and capricious
When words only betray your thoughts and knowledge only
Brings prejudice. It's better to let the crude winds roar

Everywhere and the merciless chill whip you
Until life's freshness and strength
Is instilled in your clumsy forms.

The Poems, 136–37

DIPPING MY FEET IN WATER

From its bosom the dense forest offers a narrow trail,
The trail leads toward, ah—here the ancient trees circle
        the pond, and the pond
Reflects a face, with a smile flowing all over it,
Like immobile flowers offering life to a myriad of mobile
        things.

Look over there, green oozes from the tender leaves
And blends back into the filtered sunlight. Dipping your feet
        in water
You have merged yourself with the cool
        of the woods; and in the blurred light and lines
You, young lady, are happily awaiting the other half of
        yourself.

He has come, a squirrel leaps over fallen leaves,
He is whistling. Two birds chatter intimately.
And fatigue dispels the light mist in the forest.

You dream of your transformation into a squirrel, into a tall
      tree,
And again into a blade of grass, into a water pond.
Your pale feet lie asleep in water.

                                        The Poems, 13–14

A WINTER AFTERNOON

          The painter falls asleep,
          Letting the long road lie, colorless.
          Perhaps it is in meditation?
          Dreaming of a pair of soft bare feet,
          And a plaid parasol—
          With its face bleached pale white—
          White willow complains in tears:
        "When will there be beauty again
          Now that the wind no longer sings of me?"
          A crow perches on a boulder,
          The sky droops too low.

          Solitude drips from the branches,
          I pass by a sleeping beauty
          Waiting for the spring breeze.
          Someone gently nudges my elbow,
          And gently tugs at my sleeve.
          It's a pair of tiny, timid, hands
          That seem to whisper.
        "Can't I look at her?—"
          So I halt my steps to look back:
          Not a single soul on the road.
          A branch of white rose, lean and fragile,
          Reaches over a low hedge
          Still trembling by itself. . . .

                                        The Poems, 8–10

EVENING APPOINTMENT

I don't want to knock on the door,
The noise, I fear, is too rude.
There is a little boat returning,
Its oars still,
Awaiting the evening breeze from the sea.
If you are sitting below the window,
If you hear the quiet breathing beyond the door,
Feeling the presence of someone approaching ever so
    gently . . .
Toss away your cigarette,
And push open the door without making a sound,
You'll find me, waiting at your door.

The Poems, 1–2

TU YÜN-HSIEH (1920?–   )

I STILL remember vividly the tall, slender young man, more retiring and quiet than most of us freshmen of the National Southwest Associate University. He always wore an old, long black gown. I never saw him in a civilian short coat, and I still cannot imagine how he would look in one of them. We shared a table with six other schoolmates in the mess hall, which was the open space under the stage in a temple. The temple was located in a mountain village, a temporary stop on the university's long southwestward migration from Peking. It was 1940.

He never said much, and only infrequently submitted his work to the wall-newspapers and small journals that were almost the only means of publication in those days. He was polite to the point of being a little shy. He was always the first to volunteer to buy an extra dish to supplement our meager diet, even though we were all equally poor, all subsisting on government scholarships in the form of free room and board. We took turns buying the extra dish to grace the table which otherwise was always meatless. The first week he bought beansprouts fried with meat, the second week he bought beansprouts fried with meat, the third week he still bought beansprouts fried with meat. The last picture of him in my memory is his gentle, almost delicate gait, with a bowl of fried beansprouts balanced in front of him, sailing over the broken stone pavement of that narrow street leading to our temple-dormitory.

We recognized, under the cloak of his shyness, a poetic sensitivity struggling for adequate expression. We saw him plowing through the Chinese classics, and then the Western classics; we heard him occasionally talking to himself, working over the few lines he later almost reluctantly shared with his friends. To him, at that time, poetry was something so extremely personal that it could not be easily shared with others.

He envisioned, as most of us did in our youthful ecstasy over literature, something lofty rising from the untold amount of human suffering that his artist's eyes were witnessing. There were times when he longed for the undisturbed quietude of a well where his heart could retain its "crystal completeness," allowing only momentary interference from the outside world. He admired the immense sea for its varying moods, but what stayed with him the most and the longest was the perpetual silence of the sea. He even, at times, grew impatient with all that surrounded him, just as he saw a mountain growing weary of the mundane earth:

> You pursue, therefore you grow weary, and further
> you'd pursue:
> You have no peach blossoms, no cattle, no smoke
> rising from a kitchen chimney, or a homestead;
> But you can look down from above, and have more
> air and more rocks:
> For you have to abandon what you need, and remain
> forever lonesome.

The choice, as it turned out, was not his. He had to remain with us until each of us was plunged further and deeper into the lives of others, into the war.

Once having exchanged his books for a jeep and a rifle, he sampled, for the first time in his life, the awesome feeling of trying to sleep in the woods with only his knapsack for a pillow. He listened to the "ghost that wailed in the woods at night," became excited about his role as a sniper, and learned to appreciate ever so much more than he had the life and death of a "Sandaled Soldier." He saw a soldier's glory and, even more thoroughly, he understood a soldier's fear. There was something about a peasant, as our poet observed, that would forever remain with him, defying his new uniform and his new role on the unfolding stage of a tremendous human drama.

In his poetry, he is not intense, but he can be deep. His work calls for quiet reading, even when, rarely, it deals with the roar of cannons. In his poems we find traces of Feng Chih's short poems and Pien Chih-lin's terse, occasionally stiff lines. That bit of awkwardness is like him; it seems to be the unavoidable result of an unusual sensitivity exposing itself to the world, trading its customary shelter in a long black gown for a soldier's uniform.

THE SANDALED SOLDIER

You, suffering Chinese peasants, carrying on your back a
    rotten ancient tradition
Under the quickening steps of history, you succumb in
    silence, you struggle;
Power of many kinds rises and disappears; nobody can tell
    how Tao changes;
The different types of guns uniformly rob you of life,
    like a tornado at night

Swooping down unexpectedly, but you could only grope your
    way like a blind man's bamboo cane,
Only let yourselves be kidnaped, and paraded
    through the street,
    Calling all this natural disaster willed by God . . .
That had to be accepted as winter has to be accepted. Finally
    a beautiful change arrives.
Accepting some Christian missionary's words, you believe
    that you have outlasted the days of manacles.

Still you tread in your sandals, marching toward superior
    weapons,
As if walking into a city. You fought guerrilla-style as
    though you were hunting wolves,
Bearing the "Sustained War of Resistance" like an unusually
    long monsoon.

Yet you won't boast: The awakening of a gigantic thing,
The shattering of a chain, and that the poets can now sing of
    the dawning,
All depend upon you, "Sandaled Soldiers" clad in gray from
    the muddy fields.

                        Forty Poems, 1–2

THE SNIPER

They cannot see me, I am safe:
Once again in solitude I have found a paradise of freedom;
They are waiting, searchingly: Danger!
I am waiting to find a place of "Safety."

This hide-and-seek game must be ended in gunshots
Instead of laughter, and nerves become their igniter;
A little carelessness, a lucky find, is enough
To kindle the black powder, aimed at taking a life.

But the nocturnal birds often cannot help but burst out
In a peal of weird chuckle. I grip my rifle, watching them fly
And circle; the moonlight has, for every tree,
Spread out a beautiful but dangerous round cushion of
     shadow.

I grip my rifle and gaze at the patterns on the cushions;
Perhaps the patterns will walk, and the shadows will strike
     metal.
Then I can tell the confused people who have lost their way:
"I'm here to guide you, but I prefer solitude more."

Forty Poems, 10–11

THE GHOST WAILS IN THE WOODS AT NIGHT

Death is the most meaningful moment in my life,
     It's also the happiest,
          For I have finally obtained my freedom.
The crimes would remain forever, but still there are chances
To declare to you in loud voice: We are friends.

The cherry blossoms are the eyes that make me sad.
          Together with the white hair of Mount Fuji,
          They have caused me to forget about hell.
No longer can they see me, and I can only cry;
But they continue to cheer my wife and children.

They all want to live, awaiting humiliation
  To arrive one day for the last judgment.
  Only then can Japan expect a great reunion.
Ah, all of you must forgive this dead man who can wail,
One day we perhaps will frighten you.

Suddenly I begin to like the wailing in a quiet night,
  Because I need an echo, because the police
  Would not permit me to acquire a habit of
    enjoying solitude.
Ah, don't come out on a moonlit night; we can bear no more
The sighing of our dear ones on a distant shore.

Death is my last need, no other wish have I,
  Although I may still wish to see
  If mankind will become wiser from now on.
But, ah, a gust of cold wind stirs, shaking the sobbing
    branches and leaves.
I still cannot saunter and groan here at night, all alone.

> In the Kawng River Valley, Burma, March 1945
> *Forty Poems*, 21–23

HOMESICK

The lyrical pen of the twilight after rain
Poised on a calm river bank
The whorls on water rolled on, finally sounding a note of my
    hometown,
The quiet mountains beyond the bridge were an intense blue.

The travelers all faced the smiling rainbow
And the road toward home; the cows and sheep shook their
    bells casually,
Wading into the water. Homebound birds rose and descended,
    echoing each other's call, while the clouds
Rejoiced at a distance, then suddenly started sobbing behind
    their sleeves.

Her child in her arms, a mother watched the half-moon
Floating on the broken water margin. The light through a
    little window
Approached me from the bottom of the water, and in the
    hoarse barking of a dog
Someone, with a tired smile on his face, came home.

                         Written in Rangpur, India
                         Forty Poems, 39–40

NOT A LOVE POEM

The mountains grow somber, and trees crowd together;
The flowers and herbs lose their colors.
My dear, more than ever are your eyes black
And gleaming, quickening my pulsation.
Please, won't you move your lips again;
I long for more dizziness: We have,
In the gyration of the earth,
Carried with us many a brilliant galaxy.

Forgive me for again and again giving myself an order
And canceling the order, and again and again cursing
The shouting of the policemen on guard in the city
That threatens and complains in turns.
Now, my dear, let us only soar afar,
Let us melt, let us atone
For those impatient and unlucky tears
And that shameful bit of jealousy.

Let us be like those two blossoms of light white clouds
That fly farther and grow lighter, finally to disappear
In the calm blue. Man can never again
Gossip about their romance
As untamably wild. We shall
Lean together, reminiscing of our happiness while beautiful
    dreams
Circulate through the silent contact;
We'll watch how the haze of the evening is quietly carried
    away.

                         Forty Poems, 41–43

THE SAD LOOK OF A SEASON

Drop after drop of desolation, ceaselessly plucking,
The bubbles under the eaves whirled and sank.
They were a mass of confused memories: the dead, the
      groaning,
And those who stretched themselves and yawned. Their sad
      eyes
All stared at me, asking me to sigh:
To heave a sigh cold and gray as the old tin roof.

The raindrops, crowded and unruly, flowed all over the
      surface.
And the wind, like its wintry cousin, pierced through my
      bones.
With its needle and thread. The trees bowed their heads,
Their eyes blinking, squeezing out several teardrops.
My heart was like the endless ripples on water
That mirrored nothing, except a muddy expanse of the
      battlefield.

In India
Forty Poems, 54–55

THE WELL

Silence am I. Several blades of grass,
And several blossoms of floating cloud in a little sky
Are my world, harmonious and complete.

Only when you are hungry and thirsty,
Leaving warmth behind, you come to draw water from me,
Then you catch a glimpse of your face, full of sorrow.

Yet I have to be content with being abandoned by warmth,
To be content with the desolate solitude. Only with solitude
Can I perpetually maintain a crystal completeness.

You only draw from my surface,
Leaving alone the depth of a lonely heart and soul
Where fallen leaves and petals return to dust.

And you can only disturb my surface.
My life stems from dark layers underground.
There, and only there, I am joined to the infinite universe.

You may use rubbish to cause my banishment,
Yet I shall accept and bear all in silence, cleansing it.
So forever I shall remain myself.

Quiet, pure, simple and devout
Neither running away, nor excited . . .
Only when a drizzle comes I release a chuckle.

Forty Poems, 87–89

THE SEA

Because you are infinitely deep and immense
The melancholic dark blue, a bit mysterious,
Has become your natural complexion.

As night descends, the scattered fishing lights
Vanish from the horizon: the sorrow, filling your bosom,
Condenses into loneliness, hard and black as coal.

The stars in heaven and the lighthouses on shore perhaps
Will comfort you, but you only feel this is too much ado.
Thus you turn to lean on the beaches and sigh, still more
        silent.

Only the sun and the moon can make you glitter,
Can make you show your inexhaustible gold, silver, and
        jewels.
As light breezes plume your pride with crested glory.

When the buffeting wind excites you,
You roll and roar in frenzy, waving back and forth
The white blossoms plucked from your heart.

But all these are only for an instant.
The permanent is the infinite silence
And that immense, melancholic dark blue.

Sometimes you reach into a delicate bay or lake
Where there are turf, cattle, and youthful laughter,
But it only makes you realize that this is not your world.

Forty Poems, 90–92

A DEAD SOLDIER ABANDONED
ON THE ROADSIDE

Give me a grave,
A grave like a black bun;
Even a flat one will do,
Like a small vegetable patch
Or a pile of manure.
Anything is fine, anything,
As long as there is a grave,
As long as I won't be exposed,
Like a pile of buffalo bones.
Because I'm afraid of dogs
I have always been afraid of dogs.
I'm ticklish, most ticklish,
That, my mother knew very well.
I was afraid of the dog's licking me,
It gave me goose-pimples.
And my eyes would turn red, about to cry.
I was afraid to see dogs fighting,
That noise was really too frightening,
Especially when they fought over a bone,
Their sharp white teeth were too frightening.
If one dog dragged a piece of flesh,
And another pulled a piece of bone,

With blood dripping in between them, like tears,
I would vomit and faint immediately.
I'm also afraid of the wilderness,
A wilderness with only wind and grass,
With wild animals foraging everywhere.
They all are not afraid of blood,
All laugh so strangely,
Especially when they have drunk blood.
They gnaw on bones
With their even sharper teeth.
They are a greater threat than dogs.
I'm afraid of black birds,
As large as roosters,
They scare people from the treetops at night
And their beaks are so cleverly sharp . . .
I'm afraid, I'm afraid.
The wind has run away,
The fallen leaves have also run away,
So has the dust.
The trees are struggling, shaking their heads,
And are about to run away.
Ah, give me a grave,
Just any handful of dirt,
Any handful of dirt.

Forty Poems, 110–14

WANG T'UNG-CHAO (–1957)

THE TIME-TESTED prosodic schemes of classical Chinese po-
etry have proved once more their magic and power in Wang
T'ung-chao's works. Wang wrote in the vernacular, but his
vernacular retains the clear metrical cadence of the seven-
syllable lines in China's poetic tradition. Most of Wang's lines
show a basic pattern of three stresses, each falling within a
unit of two or three syllables. The length of the unit varies,
but principally by doubling the basic bisyllabic words. Thus
often a two-syllable utterance is replaced by a four-syllable
one which maintains the same musical pattern when read in
a complete line.

Parallelism also maintains its stronghold in Wang's poetry.
Paired images appear freely and bring a sense of familiarity to
a reader versed in classical Chinese literature. Even sense im-
pressions are usually so arranged as to contrast (and to par-
allel) the ear with the eye.

This is not surprising when one realizes that Wang wrote
most of his poems in the 1930s, a time when most writers
were still trying to free themselves of the restrictive influ-
ences of the literary tradition. What is surprising is that
Wang's work shows no sign of the struggle between the
classical language and the vernacular he used. He rode on the
vehicle of musical cadence typical of the classical language
with grace and ease.

His interest in creative writing was awakened early. While a
student at the University of China, he published two stories,
"One Leaf" and "The Evening," in the leading literary maga-
zine, *The Short Story Monthly*, which won him wide recog-
nition. He was active in the student demonstrations in 1919
and became a key member of the Society for Literary Studies
upon its founding in 1921. The common interest of the So-
ciety was a serious effort to reflect the realities of life in litera-
ture. In his stories Wang tried to depict life as realistically as

he could. In his poems he tried to present scenes and characters he encountered. His "Heard En Route," for instance, written on February 23, 1925, on the train from Tientsin to Nanking, recorded the fragments of conversation among several soldiers then engaged in the civil war. But a strong lyrical element continued to echo through his lines, man's sensitive response to nature that distinguishes classical Chinese poetry. The sea, the woods, the morning mist and evening sunset in his poetry were living entities with which Wang felt empathic:

> Light clouds chase one another, wildly,
>> and pine needles compete in a singing contest
>> in green waves,
> There are lambs seeking companions, and nightingales
>> weaving their songs of love.
> The night air enshrouds strife as well as peace,
>> and the blooming of spring.
> All these sounds come to me from the slumbering
>> mountains in all directions.
>
>   (from "Night Sounds" April 8, 1925)

Wang often pondered on the meaning of life and the relation between man and the universe, and in his poems a note of quiet sorrow appeared because man seemed so feeble, and his life so brief when set against forces greater than himself:

> Is it the happenings in man's world, such hasty
> meetings and partings—"infinitely so," can we help
> but feel our hearts leap?

The traditional sentiments befitting a refined classical Chinese poet are here, and also faint traces of the Indian writer Tagore. When Tagore arrived in Tsinan, Shantung, Wang's native province, in 1923 Wang was the interpreter of his public addresses, and he was deeply impressed by the visitor.

Wang translated into Chinese many works by Byron, Shelley, and Keats. In 1934 he visited Shelly's grave in Rome and wrote a long poem in admiration of the poet's rebellious spirit. On the same European tour Wang put in verse his thoughts on the historical pageantry of Venice, Florence, and Rome. These longer poems show clearly his extensive expo-

sure to European poetry; even his rhyming schemes betray its
influence. While still relying upon the three-stress line, Wang
in these poems often doubled the units to make longer lines,
interspersed freely with alliterative rhymes.

The six volumes of Wang's poems were all published be-
tween 1925 and 1940, a period of violent war and revolution.
Although Wang's active political life seemed to have ended
with the 1919 student demonstrations, the studio he occupied
as a magazine editor, and later as a college professor of litera-
ture, was never quiet enough for undisturbed contemplation
of life and its vicissitudes. There was a constant stream of
human cries of pain and suffering, and a constant screen of
gunsmoke and flames in his writings. The majority of his
poems in the six collections deal with the inequities of life
and the effects of the war. As the title of one of the collec-
tions, *This Age,* suggests, most of his poems attempt to mir-
ror the time, and the laughter and tears (mostly the latter)
that mark it. His long poem of 199 lines, "Her Life," depicts
the miserable lot of a woman factory worker whose pitiable
existence is contrasted to the luxury and sin of a metropolis.
Another long poem, "On A Modern Battlefield," paints the
aftermath of an open military clash with the Japanese in
Shanghai. There is the desperate outcry of a peasant,

> A year like this, a time like this calls us
>   to struggle for our lives, but how?
> Can we rob? Or chase? Or dig a gold mine from
>   underground?
> Any of these will do, but the peasants who always
>   lose are struggling in vain.
> We part, we scatter, turning into refugees begging
>   for food everywhere.
>
> (from *Selected Poems of Wang T'ung-chao,* 58)

There is the fresh tear of a country ravaged by war,

> We go on, you and I both bow our heads,
> Turning to a deserted ruin, where the smell
>   of burning still lingers under the grass.
> Look: smoke columns rise at an angle from several
>   chimneys.

It's odd, why even the smoke looks so spiritless,
   so thin.

(from *The Songs of the South of the River,* 70)

And there is, occasionally, a shout in anger:

Fight!
We must use blood to bathe the soft and
   effeminate South of the River.

(from *The Songs of the South of the River,* 66)

These are what truly occupied the poet's mind. Wang was not particularly concerned with his method of expression. As he declared in the prefaces to *This Age* (1932) and *The Songs of the South of the River* (1940), he did not believe finding the best poetic language to be of prime importance. Any language could become good poetry if in its complex variations it was married happily to an unfettered imagination and a "deep sympathy with all things, sensible and insensible." And what must a poet's soul be? "At a time like this, when wild tempests are pushing endless waves, and when our lives are in deep water and hot flames . . . what author could claim to be a 'visiting celestial?' . . . Our age has no golden hue, no rosy grace, no brilliance of jade green. At a time like this what should we sing? False praises? Pretentious eulogies? Feeble curses? Ecstatic songs of feigned self-satisfaction? How indeed are we to shout aloud our true feelings about the time!"

Wang wrote much and saved very little because he was intensely dissatisfied with the quality of his own work. "Poetry, even when it is full of vitality," he said in 1940, "even when it is forcefully felt, amounts to no more than vain flowers blooming at the tip of a pen, no more than a dose of verbal satisfaction."

Yet Wang did not abandon literature, did not exchange his pen for a sword. He stayed with his books, and one of the last things he wrote shortly before his death was a poem entitled "Forty Years Ago and Forty Years Later," in which he praised the accomplishments of the new regime. Since he was a bedridden patient in a hospital when he wrote this poem, it seems likely that he was living up to his own conviction about not singing any "false praises."

A STROLL

Strolling down the path last night, I dreamed of entering a
      secluded vale.
The silver-coated moonlight spread its cool brilliance.
Light haze trembled on the wings of a returning crow.
Winding around our feet there was a splashing stream.

Strolling down the path, red candlelight flickered in my
      heart.
Should I return, but the wind was chilly; should I go on,
      but the frost was cold.
An arrow shot out of the depth of the night
Knocking out the feeble light in my heart; where could I find
      it again?

Strolling down the path, the growth and decay, the departure
      and return in the world of man . . .
Only faint footprints remained in the secluded vale,
How could the soul's mirror be found in the splashing stream!
Strolling down the path . . . have you found the prospect of
      life?

          1925 (?)
          Selected Poems of Wang T'ung-chao, 7

HOW

How could I pray, meditate—under the autumn stars,
In the sound of falling leaves, in the shadow of a lamp, to
      pursue the sadness of a vanishing dream?
How could I seize, gather up—that bitter,
Tiring, and weary chance meeting of life?

Let it go, for this sadness
Will disappear in the fading light of sunset;
Let it go, for to linger on the chance meeting
Will make you miss the late spring in the world of man.

Blood-stained thorns lie ahead,
The road is full of barbed wire.
Timid, you wasted your time in hesitation,
One day you must steel your aching heart to go forward.

The feebly flickering light in the dusk—
The hesitation of a life that has lost its way once before.
Bravely I thank the tender comfort of temptation;
Who can forever linger on this lonely roadside?

> Spring 1925
> *Selected Poems of Wang T'ung-chao,* 12

MOON NIGHT ON THE MOUNTAIN

Look up:
> The trembling shadows of pine tree spires, the
> jagged mountain peaks.

Look down:
> The pale glimmer of silver traces, the swaying
> branches.

The quiet deserted mountain slumps into a slumber;
The white-stone bridge lies silent in an ethereal light;
Two lean silhouettes, speechless, remain side by side.

Who can predict the parting and meeting in this floating
world?
The universe of this quiet night, isn't it the flowering of the
world of man?
A subtle fragrance of the night spreads from the woods,
Two lives are enshrouded in a white net that fills the sky.
The pale silver light; the misty dark of distant blue,
And a lone star smiling in the western sky.
It casts a mysterious ray
That penetrates and blends into a dream as evening draws
close.

The land, the river, all are fleeting shadows, like ripples on
water?
How much less is this pitiable, benighted entity of mine!

But there is the fragrance of soft hair in the air; and
       a whisper hidden in the night breeze,
What night is tonight? The clustering hills, the crowded
       woods, the blue sky and the bright moon.
Look up:
       The trembling shadows of pine tree spires, the
       jagged mountain peaks.
Look down:
       The pale glimmer of silver traces, the swaying
       branches.
The quiet deserted mountain slumps into a slumber;
The white-stone bridge lies silent in an ethereal light;
Two lean silhouettes, speechless, remain side by side.

            April 1925
            Selected Poems of Wang T'ung-chao, 17–18

DON'T CRY, MY LITTLE ONE

Baby, don't cry! This is not really cold weather,
It's only the beginning of September.
Mama still wears her tattered summer gown. Look:
So bright, and so way way up,
The friendly Weaving Maid star is blinking and laughing
       in the Milky Way.

Baby, since your daddy crossed the Yellow River, he rose
       high
Like a boat rising with the water. He had his fill of card
       games, strong liquor, and women kidnapped from
       somewhere.
Not that his heart is cruel, but he was a victim of his
       daredevil guts.
Who knows how many deadly games he has played?
Which man, if he is a man, has ever cast a backward glance.

"Baby, m . . . m . . . I haven't had a spoonful of rice gruel
       the whole day.
No wonder after nursing you cry so bitterly.

Look, those mountains and pagodas arranged in the mirror
Are all made of fine flour and refined sugar—they are
          pastries.
They are nice to look at, but not edible, not enough to cheat
          your appetite.

"Baby, who, having a miserable lot, wouldn't want to escape
          his destiny.
Who'd continue to think of him, that incorrigible criminal
          with no future!
Baby, this stone-paved street is for leather shoes to walk
          on, not
For you to sleep on; if the chill hurts your little stomach,
          to whom can we turn for help?
Baby, the bridge on the Yellow River . . . the murder
          knife! . . .
      Look, the moon has risen above the roof.
      Listen, a horse is neighing, and there is
          the night watchman's gong,
      Whence comes this sound of drum, of trumpet?"

          Summer 1925
          Selected Poems of Wang T'ung-chao, 21–22

BRIDGE AND WATERFALL

This stone bridge, this flying waterfall, I have seen before,
When the moon is serene, wind soft; when silvery dewdrops
          cover the mountains; when the sound
          of a bell echoes in the night—
It is the realization of a dream where I lingered in sadness—
Without my knowing it, the fine spray has
          drenched me on the bridge.

          September 6, 1928
          Selected Poems of Wang T'ung-chao, 28

THIS AGE OF OURS

This age of ours, fire and blood burn and bathe the corpses
    of the city and countryside.
Ancient trees, felled for firewood, no longer can exhibit their
    studied posture.
The bullet's flying scream has long conquered the peaceful
    fields,
And sunk in torrential waves, blended together undulant
    hatred and love.

Under the iron hoofs, epidemic, hunger, and war—a deserved
    destiny?
Honey-soft words, and full-stomached hypocrisy, are
    abandoned
To worthless dust; and dust covers the tattered clothes
That hide the ashes of the defeated, buried long ago under
    vanishing footsteps.

In secluded woods an underground spring murmurs
    perpetual harmony.
Beneath the graves of unknown heroes lie cities and villages
    beyond the reach of force,
And the glaring glitter reflects the visions of life, rocking
To the marching rhythm of the underground spring—a newly
    created world.

The disappearing bone ashes rise from the horseshoe prints;
    light appears in the distance,
A bright rainbow halfway in heaven rings clouds of black
    vapor and white lightning.
The ray of hope is a shining candle newly lit in the storm;
This age of ours, the place burned and bathed by fire and
    blood is the candlestand awaiting flame.

          August 1929
          Selected Poems of Wang T'ung-chao, 30

WIND ON AN INNER-MONGOLIAN DESERT

Yellow columns roll over an immense field of sand,
Covering and blending with the sunny sky of early spring.
The willow twigs from old faded silk paintings emerge
      faintly,
And in the vaguely defined sky metallic sounds clash.

Here there has never been an eagle's wing, weary after a
      vigorous fight,
And the shadows of a few swallows dance about at random.
Choked with the news of spring in this Northland,
How can their frail bodies face the brunt of force!
Desolate, desolate, and the biting chill of the fierce wind,
Force in sweeping movement has long banished tenderness
      and subtle grace.
Even with its pitiable submission, the small blade of grass
Cannot escape this baptism of strength on the move.

Once, years ago, there were countless armored warriors here
Galloping, tramping the land now lying still as death.
Time has destroyed the frenzied fighters,
Only the sighs of giants are heard after dusk.

The agitated calls of the chime on a deserted pagoda resound
      in the thud and thumping,
Bloody battle cries mix with the soul's response.
(The tragedy of the night is just unfolding in vigor and
      madness)
The demons are enacting an assault and bodily battle here
      in the unlimited wilderness.

Cold eyes above brute grins stare from the four darkened
      walls,
Beyond the window, ocean-churning wild waves surge and
      wail.
The tempest devours a drifting leaky boat,
The brutally grinning walls of the cabin open to tunnels of
      icy winds.

The shrill of lead wires and the crushing of fallen tiles in
     symphony
Sound this movement of weird music, together with
     chattering birds and roaring animals.
They dart, prance, piercingly scream and fiercely rush at
     each other.
This is all a lone traveler hears as he shivers in a spring night.

Time and space are filled with the movement of frenzy
     and struggle
That do not permit you to tremble, alone in hiding.
This ground swell of force once again kneads everything
     together,
Listen, the sighing of the giants—the spouting of wild waves,
     the clash of metals.

Spring 1930
Selected Poems of Wang T'ung-chao, 36–37

THE FOGHORN

Late spring on the foggy seashore,
Dark flannel wraps the tops of the buildings, high and low.
White dots of light stud the night,
Silently spreading the weariness of life.
Listen, a choked moan, suddenly released, surges forth from
     the waves,
Its suppressed quiver continues.

The sound of a bell at midnight makes one reminisce:
Sad is the sound of fallen leaves lashing at the windowpanes;
Happy songs are for the oriole in the morning sun-bathed
     willow tree;
Soft tunes from a shepherd's flute weave a cool evening.

Sorrow, love, happiness and suffering arrive through the sense
     of sound,
At times they have shattered the spirit and soul of man.
But the sound of foghorn through the waves in a spring night
Deeply stirs the soul.

Has the night sunk in the fog, or has the fog become the
    night's overture?
There is still a journey for the sleepless on the inky water.
The lighthouse has long turned into a distant star in fog, no
    longer heeding
The bravery of those in search of their destiny.
This monster draws a deep sigh in the shadow of crazed
    waves,
Light may yet replace the bewildered and lost world.

> Midsummer 1930
> *Selected Poems of Wang T'ung-chao*, 38–39

THE VISITOR

Shadow inserts itself in the windowpane whose tiny eyes stare.
Gently the sound of a violin rises in the street after dusk.
A thin layer of gray haze presses the space
    around me against my body,
The sound of the string fades and halts, slicing the gray
    mist into waving strands of silk.

I have come; this is a moment for your undisturbed
    meditation,
Let me impose myself securely on your heart.
The gray mist lifts, blends into a quiet tune on the string.
Has it stirred your sorrow, most deeply felt?

Infinite sorrow has lost its equilibrium,
Waiting to share the fate of fallen leaves.
In vain the shivering visitor struggles to keep his strength
As the leaves utter a groan of destruction.

Suddenly a storm, heralding autumn, sweeps over, urging
    along the chill,
And reducing to light smoke all illusions and sorrows.

The time permits you only to look and listen, in haste,
Who is to linger with you in vain, now that the dark shadow
    is gone?

> Early autumn 1933
> *Selected Poems of Wang T'ung-chao,* 49

BEAUTIFUL IS THE LAND SOUTH OF THE YANGTZE

Beautiful now is the land south of the Yangtze River:
Thousands of miles of green spread out in blood,
Flowing flames and flying bullets have destroyed dreamlike
    villages,
On faces of men and women are branded
    shame and hatred.
How much news of exile has been spread by the spring wind?
Beautiful now is the land south of the Yangtze River:
Blood, like peach blossoms, drowns the torn bodies of infants,
And rotten corpses, swollen with anger and grief, drift down
    the river.
Fire lights up red clouds, far and near.
No longer is the spring wind willing to transmit the soft songs
    of young swallows.

Beautiful now is the land south of the Yangtze River:
Dust of close combat everywhere fills the air,
No floating gossamer can attach itself to one's heel
    on a spring outing.
My friend, are you still drowsy with spring fever this
    long day of April?
You, lying on your motherland, also have your home, your
    dear ones?

Beautiful now is the land south of the Yangtze River:
A sign of spring, bright as the autumn burn,[1] covers all
    mountains.

[1] A common Chinese expression for the countryside under red
autumn trees.—Ed.

Whose dream still lingers on the soft rivers and warm hills?
Funeral bells are ringing high in the sky, sprinkling drops
      of red blood.
You, can you hear clearly? The sound of the bell—
Still signals the morning and dusk of the old south of the
      River?

> Late spring 1938
> *The Songs of the South of the River,* 39–40

STARS IN A MAY NIGHT

All the stars in a night of May have packed up their light
To let the storms stir up flying waves all night long.
Seize the rudder, then, and the oar; we depend on every arm
To break through the hot darkness
      to greet the moon.

Hey, my friend, are you falling back? Are you gazing at
      the sky, dreaming?
Behind you rushes a stream of blood; above, thunder roars.
Where shall we dock this boat in which we share our fortune?
Exert yourselves with us, we must protect the cabin of life.

My friend, really, can you not be a bit patient?
You are missing your chance to struggle; the end of the
      night is still far away.
I don't ask you to put back into your bosom your burning
      tears,
Why begrudge them? Turn them into a fire
      and hurl it in all directions.

The stars of the night of May still remain with you;
They remain to guide that lonely boat in its flight.
Don't blame heaven, nor regret the length of the summer
      night.
Look, the rain of blood around you. Which drop fails to
      taint your clothes?

> June 1938
> *The Songs of the South of the River,* 13–14

MY FRIEND, YOU MUST HAVE
SMELT THIS STENCH

My friend, you must have smelled this stench on the wind!
Human flesh, human tendons and bones, and human
      intestines? . . .
From the rice paddies, the marshes, the northern plains
      and valleys,
Spreads that luring scent, stretching across the sky.
Look, the white autumn stars light up bloodshot eyes.
And the crazed guns, listen, are dreaming blood-thirsty
      dreams.
No more pretense of half-sleep in a night like this,
So quiet, so serene, even a cricket could cry out its grievance.
The gust of stench on the wind blows not desolation, nor
      solitude,
Surely, you hear the groan of the wounded, and the sobbing
      of women,
But this will not shake the spirit of the brave.
You must listen and receive the message from the stench
      on the wind.

It blows over, blows over ditches of blood and pockets of fire;
It blows here as we trample the devil's footprints everywhere.
It blows over towering peaks and narrow vales, drowning
      the notes of the leaves.
Fiery rockets and deafening blasts in the air, where steel
      dances with steel.
Night bares herself under the wings of darkness,
We carry the word of the righteous to all corners of the world,
And we reach out our hands, the hands that have been soiled
      by the devil's blood.
Thank you! Immense open space above the yellow waters in
      the river, and bright moon
Whose light accompanies us in our flight over the distance.
We have our mission, and the moonlight as our witness.
We hasten to broadcast our grievance, wrath, and boiling
      blood
In the cities, in the countryside, and in the hearts of all men.

A country four thousand years old has a life undying;
The winding Yellow River, the fertile Yangtze River, so many
      miles of land,
So much riches, and so many historic heroes.
Their ancestors have left clear milestones on this land,
And never have they halted in their march, not even in
      severe storms.
As we came from the north, we saw all these milestones,
Now, the brave ones shout aloud the angry cries of an all-
      consuming war.
China! Once again this poignant word comes alive,
      throbbing,
Irresistibly plucking the chord of everyone's
      heart.
What matter if the devil plays tricks, what matter if we
      go on under strain,
For this word—China—we have our mission.
Can you resent us, though we are a gust of stench on the
      wind!

My friend, you must have smelled this stench on the wind,
You must retain firmly the message it spreads.
China—because of this word, from now on
Never will you lose your way, neither will you
Miss the source of the stench, nor the cruelty of the devil.
The call of the age will not allow us to idle away
In dream. The gleam of the sword and the shadow of fire,
      those rows of corpses
Never again will they fear the threat of sword or fire. For
      the sake of China,
For China their souls rest content, forever smiling.
They have accepted the mission enjoined by the stench on the
      wind, and they
At the juncture of life and death raise a bloody red flag for
      China.
My friend, when you smell the stench on the wind, take note
      of the word on that flag.

        1938 (?)
        Selected Poems of Wang T'ung-chao, 129–31

THE BATTLE HYMN OF SHANGHAI

Who is worried about the destruction of the riverside
      pleasure houses?
Who is still concerned about the "perpetual festival" here?
We struggle for life in the enemy's rain of blood,
Struggling for life, we fight, and shout in all directions:
      Hurry home, soul of our nation!

Look, a herd of ferocious animals harassed by a hunter;
Look, beacon flames covering the daylight sky;
And a naked orphan, covering his wound with his hand,
      in the street.
A falling white cloud explodes into many red streams.

For living room, for expansion, so many young men are sent
      to be buried in blood on the riverbank,
Expedition, conquest, depending only upon the soulless
      generals' dreams; but they, too, have their widows,
      orphans, refugees and suffering—the misfortunes of
      the ordinary man.
Why, oh, why? Truly these are confused accounts in
      blook-soaked history.
Now, our mountains and rivers hasten the enemy's cars and
      boats.
Now, we are still held under layers of chains.
Even if we could wipe out the colors of memory, forget
      the bygones,
Now—can you bear the humiliation right now?

Every night soft music floats on a spring river,
In autumn the moon shines bright and high above the water,
A gust of frightful wind descends to stir a bloody tide
      surging toward heaven,
And the soft music and bright moon all disappear in the
      flight of bullets and the flow of gun smoke.
The millions of residents here, clenching their teeth, laugh
      in unison:

For final clearance of history's bloody account, we
Patiently await our revenge, patiently await our revenge!
Pleasure and leisurely games have no claim in our hearts, not
      any more.
You and I equally taste the severity of this age.
Listen, aren't enemy horses whinnying north and
      south of the Yangtze River?

         1939 (?)
        Selected Poems of Wang T'ung-chao, 112–13

YÜ TA-FU (1895–1945)

Yü Ta-fu's life was unusual. Four years of study in Japan exposed him to an enormous number of Western novels in translation and set him on the road to a writing career. With Kuo Mo-jo he founded the Creation Society in 1922, and during the next several years he was active in politics and had many ups and downs in his personal life. He taught for a while and edited a magazine with Lu Hsün in 1928. During the next five or six years he was a central figure in the leftist literary movement, traveling frequently between Formosa and the southeastern Chinese coast where he held a government post. Discovery of his common-law wife's infidelity in 1937 drove him to despair. He tried to lose himself in the South Sea Islands and spent the war years incognito. His acquaintance with many Japanese has been a source of wild speculation as to his real activities during those years. He was secretly put to death in Sumatra on September 17, 1945, by Japanese police.

He is best remembered as a short-story writer, but his poems written in the classical style have a place in twentieth-century Chinese poetry. He once declared that he wrote poetry merely to give vent to his feeling, and he could do so with very few words in the classical style. Vernacular poetry seemed to him too tedious for his purpose.

TO YING-HSIA

Away from home
In a season when the plums are ripening,
A lone lamp lights the still of the night.
I still remember the days when we went out in springtime,
Rowing on the lake to the full of our hearts' desire.

Since our cars started toward the station of departure,
Writing poetry has become uninteresting, and drinking a
     chore.
So much boredom!
Especially now that the sail is all set to go,
And the seagoing vessel is beckoning.
This longing is already too much to bear,
Not to think
What a failure I have been.
I regret that I'm poor as Ssu-ma
And having burned myself out as Chiang Lang,
Unable to face the others as the defeated General Li Kuang.
My only comfort is your unwavering devotion,
And the depth of your feeling
Is enough for me to lose myself there forever.
I must arrange for a true likeness of you
To be framed for me to worship.

> July 3, 1927
> *The Poems of Yü Ta-fu*, 39

IN MEMORIUM
My Son Yüeh-ch'un

How can his little soul enter our dream?
So many crossroads will require his guessing and hesitation.
For fear that someone might take advantage of him in the
     other world,
We bury him near the ancestral grave, and plant an ashplant
     for him.

> May 1935
> *The Poems of Yü Ta-fu*, 25

HSÜ HSÜ (1908–   )

PROBABLY THE most popular Chinese fiction writer now living in Hong Kong, Hsü started his writing career in 1932 when he and Lin Yutang published the magazine *Lun Yü* (*Analects*) in Shanghai. The journal specialized in "light" and humorous prose. Three years later, he and Lin developed another magazine of the same type, *Jen chien shih* (*The World of Man*). This venture lasted only a year, and Hsü joined Lin Yutang's brother to produce a third magazine *Yü chou feng* (*The Winds of the Universe*). During World War II, Hsü moved himself and the magazine to Hong Kong. He has visited southwest China and spent some time in Chungking and Kweilin.

Most readers remember him as the author of more than fourteen novels, but he has also published several volumes of poetry. His verse is clever and strongly influenced by Western European literature. Chinese readers readily identify his writing as of the "Shanghai" style; but they have difficulty pronouncing his given name and often make it "yü" because it is a very uncommon Chinese character.

REVISITING THE SOUTH OF THE RIVER

Again early summer; again I visit the South of the River,
But from whom can I inquire about the peonies?
No plum blossoms on the Ku Hill;
The lake still stores my tears of past years.

Perhaps what is to come may yet be pursued,
Yet what has departed will never return;
Let not my soul be drenched in misery, please,
I'd rather let my flesh commit any unforgivable sin.

That over there is neither a man nor a ghost
Nor a statue of clay, nor a stele of stone;
It's but that my tears and blood over the years
Have reduced to ashes all my hopes and dreams.

The flowers I received have all withered,
From whom can I inquire about the peonies?
No plum blossoms on the Ku Hill,
On the lake I shed my tears of this year.

> Hangchow, June 11, 1932
> *Collected Poems at Forty*, II, 75

SECRET PRAYER

I've watched many people die
I've watched many grow old;
In the short life of man,
Are you never troubled?

All year long in the noisy city
I hear some one cry;
Should I fear the ghost's wail
On his grave under a lonely sky?

So many weird mountains
Hide bottomless canyons;
Who said whenever the sun shines
Every place is lighted?

You've your right to ban the crows
From chattering to humanity;
But many owls in the night wind
Are praying secretly.

> Chungking, September 25, 1942
> *Collected Poems at Forty*, I, 24

THE CYCLE

I gaze at the view of the evening, pretty as a picture;
I lean on a railing and drink alone.
Tipsy are the scattered stars
That I have long known.

I think of the absent that have returned,
And of the returned that are gone again,
While all the colorful clouds have
Broken apart one by one.

New flowers are not yet in bloom;
The old ones, already forgotten.
Who is there in a night like this
To remain in the garden?

Those fated to shine are about to shine,
But already faded are those fated to fade;
A morning breeze blows away the stars,
The world swings only between light and shade.

November 20, 1947
The Cycle, 11–12

UNDER THE MOON

A crowded city,
A difficult existence;
Under the pale moonlight,
Shadows and shadows!

Fitful lights,
Trembling leaves,
In the whistling sea winds,
Desolation, desolation!

This door sighs,
That window groans,
Life full of suffering,
Awaken, awaken!

The first wave is receding
The second promptly arrives;
So many layers of time
So many lives.

Hong Kong, January 5, 1951
The Cycle, 25–26

TSANG K'O-CHIA (1910?–   )

A YOUNG MAN quietly chewing over his own words, forever dissatisfied with the fruits of his own inspiration, was Tsang K'o-chia of Shantung Province in the early 1930s. Life and poetry he took so seriously that they weighed him down and gave him excruciating pain. In one of his earliest poems he complained:

"The pain brands my heart,
Reminding me, every minute, that this is life."

To tell of life and its branding force Tsang tempered his verses, with the encouragement of Wen I-to when the latter was teaching at Tsingtao in Shantung. Tsang adopted as his motto the saying of Tu Fu, "If my words fall short of startling, I won't stop even after death." His first book, *The Brand*, which shows much of his painstaking hammering, appeared in 1934.

As he admitted in a postscript to this volume, he had had a pleasant childhood until the harsh reality of life thrust bitter disappointment upon him. He drifted to Hankow in the late 1920s hoping to offer his life to the revolution. Later he went north beyond the Great Wall and devoted himself to writing. He sought to "give a forceful life to the new poetry." He wanted to portray the sinister look of life and society in words that could not be altered, even by a syllable. Consequently he often spent a whole evening working over a single line. He worked so hard on his poems that he ruined his health.

The themes in his early poems indicate a preoccupation with the Japanese invasion of Manchuria and its resultant exodus of refugees. In expressing his sympathy with them, Tsang gave vent to his anger against the chaotic forces that victimized so many helpless people. A few poems suggest his longing for a dramatic and drastic change in the lot of his fellow men, but he conceived the change too vaguely to be the herald of a revolution. In "Self-Portrait," a long poem published in 1936, he attempted to reflect the background and history of the violent and troubled times around 1927.

After the outbreak of the war with Japan Tsang went to the war zone, spent some five years with the soldiers, and traveled from trench to trench. A wider range of characters and settings entered his poetry. Allowing his enthusiasm to carry him along, he broke away from his earlier habit of meticulous concern for diction, and wrote much more freely and loosely. As time went on, his initial wild enthusiasm was tempered by an increasing depth of understanding of the people he met, and he sometimes returned to his original practice of polishing his lines.

The end of his five years in the war area found him back in the capital, Chungking. The worsening political situation drew his attention to the comedies and farces that highlighted the foibles of man. He wrote a number of satirical poems, such as those collected in *The Zero Degree of Life* (1947). In them, he again shows that he could, when he chose, free himself from his preoccupation with excellence of texture to capture an outburst of uninhibited feeling. His post-1949 writing has been a serious attempt to make use of the form and prosody inherited from folk songs, but his diction remains more polished than that of most of his fellow poets.

LIKE A GRAIN OF SAND

Like a grain of sand, the wind carries you along,
Without your knowing where you are going.
Don't keep thinking that you have your own strength,
Nor mention the direction you have in mind.

Since the sun turned red you have been following
The wind until dusk casts dark shadows around.
Now there is not a single star in the sky;
You may cling to the grass root to stay still for a while.

March 1932
The Brand, 21–22

INTERNATIONAL CEMETERY

Perhaps while living none heeded the other,
But now all have drifted to this space.
No longer strangers, nor harboring any dislike,
The blossoms on this grave spread over to that grave.

A tablet in front bears fine inscriptions
Pointing out the glory of a past life for others to see.
Little by little the lichen hides the words
But he has never had the heart to rise in protest.

Some have no more than a mound of yellow earth,
Yet insignificance causes them no sorrow.
They seem to bury their history purposely
Just to keep themselves perpetually free.

However sweetly spring birds may sing above,
No smile will ever again appear on your face;
Nor can the crickets' mournful chirp under the moonlight
Call forth a drop of your tears.

You have at one time lived in the world,
And have been friends, or perhaps enemies.
Now that dirt has sealed everyone's mouth
You have to keep to yourself, even if you have something to
    say.

May 1932
The Brand, 28–30

SLEEPLESSNESS

I can't hear any sinful noise,
Nor catch a glimpse of any light;
My heart, dripping blood,
Shines bright in the depth of the dark shadows.

In a stretch of indescribable sorrow—
Silent raindrops arrive.
Ring upon ring of gray blossoms
Bloom toward the unlimited distance.

June 1932
The Brand, 19–20

THE BRAND

Afraid of looking back at what has passed by,
I cleverly tell myself, "Life is a lie."
The pain brands my heart,
Reminding me, every minute, that this is life.

Ceaselessly I feel this brand,
All of a sudden poisonous flames leap up from its red light,
And out of the sparks bursts a peal of songs,
Each singing of life's misfortunes.

Never have I told others of my suffering and sorrow,
To do that is a crime, I know.
Live on, then, without thinking, or feeling anything,
If it's a riddle, one mustn't divulge its truth.

I make a living chewing bitter juice
Like a worm gnawing a croton bean.
High in the sky I lift my heart,
Even breathing feels hard and heavy.

1932
The Brand, 14–15

FIRE IN THE SKY

You exaggerate, saying how beautiful life is,
Like a blossom newly picked from a branch.
On it there gallops your spiritual and imaginative light
That paints one dream after another dream.

Perhaps you, it may be said, simply don't understand:
Dark clouds note the pent-up feelings in the sky.
Listlessly the schools of dragonflies fly.
What kind of omen does that portend?

A young girl cannot sell enough for a meal,
As human flesh and pork both come into the market.
These facts are truly shocking, and fresh,
Yet you only cover your eyes and say you saw nothing.

I know that you are familiar with everything,
And of what you pretend to be unaware.
You place one hand over the facts, and say
To the others, "There is nothing at all."

When people get a bit restless
You behead them, labeling them criminals.
Everybody sees what this means; clearly
You wish to force a spark out of dead ashes.

But when that times arrives you'll have to die,
The world already is no longer yours.
At that time flames will burn bright on the plain,
And you surely will exclaim, "Such strange fires in the sky!"

1932
The Brand, 16–18

THE RICKSHA PULLER

The wind roars and rocks treetops;
On the tip of his nose raindrops gather in a growing trickle.
A pitiful, small lamp on his ricksha
Cannot dispel the dark shadows around.

A strange puzzle is his thought.
Unmindful of the raging storm,
He sits still, like a drenched hen,
The night is growing old; what is he waiting for?

1932
Selected Poems of Tsang K'o-chia, 8

NIGHT IN THE CITY

Troop after troop of large and small lamps
Compete with each other, their excited light blooming,
Like a flock of moons and a sky full of stars
Descends from above to keep man joyful company.
Ghostlike crowds of men, each carrying an empty shell,
Drifting and mixing, pass through these waves of silvery light.
A school of silvery fish on the sea's bottom, awakened by a
        moonbeam,
Darts away in fright, pursued by their slim shadows.
The glum and somber shadow of a bank
Lies in the street, like a giant bear.
The shadow of one person, with a dream,
Melts in the depth of this fearsome dark shadow.
It appears to be a young girl
With dewdrops glistening on her flowing hair.
And her torn clothes, torn and fluttering in the wind,
Resemble a cluster of black butterflies darting toward the
        light.
To her, is every lighted object but an illusion?
Look, before all this elegance she closes her eyes.
She lets the moonlight shine on the cheeks of other people,
And in her sleep she timidly stays in shadow.
The break of dawn cuts through the night scene of the city
And lifts up a heavy universe. She wakes from her dream.

February 1933
The Brand, 31–33

THE STREET ANGEL

A pair of feet, born so nimble,
Whirl around like the wind.
A soft scent wafts from the hem of her clothes;
Love blossoms all over the patterns of the carpet.
(She never said that she was tired.)

She knows how to use clever words
To coax the awkward pleasure of a patron.
She knows, too, how to use her wordless glances
To coat other people's hearts with honey.
(She never revealed her own heart.)

Red-colored and green-colored wine
Pin a spring blossom on her cheeks.
The scent of flesh intoxicates more than the wine's scent,
While her youth burns brighter than fire.
(Youth flees so fast she has no time to reflect.)

Her throat is gifted for singing,
Note after note draw an echo from your heart.
Joy, sorrow, she knows how to sing them all,
You need only name your choice.
(She never sings her own song.)

Alone she bears a night of solitude,
The lamp shines on four walls of quiet grief.
Memory lights up the way from the beginning,
She heaves a deep sigh and closes her eyes.
(This moment she has only herself in the world.)

1933
The Brand, 47–49

THE HEART OF THE WARRIOR

The night grows old at a riverside temple with its
          oil lamp.
The dream of the warrior is blooming bright.
He pillows his head on a soldier's book and a sword,
The lamplight falls on a mass of white hair.

Suddenly he opens his eyes wide—a battle drum is urging him,
(From the depths of the hall comes the beat of a prayer
          block.)[1]
As he steps out, the stars look like those of the old days,
When the chilly wind of the northland rattled his iron mail.

Before his eyes gallop ten thousand war horses;
He issues a battle cry, lifting his sword up high . . .
Never has the warrior returned since then
But the river beyond the gate roars on, night after night.

                    Tsingtao, January 11, 1934
                    The Black Hands of Sin, 33–34

THE CALL OF LIFE

Rising high, then plunging low
Rings the call of a street hawker—
A note that floats and sinks
Measuring this bottomless night.

Will the sleepless heart in a sequestered boudoir
Make it the haunting refrain of a poem?
Oh, no, this is the call of life,
With a mouthful of blood to each call, shattering the heart of
          the night.

                    Hsiang-chou, April 5, 1934
                    Selected Poems of Tsang K'o-chia, 40

[1] A "wooden fish"; see footnote on p. 161.—Ed.

AUTUMN

I believe there must be someone, with a cigarette between his
      lips,
Gazing through the crack in the paper windowpane at the
      courtyard in the rain.
Shreds of chilly rain drift in the sky;
The threads of man's sorrow blend into the rain's shreds.

There must also be someone, facing a red setting sun,
Thinking of the cloud and haze of his hometown far away,
Or with a lonely shadow trailing behind him,
Searching the wilderness for his childhood long faded.

Is there anyone who recognizes the autumn right now?
How brightly it appears on the faces of the poor!
Desolately everywhere flows the sound of sobbing at night,
And the night quietly smothers it.
Cool breeze in the wilderness displays a heap of bleached
      bones.
Who has ever thought:
The autumn colors of the Yalu River,
Can no longer come through the Shan-hai Pass.

October 2, 1934
The Canal, 6–7

THE TOP

Top under whip's tip
On night's peak turning
Pulled by pain I go
Soundlessly round in this windy and dewy garden.

Swell of the waves of the dead night.
Bright moon above
Myself below
Eyes of the universe ever unclosing.

July 18, 1935
The Canal, 45
(Translated by Cyril Birch)

THE EXECUTION GROUND

Carrying on its back an ancient city wall
To make a dark, shadowy, screen,
This place faces a row of withered willows
On which hangs a sinking sun.

The graves in formation
Wear a coat of yellowed grass,
Like comrades they huddle together
Arm in arm.

Past Easter, past midautumn,
No paper money for the dead ever appeared at the graves.
Nobody ever came here to mourn the departed,
Only waves of crows cover the sky, dusk and dawn.

Night falls into a chilly pool under the willows,
Fireflies guide the ghosts to talk of their loneliness.
The bosoms full of grievance will never hush,
They shout in unison, in their hoarse voice, "In Twenty More
    Years!"

January 15, 1937
Selected Poems of Tsang K'o-chia, 103

PORTRAIT OF LIFE

Two old bullocks
Work in the field.
With one hand on the plow handle
He follows behind.
Waves appear on the freshly turned soil,
Emitting the fragrance of earth.
A puppy lies in the corner of a field
To keep the little child company.
Above the plow crows beat their wings
Slowly
To land on the backs of the bullocks.

1942
Selected Poems of Tsang K'o-chia, 157

ARREST

Violent fists
Pound on the door!
The stars so shaken,
Are about to fall.
The dogs bark wildly,
Threatening to raise
The entire mountain village!
A brief pause of dead silence,
The pounding returns with greater strength.
Now fists are no longer used,
The thud is resounding.

After hesitation, more hesitation,
The door,
Amid curses,
Finally is flung open,
Footsteps enter the gate.
Also heard is
The search in every corner,
Followed by the sound of ropes.

At last, a feeble struggle
Like that of a small bird
Gripped in a huge hand.
Confused footsteps
Pass through the tiny courtyard.
Torchlights flash beyond my window.
Frightfully, for a moment,
An old woman's piercing, sad wail,
Like the ripples on a sea of darkness
Where someone has just cast a pebble,
Gradually recedes afar,
Gradually fades.

> 1945
> *Selected Poems of Tsang K'o-chia*, 201–2

THE STARS

I like to hear
People call the stars
"Little stars."

The sky at night is another world
Where the stars are the people.
Nobody pushes anybody;
They stay so closely together.

Little stars they are,
So little they have no names.
They use only their own rings of light
To assert their existence.

Raise your head and look
At that glistening Milky Way,
One, two, three, you count,
Ah, they are so many, so very many . . .

> Shanghai, August 4, 1946
> *Selected Poems of Tsang K'o-chia*, 231

THE ZERO DEGREE OF LIFE
A Recent News Headline

"Storm the day before yesterday,
Eight hundred children dead last night."

Over eight hundred of them, once full of life,
In the "local news" column of the paper
Occupied only a tiny corner.
Nameless,
Ageless,
Homeless,
Even the way and the place where they froze to death
Received no description or explanation.
Such news items,
Glanced at under the people's eyes only a moment,
Were quickly passed over.
At most they earned several sighs.
What the papers like to print are:
A young girl ravished, a spider with a human head, a baby
        born with two bodies,
And a robber getting his loot or losing his life.
Your deaths
Are as unnoticed and unknown as your births.
You, such tender buds of man,
Before you could wait for the arrival of spring,
Hunger and cold
Have already nipped your life line in one snatch.
Where did you come from?
Under the whips of the landlords?
Or from the land of a barren village?
Did you come together with your parents,
Harboring a hope to seek life from within death,
To plunge into this largest metropolis of East Asia?

You were lost in the maze of towering buildings,
Your mouths watered at the scent of feasts.
The city's noise drowned your wailing,
Here every conscience is rusty.

Your look of dirtiness
Made dignitaries and noble ladies dodge.
Your trembling bodies and voices
Begged curses and nasty stares rather than sympathy.
The great Shanghai is immense
And warm,
And bright,
And rich.
But you,
Assailed by cold and hunger,
Retreated in defeat to the dark corners,
With empty stomachs, and chattering teeth . . .
Northwest winds roared all night long,
And snow churned.
Your bodies
Like so many thermometers,
Dropped little by little
Until they reached the zero degree of life.

You died,
All eight-hundred-odd of you, as if by previous agreement,
Clutching the same despair,
Passing out of this world in the same night.
I know, you were unwilling to die;
You tried to resist,
But from a stretch of pale imagination
You could grab
No weapons.
One by one the naked bodies,
And one by one the naked hearts,
Were rapidly knocked down
By the coldness of the world of man.
In a society where man eats man,
You have always
Existed only from hour to hour.
Wherever you dropped,
That was it!
I hate those philanthropists,
Who, after your death, picked up your bodies here and there.

Let your bodies
Stay forever
On those three feet of land.
Let those scientists who invented central heating
Look at you once
As they pass by.
Block the rich magnates' private cars,
Let them spit once or twice.
Let the fashionable ladies step on you,
And scream.
Let those corpses bleed, and rot,
Sending their stench to mix
In the breathing of the great Shanghai.

> Shanghai, February 6, 1947
> *The Zero Degree of Life,* 45–51

SHORT SONG TO GREET THE NEW YEAR
CELEBRATING THE POETRY CONTEST IN HOPEI PROVINCE

In the year nineteen fifty-eight,
Achievements pile mountain high.
Grains and steel are two peaks
Towering up in the sky.

The red sun shines on New Year's Day
As we gaze at the far distance.
Two feet straddle the two peaks,
From one the other always looks higher.

We used to write poetry in the study,
Now we write it in the factory.
We used to write it all alone,
Now a crowd competes for victory.

When we open our mouths, good verses are written,
Why should we tinker with them long?
The materials for poetry fill the bosom,
No need to search for them everywhere.

The enthusiasm for labor rises high,
Poetic ideas surge in full tide.
As the east wind urges the flower to bloom,
Songs flow from everyone's lips.

December 1958
The Wind of Spring, 39–40

LISTEN

Listen,
What is the rumble
That rocks the mountains and shakes the earth?

Is it the surging surf,
Or rolling thunder,
Or armies marching?

Before my eyes, a sinewy horse
Gallops toward a destination;
Far and farther away waves its red mane.

1958
The Wind of Spring, 2

AI CH'ING (1910–   )

"WE MUST persist in the revolution brought into poetry by Whitman, Verhaeren, and Mayakovsky. We must make poetry into something that adequately meets the needs of a new era, without hesitating to use whatever poetic form is most suitable for this purpose."

Ai Ch'ing wrote these words in his *On Poetry* in 1942 when he was at the peak of his poetic career. It had been his credo since his early exposure to Western poetry at school in Chekiang, and later in France. While in Europe he worked in a small factory to support himself and became acquainted with the works of French poets, of whom he particularly admired Verhaeren and Apollinaire. An active mind and a restless soul prodded him to turn away from a medical career and from his old landed-gentry family, the Chiang family of Hangchow, Chekiang Province. (Ai Ch'ing is his pen name; his original name was Chiang Hai-ch'eng.) An intense interest in color and line augmented the sensitivity of his observation. And when he saw the immense northland of China, with its vast canvas of bold lines and hues, he virtually renounced his Eastern Chinese background and declared North China his first love.

An autobiographical poem, "My Father," sketches his early life and intellectual development. He tells us that immediately after his return from France to Shanghai in 1932, he was detained for a number of months in jail in the French concession under the charge of harboring dangerous radical ideas. Prison life spurred him to write poems. One of them was dedicated to Apollinaire:

> I'm madly in love with your Europe
> The Europe of Baudelaire and Rimbaud
> Where

I proudly played my reed flute
With an empty stomach

. . . .

Today
I'm in a Bastille.
No, not the Bastille of Paris,
And the flute is no longer with me,
While the iron chains rattle louder than my songs

. . . .

After his release, he traveled in North China and later
stayed in Yenan to teach at the Lu Hsün Academy of Arts.
Living up to his own dictum that the new poet must come
from the ranks of the ordinary people, he went to live with
and learn from country people and workers. His first major
poem, written in 1933, was dedicated to the illiterate nurse,
Ta Yen Ho, who had raised him. The poem is full of intense
feeling expressed in plain, straightforward words. "If it is to be
fine and feeble, I would rather have it crude and rough, as
the latter often indicates an overabundant force of life," he
said in 1942. And the force of life is readily felt in his poetry.

He has continued to edit literary publications and write
poetry, and to devote much of his energy to encouraging
younger writers, quoting the motto which he paraphrased
from Byron: "A robust, outstanding, original and beautiful
poetry can be born from rich and real life upon cultivation by
numerous young writers." He strives for the same goal in his
own work, asking himself,

China,
Can my feeble poems written
In the dark night without any light
Offer you a bit of warmth?

CLEAR NIGHT

1

Clear night
—Broad laughter leaps up like flames
        on the paths in the countryside—
A crowd of drinkers rushes toward the
        sleeping village, trailing a loud noise.
In the village
The dogs' barking
Shakes up the stars in the sky.

Through the village,
Through the slumbering streets
And the slumbering wide-open space,
The drinkers dart
Into a wide-awake tavern.

Wine, lamplight, and wine-flushed faces
Are blended in a single patch, together
        with unrestrained laughter . . .

"Let's go
  To the slaughter house,
  To drink beef soup. . . ."

2

The drinkers walk toward the edge of the village
And enter a lighted open doorway.
The smell of blood, the pile of flesh, and the tangy odor
Of warm, fresh hides . . .
And the people's noise, and the people's noise . . .

The oil lamps, a bright brush fire, light up
The dozen mud-colored faces
That have lived on the prairie.

This is our paradise,
And all of them are faces so very familiar.
We grab
The steaming hot beef bones,
And in our wide open jaws we gnaw them, we gnaw
       them . . .

"Wine, wine, more wine.
 We want to drink."

The oil lamps, a bright brush fire, light up
The ox blood, and the blood-stained arms of the butcher,
And the blood-splashed
Butcher's forehead.

The oil lamps, a bright brush fire, light up
Our flesh and skin that burn like fire, and
—Hidden in them—
The pain, and the force of hatred and anger.

The oil lamps, a bright brush fire, light up
—Those coming from all corners—
Those who stay awake at night,
Drunkards,
Vagabonds,
Transient thieves,
And cattle rustlers. . . .

"Wine, wine, more wine,
 We want to drink."

3
. . . .

"While the stars are bright, and shivering
 Let's go . . ."
Broad laughter leaps up like flames on the paths
       in the countryside . . .
A crowd of drinkers leave
The slumbering village

And rushes toward the slumbering wilderness
Trailing a loud noise behind . . .
The night, the clear
Night!

> September 10, 1932
> Wen, *Complete Works, Hsin,* 551–54

LISTEN

Galloping along,
Galloping along.
The roar of the Southern France Power Plant
Goes on and on. Night
Sinks in the prison cell.
Like an ocean liner,
Rocking
Together with the snoring of my cell mates,
Night
Sails along
Slicing the waves with its momentum
On the sea of dark, dark blue.

> Shanghai, 1932
> Wen, *Complete Works, Hsin,* 554

THE SONG OF YOUTH

A canoe, still smelling of new wood,
Leaves a tiny barren island;
A melancholy but warm-hearted youth
Thus left his little village.

I disliked that village—
As ordinary as a banyan tree,
As slow-witted as a water buffalo—
Where I spent my childhood.

Those who knew less than I made fun of me,
I said nothing, but kept a wish to myself.
I wanted to go away to see more and learn more,
I wanted to go far away—to places never dreamed of:

There everything would be much, much better than here.
There people would live like gods.
There no heart-rending sound of the ceaseless pestles would
        be heard,
And the annoying faces of the monks and nuns
              would remain unseen.

Father counted the silver dollars, five by five,
And wrapped them up in red paper, handing them to me
            with a lecture,
While I was thinking about things a world apart,
About the harbors reflecting the glitter of the sun.

You, chattering sparrows, what are you talking about—
Don't you know that I am about to depart?
And you, simple and honest hired hands on our farm,
Why do you always wear a look of sorrow on your faces?

The morning sun shone on the stone-paved road,
My heart went out for my poor village.
It stood beneath the mountain of twin peaks,
Like an old man, wrinkled and failing.

Good-by, my village of poverty,
And my old dog, please hurry home.
The Twin Peaks will protect you from misfortunes
I shall return, when I grow old, to be with you.

Yenan, 1935 (?)
Selected Poems of Ai Ch'ing, 88–89

HE GOT UP

He rises—
From the decades of humiliation,
From beside the grave the enemy dug for him.
Blood drips all over his face,
And all over his chest,
But he is laughing—
As he has never laughed before.
He is laughing;
His shining eyes gaze forward,
Searching for
The enemy whose blow felled him.

He has got up.
Once up, he is
More fierce than all wild animals,
And cleverer than all men.
For he must be so,
For he must
Wrest his own life
From his enemy's death.

                              October 12, 1937
                              The Flowers of Man, 45–47

THE NORTHLAND

One day
That poet of the K'o-erh-ch'in grassland
Said to me:
"The Northland is sad."

Yes,
The Northland is sad.
Blowing over from beyond the Great Wall,
The desert winds

Have already swept away the green life of the North,
And the light of the day
—A dusty yellowish gray,
Covered under a dust film that cannot be removed.
The roar that rushes from over the horizon
Bringing terror with it
Madly
Sweeps the entire country.
The deserted wilderness
Freezes in December winds;
The villages, hills, and riverbanks,
Toppled walls and abandoned graves
All don a coat of sadness, the color of earth . . .

A lonely traveler
Bending forward,
Shielding his face with his hands,
Breathes with difficulty
In the sand and wind.
Step by step
He struggles forward . . .
Several donkeys—those beasts with sad eyes
            and tired ears,
Bear the painful burdens
Of this land,
Their tired steps
Tread slowly
On the long and lonely road
Of the Northland . . .

Those little creeks have been dry for a long time,
And cartwheel ruts crisscross the river beds.
The land and people of the North
Are longing
For the trickling water that nurtures life.
Withered woods
And squatting houses
Sparsely and somberly
Spread out under a lead-colored sky
Where no sun
Is seen.

Only huge flocks of wild geese,
Scared and disorderly,
Beat their black wings
And announce their unrest and unhappiness.
They flee from this deserted land,
Winging their way
Toward the South shaded in intense green . . .

The Northland is sad,
And the Yellow River, thousands of miles long,
Rolls with its muddy billows
To pour onto the immense Northland
Disasters and misfortunes.
The wind and frost of the years
Are carving out
Poverty and hunger
For the immense Northland.

But I
—a traveler from the South,
Dearly love this sad Northland.
The wind and sand that cut one's face,
And the chill that pierces one's bones
Never, never let me rest.
I love this land of sadness,
The stretch of unlimited desert
Awakens my respect.
I see our ancestors
Leading herds of sheep
And blowing their reed flutes,
Submerged in the dusk of the great desert.
In the ancient, soft, yellow earth
That we are treading,
Are buried the bones of our forefathers.
—They first tilled this land.
Thousands of years ago
They were here
Battling nature that frustrated them.
For the protection of their land
They never surrendered.

And they died
Leaving the land to us.
I love this sad country.
Its broad and lean space
Have offered us a simple language
And a generous stance.
The language and stance, I believe,
Will live stubbornly on earth,
Never to fade.
I love this sad country,
        This old country,
—For this country
Has nursed the world's oldest
And most hard-working people
Whom I love.

T'ung-kuan, February 4, 1938
Selected Poems of Ai Ch'ing, 126–30

HE DIED A SECOND TIME

1. On the Litter

When he woke up
He was already on a stretcher.
He knew he was still alive.
The two buddies carrying him
Said nothing.

The day was frozen in biting winds;
The clouds, low and heavy, moved slowly;
The winds shook the tree tops in silence.
They moved fast
Carrying the stretcher
Through a forest in winter.

After the intense, burning pain,
He was now calm in his heart,
Like a battlefield after a fierce battle,
Returning to undisturbed quiet.

Yet his blood,
Oozing through the bandage on his arm,
Continued to drip, drop by drop,
Falling on the frozen road of his fatherland.

On the same night
In the reverse direction
A troop ten times stronger than the earlier one
With their ten thousand footsteps at once,
Wiped away the purple-red stains left by his blood.

2. Hospital

Where were our rifles?
And our blood-drenched clothes?
Other comrades had put on our helmets,
We put on cotton jackets with a red cross embroidered on
        them.
We lay in bed, lay in bed,
Watching the numerous bodies chewed by molten metals
And poison gas.
Each man, his eyes sunken and black, fearful,
And his groaning ceaseless,
Greeted the passing of countless days,
Like so many black coffins in procession.
Here
No one was suffering
Less than any other.
To stop the enemy's attack,
Everyone met the merciless gunfire
With his life, his only life.
All of us had shed our own blood
On the land which we defended.
But today, we lay down, we lay down again.
Others said this was our glory,
We wanted none of it.
As we were lying there, our hearts were on the battlefield.
More than in our native villages.
We still would like
To dash forward into the smoke and fire of the war.

Today. Ah, today
We were like animals, tied with ropes,
Groaning on metal beds.
—We bore pain, and we waited,
But how long must we wait?

3. The Hand

Everyday at a fixed hour
The nurse wearing a white cap and a white uniform,
Silently walked out and returned
To remove the bandage from the wounds of the injured
        soldiers.
She gently pulled away the cotton and
Cleaned the unpleasant pus and blood around the openings.
Her dainty fingers were so nimble.
We could never have such wives;
Neither were our sisters like her.
She cleaned the wounds and bandaged them again,
So gently, doing all this with her ten little fingers
Doing all this with her dainty white fingers.
On one of them glittered a touch of gold.
The glitter danced on our wounds,
And danced in a certain corner of our hearts . . .
She left, keeping her silence.
After her quiet exit I gazed at my own hand
That had held a hoe and a gun before,
That had been worn rough and clumsy by hard labor.
It lay limp on my chest,
It grew on the end of my wounded arm.
I looked at my own hand and looked at her hand.
Thinking about all this, I fretted,
And fretting, I thought again—
What karma was this
That had brought these two hands together?

4. Healing

Time passed in the void.
He was discharged from the hospital
A prisoner leaving his jail cell,

He removed the heavy cotton-quilted jacket
And put on a thin gray uniform
That still had a red cross in front.

Free, and bright, the world had arrived at spring
There were countless people in the street.
They made him feel strange as well as welcomed,
The bright sun shone on the street.
Life, startled from a long sleep,
Pranced in the glaring light.
People walked by hastily,
He, alone, was still so tired.
Nobody noticed him—
A wounded soldier, today his wounds
Had healed. He was happy
But he knew, even more seriously,
The deeper meaning of the healing.
Only now he felt
That he was a soldier.
For a soldier must be wounded on the battlefield,
And there he must return when his wounds are healed.
He was thinking as he walked along;
His pace was strained.
The color on his cheeks was gone.
People passed by, none noticing
The pain in his looks.
Only the sun stretched its
Glaring fingers down from the top of the telegraph pole,
To touch his pale face,
Smiling in pain . . .

5. The Posture

He draped on his back the gray cotton uniform with a red
    cross on it,
Unbuttoned, and two sleeves dangling.
He walked down the wide and straight street in the city at
    night,
He walked down the city street that made him feel drunk.
Around him, the bubbling noise of the crowd,
Of the cars, horns, and whistles

Pressed itself upon him, pushed him, and prodded his senses.
On those smooth sidewalks,
Under those glaring electric lights,
And over the shining tar-paved roads,
Beside the rows of modern cars,
And in front of the fashionably dressed women,
He appeared so pitifully shabby.
Yet he seemed to have thought, suddenly, of lifting his feet
        proudly,
(For today he wore a robe of glory)
He felt he should walk in the world in that manner,
And only a person of his kind
Should walk in the world that way.

Yet as he felt himself walking this way
—with his chin up, his gray uniform on his shoulder and his
        strides long,
As he felt people watching his steps,
His face, bathed in electric lights,
Blushed in shame.
For he was afraid people
Had already guessed the secret in his heart—
In fact, of course, nobody noticed him.

6. In the Countryside

It was a sunny day.
He walked toward the countryside,
Something there seemed to be beckoning him.

Today his feet stepped
On the soft warm soil of the paths in paddy fields,
He felt an indescribable joy.
He removed his shoes,
Dipped his feet in the shallow creek,
And splashed the water with his hands.
For a long time he had been passing his days
Controlled by numbers only.
His future days were also to be
Controlled by numbers.

But today he felt compelled to search
In the countryside, even for the last time,
For that which was beckoning him.
He knew not what it was.
He saw the waterlogged rice paddies.
He saw the buffaloes pulling plows,
Everything was like this,
And like this it was everywhere
—Ah, people said this was China.
The trees turned green, and grass covered the land, all over.
Those adobe walls, those faraway places,
Those tile-roofed houses, and those people walking by
—He thought of what people said, that this was China.
He walked along, walked along.
What kind of day was this
That made him so silly and yet happy.
Even the New Year festival was not so joyful.
Everything was bright and shining
And bright and shining it was, everywhere.
He smiled at the farmers busy in the fields,
Without knowing why he smiled,
Nor did the farmers notice the smile on his face.

7. A Glance

Along that tree-shaded road stretching toward
The suburb, he walked in the shadows of intense blue
To avoid the sun's glare. From the shaded place he saw
Horse-carts jauntily
Rolling by, carrying
Young men and women neatly dressed.
From their mouths drifted peals of laughter
And loud chatter that made him feel uneasy.
He walked like a withered old man,
Slowly approaching a park.
At the park's entrance,
At the foot of the marble archway
He saw a disabled soldier.
A strange sensation jarred him wide awake,
And he thought to himself, perhaps this maimed comrade

Has been braver than everyone else, perhaps
This soldier has also wished to have his remains
            buried on the battlefield,
But had had to lie helpless here, groaning,
Groaning and lying down,
To pass his remaining days.
Ah, who can bear this sight?
And seeing it, who would not feel hate
            burning in his heart?
Let us do battle again,
Let us die happily in action,
But let us not return with only one leg
To shed tears before other people
And beg a sympathetic donation
With our out-stretched dirty and bony palms!

8. Exchange

He took off the gray uniform with a red cross on it
To put on again the olive green of several months ago.
Where had the blood stain on the uniform gone?
The bullet holes in it also had been mended.
Wearing it his heart throbbed violently,
More violently than when he first joined the army.
He seemed to perceive a perpetually inseparable relation
Between this uniform and the red cross uniform.
He was to wear them by turns forever;
Yes, exchanging one for the other, this is the way it ought
            to be.
For a soldier, before the end
Of the war for the liberation of his fatherland,
These two kinds of uniforms are the banners of his life.
The banners should vigorously
Unfurl and flutter on the downtrodden land of his country.

9. Send-off

Led by ceaseless sounds of firecrackers
Led by the sound of bugles vibrating down the street,
Led by the cheers of spectators along the sidewalk,

Let us march down the road paved with the wishes of every
      one,
Let us march down the road leading from the world of today
      to the world of tomorrow.
Let us march down the road that will be remembered
      with gratitude by posterity.
Our chests out,
Our steps in cadence,
We marched between the walls of spectators,
We marched with confidence and pride.
In our hearts there was only glory,
And we were pursuing only glory.
To die happily in pursuit of glory was the only thing
      in our minds . . .

10. A Thought

Did you ever know
What death was?
—Living, and dying
Insects and plants
Are also going through life's metamorphosis . . .
In this, what can you
Think of?
To be a soldier, yes,
Offering life to the war,
And dying on the riverside
Or in the wilderness!
Cold dewdrops freeze into ice over our chests
Our remains rot in the weeds.
For so many ages
Man has used his own life
To enrich the land
And used the land
To nourish his own life.
Who can escape from the rhythm of nature?
—Well, then what is wrong
With our death for this cause?
Guns on our backs
We walk in a long column

Isn't your heart also often disturbed
By something more intense than love?
When one day you are ordered to the front, to the battlefield,
Don't you often
Feel that you have had your life already,
And now you should die,
And your death is for
The countless future generations
To live more happily than you?
All the glories
All the songs,
To what avail are they
If we fail to remember
That we are dying of our own noble will?
—Which is also the irrevocable will
Of our nation.

11. Forward March

Forward, March, Be Brave, O
Comrades, Fix bayonets!
Let us tie our hearts
Together in one will:
For the liberation of our fatherland we fight.
Of what should we be afraid
As we have already known that to die in action is glorious?
Forward, March, Be Brave, O!
Toward the place where gunfire is most intense,
Toward the bullet-spitting trenches,
Look, the frightened enemy
Is already trembling at the footsteps of our march straight
        forward.
Forward, March, Be Brave, O!
Humiliation and shame
Must be brought to an end now.
We must wrestle from the enemy's hands
The destiny of our fatherland,
Only this sacred war
Can bring us freedom and happiness . . .
Forward, March, Be Brave, O!

This radiant day
Is in our grasp.
Our lives can
Resound and glow
Only through stubborn struggle.
Comrades, Fix bayonets!
Be Brave, Forward March!

12. He Fell

It all happened so suddenly
Allowing no time even for a fleeting thought
Or for a flashing question of surprise and wonder.
As a burning bullet
For the second time—also, ah, for the last time—
Pierced his body.
His life
Having been through this world (so they say),
Fell
Like a tree at the stroke of a gigantic ax.
At the split second before he closed forever
The window through which he used to view the world—
The eyes which at the moment were dimmed by tears of joy—
He could think of nothing.
His mother had died long ago,
And he had no intimate memory of any woman,
Everything about him was so simple, so very simple.

A soldier
Knows very few things.
He recognizes only
That he should die for this war of liberation.
When he falls
He only realizes
That the land where he lies is his fatherland,
Because other people, those who know better than he,
Once upon a time told him so.

A few minutes later his comrades
Went out searching for him:
This must be life's last visit with him.

Only that this time
They brought no stretcher,
But a short-handled spade.
Without choosing,
They dug a shallow hole
Near the spot where he guarded
The bank of a river.
The dirt, mixed with spring grass,
Having thus covered his body,
What he left to the world
Was but one of those pitiable mounds.
Those numerous mounds scattered like stars in the wilderness.
On those earth mounds nobody ever
Marked the name of the dead beneath
—Even if they did
What would be the use?

> The end of spring 1939
> Wen, *Complete Works, Hsin,* 538–51

AUTUMN MORNING

Fresh and cool morning,
With the sun just rising,
A dawning over a pitiful village.

A little bird with white rings around its eyes
Stands on the black tile of a roof
Pensively
Gazing at the high sky full of colored clouds.

It's autumn
And I've been in the South for a year.
There is no tropical breath here,
No towering coconut trees to be seen.
An inexplicable sorrow has already claimed my heart.

Yet, today when I am about to go away
My heart is curiously troubled
—The villages of China
With their poverty, filth, and shadowy gray, everywhere
Still never fail to make me linger.

> In Kweilin countryside, September 1939
> *Selected Poems of Ai Ch'ing*, 175–76

CARRY

Please move over,
Please stay on the sidewalk,
Let us get them up from the ground.
Please don't push,
Please stand on the side,
Let us get them up from the ground.
Please don't yell,
Please show your sorrow in silence,
Let us pick them up.

This is a woman
Her chest has been blown open,
Let her sleep with her eyes well closed.
Let her wake up gently a little later.
Let us carry her to her home,
And let her family, in bitter tears, arrange things for her.

This is a member of the Service Corps;
There is still an arm band on his uniform.
Do you know him—his face is covered with dust.
Merciless shrapnel broke his arms.
Please move over, please show your grief for him.
He died because he wanted to keep you from injury.

Please don't push, there are more here.
They are all wounded soldiers staying in the veterans' hospital
They were wounded in action, and then confined to bed,

Waiting for the wounds to heal so that they might return to
　　　the front.
Now that the shameless enemy has already destroyed the
　　　hospital with bombs,
More injuries have been added to their injuries.

Please move over,
Let us pick them up.
Please stand aside,
Let us get over here with our stretchers.
And remember, please, everybody remember,
All these are the enemy's debts of blood.

Chungking, June 11, 1940
Selected Poems of Ai Ch'ing, 81–82

WILDERNESS (II)

On a day when the corn is ripe, as if burned in fire:
Near a field where a crop of hemp has just been harvested,
A farmer, under the scorching sun,
Bends his straw-hatted head
To gather the tender leaves of the beans.

In the emptiness, immense and quiet,
The soft but complex chorus
Of the thousands of insects
Is singing grand hymns of nature.
The cicada's ceaseless squeal
And the inviting earnest calls of the cuckoos,
Arrive from the thick brush
Below the hills . . .

The murmur of the water in a narrow valley
That I heard yesterday at dusk,
Has already halted.
As I walk by the meadow through the shadowy woods
I hear only a hurried and brisk knocking—
A woodpecker hammering on a hollow tree.

Sunshine filters through the openings in the foliage,
Sunshine darts down from a height beyond our reach,
Sunshine broadcasts heat that makes man bow in gratitude.
Sunshine sets all lives aglow,
And gives warmth to all lives.

Ah, sweat has already drenched my back.
I pass by the long, long rows of beans and melons
That cling to the hedges with their tendrils,
(I feel so humble, and yet so proud.)
Once again I walk on the hill,
Wiping my brow,
I rest under an elm.

The simple, clumsy,
Towering and unpopular
Elm is my friend.
I never miss a day coming here.
Often I stay in its shade
Gazing at the wilderness,
Wordless, for a long time.

The wilderness—so immense, so savage . . .
So familiar and yet so fearful,
A ferocious sea
Of galloping earth, and rocks, and trees.

The untamed hills,
Defiant green waves
Rise and fall.
Black rocks
Pile high in an inseparable tangle.
Many trails
Appear inaccessible to each other
And yet are twisted together in a phantasma.
Small hamlets
Humble and pitiful,
Scattered about, each by itself.

Their windows
Stare at each other in spite,
And yet with indifference.
The mountain peaks stand
Face to face, charged with anger.
Wild woods far and near,
Like the thick curly hair of Africans,
Like their unkempt curly hair,
Harbor a quiet sorrow of thousands of years,
In their frightful silence,
In the depth of their unfathomable shadows.

Below,
In the deep, sunken valleys
Lie adjoining fields.
There, man lives, obeying predestination,
Imprisoned in the mountains.
From childhood to senility to death,
He bends his body to till
The stubborn earth, without stop.
Everyday he sweats
And pants
Under the heavy yoke of poverty and travail.

Tossed by a rebellious fate,
Once I abandoned my declining village,
But now here I return.
How could I hide—
I'll always be a son of the wilderness.
The way I, alone, walk on the hills,
Moving my legs slowly and with difficulty,
Much like an exhausted draft animal.
Inside my body, unvisited by the sun, like the pine tree bark,
Flows a weariness of life, and also a stream of stubborn blood.
Often like the moon I gaze quietly
At the immense and robust wilderness.
And often like a beggar, I
Humbly pass by
Those threatening mountain trails
In the closing dusk.

In my bosom that hides a pain
Perpetually surges
The desire of life, burning, unrestrained.
And everyday
When troubled by uncontrollable sorrow
I lie on my back on the hill,
To gaze beyond the horizon of the wilderness
From under the elm's shade.
For a long time, and without a word,
I let my flaming thoughts and feelings
Melt in the boundless space
With its undulating haze,
And sunshine, and rocks.

Szechwan, July 8, 1940
Selected Poems of Ai Ch'ing, 161–65

ON A CHILEAN CIGARETTE PACKAGE

A goddess of liberty,
Painted on a Chilean cigarette package,
Although she holds high a torch,
Only a black shadow of her is seen.

For a trademark, for advertising,
A bit of space is offered her.
You can buy it with small change
And after you are through, it vanishes in smoke . . .

The package is tossed on the roadside,
He steps on it, and you spit on it.
Whether it's a fact, or merely a symbol,
The goddess of liberty is but a pack of cigarettes.

Santiago, August 1954
Selected Poems of 1953.9–1955.12, 474–75

TO HIROSHIMA

You should be a beautiful harbor
With mountains on three sides, and one side open to a plain.
Embraced by the hills, your city
Spreads like a fan southward.
Seven streams feed the bay,
Warm and moist sea breezes come from the south
To cheer the blossoms blanketing the seashore,
Where seaweeds drape their tassels and ribbons.
Hiroshima, you are an ancient city
Scented with sandalwood.
Over the years your thousands of residents
Have worked diligently, like bees.
The noise of berthing boats filled the days,
And songs and music accompanied the long nights.

None of them ever wanted war—
These common Japanese workers and farmers,
Of Nagasaki or Hiroshima,
None of them ever wanted war.
They nursed no hatred
Against the Chinese or the Malayans.
The Japanese never sought a rubber plant in Ceylon,
Or a coconut plantation in Java,
Or a colony on the Mekong River,
To support any claim to a conqueror's fame.
These people gained nothing from the war;
The war fattened other people,
Not them.
Yet, one morning
When sirens had just stirred people awake,
A sudden flash, without any noise,
Slashed the sky from the east westward.
Everyone knew disaster had arrived.

The survivors
Have become deformed, mostly—
As if meant to tell the world
Of their experience of horror.

They have seen so much, so much,
Beyond what anyone could have seen.
The light so intense,
The wind so violent,
The explosion blasting granite into powder,
And more explosions turning steel rods into fragile strings.
Over a hundred thousand lives
Perished in the same instant.

Love, art, poetry and music
Turned into dust and ashes in that instant . . .
A city destroyed,
With its pain lingering so long,
Even today—when ten years have passed,
Heart-rending cries are still heard.

. . . .

Hiroshima, you are the eyewitness,
You must rise from the disaster.
Your existence itself is a declaration,
For you have recorded the cruelty of war.
You must speak in defense of peace,
And tell the world,
How the dead died,
And how the survivors live.

Today—Silence, please, everybody,
Let Hiroshima speak.

> Early August 1955
> *Selected Poems, of 1953.9–1955.12*, 466–70

T'IEN CHIEN (1914–   )

WHEN T'UNG T'IEN-CHIEN (his original name) first wrote poetry at fourteen, he was impressed by the experiments of the Crescent poets and works translated from the European masters. Among his very early published poems is one describing the life of the farming population, written in neat stanzas with over fifteen syllables to each line. The cadence and diction in these early poems give little hint of what he was to become later—the trail blazer of a new direction for modern Chinese poetry, the champion of a nervy, drumbeat rhythm in verse, and the generally accepted "herald of the new era" into which China was evolving.

A dramatic change in this son of an eastern Chinese (Wuhu, Anhwei Province) landowner came about when he went north and plunged into feverish activities with leftists and anti-Japanese underground workers. The occupation of Manchuria by Japan fired his youthful zeal and the resistance movement kindled his imagination. He became a close associate of the veteran leftist woman writer Ting Ling (the pen name of Chiang Ping-chih, who won a Stalin Prize in 1951, but was "purged" by the Communists in 1957). "His poetic mind has become intensely united with life as it truly is," said Hu Feng, and T'ien Chien seized upon a new technique to give expression to what he saw and felt. This was his "drumbeat" poetry with two or three syllables to the line, which appeared in his first collections, *It Is Not Yet Dawn* and *Chinese Ballads* in 1936.

T'ien Chien said that he welcomed such models as he found in Mayakovsky's works. Whether he consciously imitated the Russian writer or not, T'ien Chien certainly made a drastic departure from the Chinese poetic tradition, including the new trends established after 1919. He believed that the true and most intense feeling of man can best be expressed by the pauses and halts in his speech. The accen-

tuation of the elements that are significant in a line calls for
stressed syllables, which T'ien Chien indicated by placing
them at the beginning of a line. Hence the breathless pace of
the drumbeat.

The ten years when he was most active in writing poetry,
from 1936 to 1946, certainly were an appropriate time for
drumbeating. Wen I-to praised T'ien Chien as the "Drummer
of Our Time" who had restored to Chinese poetry the ro-
bust spirit of the primitive songs, which Wen felt the Cres-
cent poets, including himself, had not done.

T'ien wrote to be read aloud, and when his poems are so
read their powerful rhythm is palpable. The pitch of certain
lines sometimes rises so high that they seem to shout. But
they are never mere slogans and they speak for a disturbed
generation.

The feverish battle cries of the early 1940s subsided after
1949. T'ien Chien's drumbeat lines, once popularly and af-
fectionately called "postcard poetry" because he made a habit
of writing his postcards in the same style, immediately slowed
their pace. "I Sing of My Fatherland" of 1954 shows that he,
too, has turned to the folk song tradition and stopped
shouting.

TO THOSE WHO FIGHT

Prelude

In a dark
And cold night,
The Japanese robbers
Came,
And from our
Hands,
From our
Bosoms
Seized our innocent comrades
And locked them behind a fence of violence.
Their bodies
Showed
Angry scars,

Their hearts
Throbbed
In grief and hatred,
They shivered
In Dairen, in the camps
Of the Manchurian wilderness,
Waiting for the drunken,
And meat-gorged brutes,
Wielding their swords
To tease
These abandoned
Lives
And their hungry
Blood . . .

1

A glorious name—
The people!
O our people,
Stood at the Marco Polo Bridge,
Facing the buffeting winds,
Blowing their bugle of assault.
O our people,
You have stood up
Like a giant,
On this immense land.

2

It was July, the July
That saw the beginning of the great war.
In July
We
Stood up.

We
Rose
And opened our grieved and angry
Eyes.

We
Rose
And rubbed our red, chafed heels,
And our black, soiled
Fingers.

We
Rose,
On the blood-covered wilderness,
On the blood-drenched desert,
On the blood-filled river,
We guarded
The center of our country
And its frontiers.

Through ice and snow, smoke and haze,
Over a great distance,
A great distance,
We raised our heads,
To summon
Love and happiness
Freedom and liberation . . .

In July
We
Stood up.

Resounding bugles
Were calling day and night,
Calling,
And calling.
We rushed to the battlefield together,
Determined to wipe out the aggressors!

We swore
We pledge our lives
To the defense of China.

In China,
The people's
Children

Need feeding and care,
The people's cattle herds
Need care,
The people's
Woods
Need thinning and attention,
The people's
Crops
Need harvesting.

In China
We remember fondly—
The wine
We brewed ourselves,
And the melons and beans,
All home-grown.

Each day
And every day,
We want
To pack away
Those things woven on our own land—
The white muslin
Of our fatherland
And the blue cloth
Of our fatherland.

In China,
The broad land here
Is a magnificent picture.
On it
Our souls
Are clean.

We want to live
In China!
We want to live
Forever!

3

We are laborers
Great sons of our great fatherland.
We have
Rowed
Our fishing boats
On the impatient
Waters
Of the Yangtze and Yellow Rivers.

We have
Carried
Our hunting gear
On the Southern grassland
And on the sand and rocks of Ulanhot.

Robust
Young girls
Have worked
Diligently
At their spinning wheels
Near the leaping flames
Of a wildly burning
Fire in the Asian night.

We have
Pioneered
A rough
And tough life
With our muscles and backs.

4

Ah, fatherland, our fatherland,
Gunshots rang out . . .

The enemy
Is breaking through
The beachheads and strategic paths,
Through Tientsin
And Shanghai.

The enemy
Is spreading
Bombs and poison gas
Over the fields and rice paddies
And the water ponds.

The enemy came,
An ugly grin on his face,
Marching
Toward us.

With an ugly grin on his face,
He strafed
And strangled.

Today,
You must tell us
Are we to fight, or to surrender?
Ah, fatherland, our fatherland.

5

We must
Fight on.
Yesterday we were an enraged,
Shouting
And writhing
Nation of 450 million.

Struggle
Or die . . .

We must
Yank out the enemy's swords
That have been stabbed
In our veins.

Our breathing—
That of human beings—
Cannot be stopped.
Our formation—
That of flesh and blood—
Cannot be torn apart.

Our
Vengeful
Guns
Cannot be snapped.
For we know,
This ancient nation
Simply cannot
Live in humiliation,
Nor die in humiliation.

We must
Raise our arms high
To greet—freedom.

    . . . .

The sun is hidden now,
But look, ah,
The smoke and fire and war on this land
Have already become the second sun.

The outposts have been destroyed,
But look, ah,
Our comrades' banners
Have been planted on the broad road.

A glorious name,
—The people!
Ah, our people,
Still more stubborn,
Still more resilient.

6

. . . .

Where
Shall we go?
If in this world
There is no land,
No rivers or seas,
No will of man,
Just living
Like a worm
Is the same as death!

Ah, today
Let us
Die.
Will we die?
—No, never!

Together we are a giant,
To live means to fight.
Noble souls
Prefer death to surrender.
Reach out
Both your arms
To greet—freedom.

A glorious name
—The People!
Ah, our people!
Victory is directly ahead.

People, our people!
Get hold of
Our weapons
From our carpenter shops,
From the corners of the walls,
From the muddy ditches,
To strike at the murderers!

People, our people!
Raise up high
Our laborers' arms
That have been burned,
Weathered in storms,
And flailed by whips,
To struggle.

In the struggle
We triumph
Or die . . .

7

In the book of epics
The graveyard of a warrior
Is warmer
And brighter
Than a country of living slaves.

Wuchang, February 24, 1937
Selected Modern Chinese Poems, 148–60

FREEDOM IS WALKING TOWARD US

A sad
Nation, ah,
We must fight!
Beyond the window, in autumn,
In the field
Of Asia,
Freedom, ah . . .
Is walking toward us
From beyond the blood pools,
From beyond the dead bodies of our brothers—
A wild storm,
A swooping sea swallow.

Wen, *Complete Works, Hsin,* 570–71

SOME MORE

"One more grain of food
One more bullet to kill the enemy!"
Do you hear?
These are nice words.

Do you hear?
We must
Mobilize our own hearts
To go to the fields!

We must demand that the land
Yield wheat,

Demand that the land
Yield millet,

And we must use these things
As
Weapons for a long and bitter war.

(Some more!
Let's have some more!)

More food
More victory.

> Wen, *Complete Works, Hsin,* 572–73

HUA-LA-MA-CH'AO

1

A dark red horse
Lifts its hoofs from the undergrowth;
Ahead of all other horses
It takes off in flight from the grassland.

The dark red horse darts up the hill
The little mirror it wears glitters and dust flies.
Hua-la-ma-ch'ao straddles its back
To jump over the pools and marshes.

The prairie land of two thousand li
Rushes and flies after her
Is she riding horseback
Or driving a flying grassland?

The grassland, a stretch of brocade,
A scroll painted by nature,
Under her streaming hair
Rolls in ground swells.

2

Under the round, round sky
A shepherdess appears in the clouds.
If you want to ask her where she lives,
Her home is in the clouds and on horseback.

If you ask her how old she is,
She is seventeen this year.
If you ask her who she is,
She is a member of the commune.

Is she riding on horseback,
Or driving the grassland itself?
She carries the grassland on her saddle,
And the clouds on her shoulders.

The fastest bird is she
Flying this way from the far horizon.
Suddenly she descends
Landing beside the red flag.

3

I want to sing of Hua-la-ma-ch'ao,
She makes the grassland greener;
I want to praise Hua-la-ma-ch'ao,
She makes the sky brighter.

Her spirit and her face
Never, never can I forget,
Her scarf, kingfisher's color,
Flutters behind her head.

The ground swells of the grassland halt,
Now she is all tenderness and grace.
Anyone feeling her hand knows
Her hand is as light as silk.

Ah, glorious Mongol people,
She is brave as a lioness;
Ah, lovable Mongol people,
She is sweet as a pigeon.

4

Is she a mountain eagle? Oh, no!
The eagle's feathers are too weather-beaten.
Is she a swallow on the tree? Oh, no!
The swallow's wings are too short.

She is a skylark then?
No, the skylark is too delicate.
If anything is better than she
I have never seen it.

Hua-la-ma-ch'ao rides horseback,
The steel-like hoofs strike the grass.
Her green robe flutters in the wind
Sweeping the grass, sweeping the great earth.

A dark red steed
Darts through a herd of horses
Like a mighty wave
Rolling over a sea of grass.

Selected Short Poems, 110–14

MAN AND MOUNTAIN
To Those Building an Electric Power Irrigation Project

You see, is that a mountain?
It wears blue costumes
And the red scarves of women of the commune flutter
Like red sunset unrolled on the mountain top.
That's a mountain of men
Rising suddenly on the lake shore.
More magnificent than a mountain of rocks and trees
Are those two thousand heroes.

1953 (?)
Selected Short Poems, 140

I SING OF MY FATHERLAND

1

My fatherland, its blue sky
And its golden land
Have become independent and free,
Have emerged from clouds and haze.

This is an era of glory,
Mao Tse-tung has drawn up a blueprint.
Ah, fatherland, we cheer and rejoice
And proudly march on the broad road.

2

The new Constitution is shining
Upon our great nation.
On the giant pillars, red in color,
Are hung words powerful as steel.

The entire country cheers and cheers
Determined to walk one road, one road alone,
To build toward socialism
And heighten the value of labor.

3

Ah, fatherland, your mountains and rocks
Are also rumbling, rumbling aloud,
As in the hills and on the Hwai River
Now we have built reservoirs.

Who are shaking the mountains and rocks
On the immense land of our country?
Not wild winds, nor pelting rains,
But the footsteps of the working people.

4

On our mountains and near our lakes,
Resonant songs of construction are sung.
These songs are worth more than jewels,
And even for jewels we won't exchange them.

Ah, fatherland, on your immense land
There is the greatest wealth.
It is called courage and industry
And brings us undying honor.

5

Ah, fatherland, your people
Number over 600 million,
Who, for the future of their country,
Shall not fail their glorious duty.

We shall raise the flag of our nation
High, and still higher.
Look, over this great land of ours
Has risen a sun, red and bright.

June 17, 1954
Selected Poems of 1953.9–1955.12, 20–22

TSOU TI-FAN (1918?–   )

TSOU TI-FAN spent a childhood of considerable poverty in
Hupeh Province and went to college in Chungking during the
early part of World War II. His familiarity with manual labor
is reflected in his sinewy poetry and also in his ideological
development.

Upon entering Fu-tan University he took poetry as seriously
as Tsang K'o-chia, and painfully worked over his words again
and again. Then he met a girl whose vivacity was in sharp
contrast to his reticence, but in whose leftist leanings he
found a common ideal. Together they moved further and
further to the left.

Most of his works are long narrative poems with a number
of characters. *The Carpenter Shop* exemplifies his style very
well. The setting, a sweatshop that engulfs the lives of a team
of carpenters and their apprentices, must have been familiar
to Tsou for he describes it with authenticity and feeling.
Against the noise of hammer and saw, the smell of sawdust,
the odor of drunken workers on rare festive occasions Tsou
calls back a dead man to tell of his life and disappointment.
A later story of a man "Who Hanged Himself" is enough to
explain why Tsou took off the first chance he had, "Marching
Toward the North," without ever turning his head.

His language flows easily and forcefully. His rhythmic pat-
tern is not always easily discerned, but jarring notes are few.
Tsou is perhaps the most successful writer of narrative poetry
in modern China.

By 1949, Tsou had adopted satirical themes as his main
interest. Works like those in his *All-out Attack* are meant to
be read aloud, and their neat cadence, ringing alliteration,
and short repetitive lines, enforce the message each poem is
designed to bring to the hearer. Listen to this:

Brothers,
Comrades,
Tell them,
We shan't permit!
Tell them,

. . . .

(from *All-out Attack*, 24)

Many critics say that Tsou has gone overboard and lost
himself in politics, that his works now have entirely lost the
real quality and freshness his lines once had. Unfortunately
political attitudes have been allowed too much weight in the
aesthetic judgments of both critic and criticized.

THE RIVER

The muddy river swells in summer,
The torrents, dancing and prancing, spreading over
      ten thousand acres,
A battle horse carrying a full load of wind and sand,
Gallops down
From the prairie land of the Bayan Kara Mountain;
Having bitten off its rein.
Its red mane defies the restraint of the Three Gorges
As it darts toward a destination faraway.

Eagles scream above
And gibbons in the gulches and creeks scream in unison.
The boatman with two bright eyes
In a dark brown face,
A pair of dark brown arms,
And a blue turban,
Poles his raft.
He pushes his pole against the rocks,
His body bent double,
In combat with the river.
The spray of the waves fall off the rock,
An eagle lands on it;
And again the waves roll over the rock,
The eagle takes off in surprise.

A stormy rain descends.
More loudly roar the waterfalls on both banks,
The rain boosts the waves,
And the waves, with their sharp tongues
Lash against the rocks,
Leaving endless rings of eddies whirling by.
The river calls
And howls
And laughs without restraint.

The river rushes over the grassland of the south,
Whipped by willow trees along the way.
The whistles of river boats
Echo each other.
And the river on its laborious journey,
With its mane and tail flying,
Neighs and gallops on the high wind.

Ah, river—
I love your robust strength
That carries you thousands upon thousands of miles.
No dike can stop your surging billows
From irrigating the land and feeding the people along your
          course
For thousands of years without end.
Today the fortune of our fatherland is so pitiable.
The refugees fleeing disasters upriver
Are like the flood that rushes downhill.
Ah, river—
You will hear
And see
How those suffering people groan and grieve
All around you.
Ah, river—
I'm grateful for your revelation,
For I too shall offer to our fatherland a bit of service
And a bit of warmth.

I shall mount my battle horse
To gallop after your huge roaring waves without stop,
Leaving a storm of dust that trails my horse's hoofs.

June 1938
Northward March, 2–5

NORTHWARD MARCH

Through the woods where rich green drips,
Over the ink-wash distant hills,
On the dark brown road
Our heavy footsteps
March toward the north.

The northland is immense.
Those places only dimly sketched out,
We have neared, and reached,
But we long for
The black roofs studded with cactus shoots,
And the ancient city clothed in green lichen
Under white clouds
Still farther away.

Everyday
We trudge
On the hot and dust-clad road.
Sweat and dirt pile thick behind our ears.
Sticking to our backs
Are slimy shirts.
Gravel drills through our sandals.
Day after day
The bottoms of our feet become more calloused,
But we shall use our calloused feet
To walk every road of China, freely and happily,
Stepping again in the footprints of our ancestors.

At night
We find shelter
In a room with dank walls.

Sitting around a flickering candle,
We wash down stale stiff wheat biscuits with cold water.
We remove our muddy sandals
And lie down on straw mats.
To count our footprints on the road in memory.

The candlelight dances,
Our burning hearts also dance with the flame!
Ah, our fatherland,
To bring you light and make you free
Our burning hearts pursue the wind and sand in the distance,
Hastening our steps without fear of the long journey.

The feeble light of the candle
Splits the darkness.
With a red pencil
We sketch out our plans and our journey for tomorrow.
For tomorrow
We shall, still more resolutely, march toward the north of the
     northland.

                July 1938
                Northward March, 6–8

HE WHO HANGED HIMSELF

In the first shadow
I see an old man dangling at the end of a rope.

It was winter:
From the lonely villages,
Over the immense wilderness,
The north wind roared
Coming like a flash flood rushing down from the mountain,
Sweeping over the roofs, over the plain,
And rushing away, leaving a wave of tumult in the distance.
The sound of the wind receded, farther and farther away.
Chunks of snow fell from the tree
To pommel the straw-mat door.
The white dog lying by the door started barking.

In the snow-filled night the north wind marched
Wantonly snatching things from man.

A shower of sleet tapped on roof tiles,
And the wind drilling through the cracks in the wall
Cut and peeled away the little warmth in the room,
Like a sharp knife.
The old ones
With their warm flesh pared away by months and years
Kept only dry bones—
Those nuts and stones of men.

The old carpenter
Hard-pressed tonight
Had only a torn old quilt over him.
Cold whipped him
And he surrendered,
Trying to curl up like a ball.

The north wind, like a mountain flood,
Roared
And swept over the roofs and plains.
He dreamed of his hut as a small boat,
In a cold night like this
When ice and hail matted the sky,
The tattered sail of the boat was hopelessly tangled
And its oars unable to break the ice sealing the river.
Even if fires were lit by his fellow fishermen on shore,
Tonight would still be a hard night for the old man aboard.

And he thought:
If I could only lift my ax and saw tomorrow,
The chill would be chopped away just the same.
But he could not forget
How frozen he had been the night before.
His arms and legs ached
Unable to lift his ax
Or move lumber,
No matter how the boss scolded and ridiculed him.

But he had had his youth once,
And his strong body,
His arms, agile and muscular.
Once he was resolute, hard-working, and devoted to his duty
Which he knew well.
In his heart, in those days,
He always kept the medal that his boss had given him:
"What a strong arm!
   You don't need to worry about not getting rich in three
      years."

Forty years of work,
His finger marks sank deep into his ax, his saw, his plane
      and chisel.
The tree outside grew tall, and then grew old.
The money—the old coins with square holes, copper pieces,
      silver coins, and banknotes, that passed through
      his hands—
Also changed their looks a number of times.
Today
He could not get used to the ridicule and scolding.
Tonight
Cold again whipped him.
But tomorrow
Who would know if he could again open his eyes?

The cold was unbearable
He suffered, he shivered.
Tossing in bed
Made his old bones sore.
Suddenly he opened his eyes wide
As he recalled the cotton
His boss had stored upstairs in the back.
In the dark of the night
He gently pushed open the door to the storeroom upstairs.
A dark deed done in the dark,
Made his heart throb violently.
He grabbed a handful of cotton and tucked it under his
      quilt.

Strange feelings surged in his heart:
Some day I will grow still older,
Some day I shall lift my ax and saw no more,
Who then will look after a wretched old man?

A dejected sigh
Accompanied him into a fitful sleep.
The next day he lifted his ax,
And the next night under the long-legged turtle-shaped oil
      lamp
The boss clicked his abacus:
"Look for a greener pasture, man,
This is your pay.
Think carefully about what you did last night."
Suddenly he felt
Perhaps this was only a nightmare:
As if he were walking on a frozen river
Treading the ice step by step
Hoping to reach the other shore.
Then just as he arrived at the middle of the river
The ice cracked, piece by piece,
Dumping him in the cold water of December . . .

There was nothing to say,
And no light to be lit,
In the darkness he saw a ray of light,
And yet again in the darkness he saw things darker than
      before.
Dark night,
The north wind again paced the land
Snatching things from man.
He lay quietly on the hard board in his hut . . .

· · · ·

And then he felt
The white cotton was colder than snow,
And chillier than snow was the world of man.
Almost piously, he felt regret . . .

· · · ·

So immense was the snow-clad plain,
And so warm the fluffy fresh snow seemed.
Reflection from the snow lit up the silvery night,
Spreading over a limitless space, white-covered.
He smiled,
And the broad laughter of the wind approached from the
      far end of the snow plain . . .

          . . . .

Dawn broke
The rooster's crow woke me up.
Ai ya,
I must hurry to make tea and heat water
And pull open that heavy door of the shop.
I wiped the sleep from my eyes,
Hastily threw off my quilt,
And scampered out of my hard-board bed.
Something kicked in my chest.
"Ai yo," . . .
I yelled as I saw
That ashen face
With its tongue protruding
And its eyeballs turned upward,
On top of a body dangling from the rafter.

At once the workers all got up,
They moved fast, untying the rope from the neck of the
      hanged man,
And laid him down on the floor,
Someone immediately slapped him on the cheeks.[1]
Another undid his buttons
To feel his chest.
"He's gone," . . .
Tears fell from all the faces around.
On that very day
They sold his ax, saw, plane, and chisel,
And bought several straw mats
To wrap up his remains.

[1] Done, not with the thought of resuscitation, but to prevent the
ghost from haunting anyone at hand, in accordance with Chinese
folk belief.—Ed.

Two fellows carried him
To the paupers' graveyard.

No monks or nuns in Buddhist robes to say prayers for
          him,
No survivors wearing mourning to shed tears over the dead.
The wind churned the snow
With a heart-rending whistle resounding through the land.
The fellow workers of the carpenter shop bent their heads
Sadly following him, tossing a sheet or two of ghost money
          along the way.

Through a white-turbaned cypress grove,
And past a village where icicles hung under thatched roofs,
The procession went toward the graveyard.
A pick broke the snow cover on the ground,
To rest him in the black earth.
Snow flakes lashed their faces,
Snow flakes soaked their clothes,
With their heads bending low
They trudged along in heavy steps.
Their footprints branded the snow-paved plain,
Dragging iron-colored chains
From the carpenter shop . . .

Coming back from the burial
They said:
"Through his life he was hard-working and thrifty
Still he ended up this way.
It's frightening to think what's waiting for us all." . . .

After a little while
The boss scolded me again.
He said the rope of the hanged man
Should have been cut up before burning.
Now, the ghost of the hanged man
Would surely find his substitute[2] in the shop.

[2] In order to gain deliverance, a ghost with a grievance will return
to find his substitute. The substitute will then be haunted to death
and he in turn must find his own substitute.—Ed.

Nobody said a word,
Still I could not understand this riddle.
Why should he look for his substitute back here?
In silence I prayed to him:
"In your life you made no enemy among them.
After your death they buried you.
This was enough friendship.
They have done nothing dishonest, nothing at all.
Please, oh, please, don't look for your substitute here,
Because all of them are as poor and hard-pressed as you."

Buried deep under the snow
Was that dead body,
But in front of my eyes
Perpetually remained that shadow dangling under the rafter,
Its tongue protruding
Eyes turned upward
On an ashen face.

1940
The Carpenter Shop, 81–100

FIVE SHORT STANZAS

I. Chariot

Time will come when there will be no dark night,
The blue sky will be our shelter,
The sun, our wheel,
And a lofty ideal will pull our chariot.
We shall ride in our own chariot toward
The apex of time
And the edge of space.

II. The Morning Glory

Morning glories, blue and red:
You climb a tree,
With unshakable faith,
Advancing forward.

You are a brave bugler
Who ascends the highest peak
To sound reveille.

III. Spring

Let the trees clap their green palms,
Let blood-colored blossoms raise their glowing torches,
Let the wilderness swell in a sea of turquoise,
Let the cuckoos sing to herald the spring,
Let our battle hymns, ah,
Spread out together with the immense blue of the sky.

IV. A Bud

A youthful laughter,
A nurtured love,
A bottle of wine under its original seal,
An ideal yet to be attained,
A heart awaiting the kindling.

V. Dark Night

It's no crime to light a lamp at night:
Aren't swallows entitled to the blue sky of March,
And the bees, the blooming woods?

> Spring 1942
> *Selected Contemporary Chinese Poems*, 185–87

WANG YA-P'ING (1910?–   )

As a young high school student in the southern Hopei city Hsing-t'ai, Wang Ya-p'ing turned to poetry to tell about himself, his family in the country, and some of his painful experiences. The time was shortly before the 1927 political and military upheaval, and the setting was a countryside beset by crop failure and abuses of the local power hierarchy. The village that used to present a "pretty picture, with green fields smiling at the blue sky," to the poet in his childhood had become a scene of misery. It was another re-enactment of the proverbial "thirty million refugees" fleeing a barren land. And the poet's own family had to face a heartless landlord who resorted to pressures and tricks to take over their last small patch of land. The deepest gash in the poet's memory was the humiliation he felt at fifteen when he had to beg the landlord, with a gift the Wangs could ill afford, to forgive their misbehavior—"because we had protested against his dishonest treatment."

There was also the lure of fame, of course, as Wang admitted in 1953. In his high school there was a group of students interested in the then budding new literature. They studied Kuo Mo-jo and Lu Hsün, and used these writers as their models. The radical expressions in a mimeographed pamphlet put out by Wang and his friends got them in trouble with the local authorities. Three of them went to jail and Wang fled to the large cities, from K'ai-feng to Peking, and later to Tientsin. Ill-prepared to find his way in a new environment that was anything but hospitable, Wang wrote:

> "Trusted my footprints to the great earth
> And let difficulties tear away my life,
> Day after day."

In his drifting he found himself not quite alone. Many like him were equally restless in Peking and Shanghai, where young writers' groups were braving the political storms in order to remain active. The 1927 coup in Shanghai drove the leftists underground. In the north the worsening relationship with Japan led to the latter's occupation of Mukden in 1931. From Tientsin, Wang traveled to Tangku where he heard a child asking his father:

> "Isn't this railway station our place?
> Why are the Japanese sentries on duty here?
> The other day one of them kicked my playmate,
> And today one of them aimed his gun at me,
> That's really terrible, Daddy."
>
> (from "A Child Asks," 1933)

And as he strolled along the docks at Taku, he learned from an old fisherman the history of the Chinese cannons half-buried in sand there. The old man told him:

> "All Chinese troops fell back from the front line,
> As the Japanese soldiers broke through the Great Wall.
> Bombs fell as far as Lu-t'ai,
> You could see black smoke from here."
>
> (from "The Port of Taku," 1935)

Unable to continue publishing their poetry journals, Wang and several of his friends fled to Tsingtao. Wang pondered on what he had seen and decided that he must dedicate himself to his fellow men and his country.

Tsingtao provided him with some peace and quiet to study. He became well acquainted with the poets Wang T'ung-chao and Tsang K'o-chia. He read and re-read the masters of classical Chinese poetry, and studied Byron and Pushkin. He took time off to roam the countryside, collecting folk songs and listening to the country people talk. His work in this period resulted in three volumes: _The Winter in The City, The Song of Sea Swallows, The December Wind._ These poems describe the people's suffering from the war and their anger, the miserable lot of the woman worker in Shanghai textile mills, and "innumerable skeletons arrayed on the shore" of the Huang-p'u River, once a romantic setting for stories.

Shortly after war was declared in 1937, Wang went to the front to work with the troops. He wrote short rhymes in folk-song style for his unit of "war area service" workers, who entertained the troops to boost their morale, to use in songs and skits. Two years later he returned to the wartime capital, Chungking, and wrote poems full of the images he brought back from the field—the simple peasant-turned-soldier, the life in a crudely dug trench . . . all completely alien to the atmosphere in Chungking. His language became plainer, but, as he admitted, his imitation of peasant speech was not entirely successful. On the other hand, his short poems decrying a metropolitan life remote from the life-and-death struggle on the war fronts, achieved a high degree of lyrical quality.

Chungking was too sedate for Wang and he waited for an opportunity to go back to the North. In 1946, he returned to his native village where he joined the Communist units wresting the land from the Nationalists and resumed his work with the soldiers, publishing propaganda pamphlets and staging plays for the troops. He worked on the Yellow River with thousands of Communist militia and villagers to protect a strategic dike the Nationalist troops were trying to dynamite. He helped to establish Communist control in many villages, and began writing story poems in the folk-ballad style. His works continue to appear in mainland Chinese publications.

WINTER IN THE CITY

The moon has not yet risen
A chill wind brings in the shadow of evening.
Layers of dark smoke spill over the street,
The low houses, and the roofs of Western-style buildings.

Faded banners drape the store fronts,
The face of a policeman retires into his fur collar.
Blurred words on a bulletin board say
"Shake up city administration, restore prosperity."

Packed snow continues to await the thaw:
Cold, the streets lie desolate;
Dry leaves shiver on barren branches,
Murmuring: "It has come, the winter in the city."

> Tsingtao, December 1934
> *Winter in the City,* 21–22

THE LIGHTHOUSE KEEPER

White gulls fall asleep behind the curtain of the night,
Not a shadow of a sail floats on the Pacific.

Dark clouds rob the moon and stars of brilliance,
A towering lighthouse rises alone in the sky.

The frightening roar of the wind comes from afar,
Angry waves are thundering all around.

In the darkness when dawn is about to break,
I offer myself to the task of bringing about the light.

> January 5, 1935
> *Winter in the City,* 82–83

NEW YEAR

New Year brings with it no new look,
On everyone's face hangs a forced smile.
Red scrolls signify good fortune no more,
Neither do yellow ritual papers again summon luck.

Palace lanterns have disappeared, streets lie unswept,
Several firecrackers break through loneliness.
The sound fails to dismiss real poverty,
It only brings about heart-rending desolation.

No noise of New Year celebration is heard in the street,
No girl in new clothes is seen in front of the door.
One's heart aches at the depressing scene,
On an abandoned swing spiders have spread their webs.

Only the bulletin board of the village office is crowded
With many papers bearing big red seals,
There are also a few freshly written characters
"By order of the Provincial Government, Deadline for the
    first-quarter taxes must be met."

New Year brings with it no new look,
Sorrow weighs heavily on every heart.
For a fresh beginning of this life,
They set up a future hope out of the present despair.

                          Spring 1935
                          Winter in the City, 64–66

THE NIGHT OF TERROR

Cold wind blows from the ruins,
Pale starlight shines on the straw-thatched shack.
She carries in her arm a child, thin from hunger,
And listens, with one hand clenching the window sill:
Po, po, po . . .
Gunshots ring out again down the street.
No dog barks, roosters dare not crow.
Ts, ts, ts . . .
Trembling bullets pierce the air,
The guns fall silent
A spell of dog's barking
Accompanies a woman's weeping.
Suddenly, from outside the short wall
Leaps the shadow of a man.
She knows it is the father of her child,
Liu Ch'ing, driven crazy by his debts.
"You still haven't gone to bed yet? It's very cold."
"Sleep, how can I sleep? I'm afraid
    You will do that again, even though it's because we are poor
        and hungry."

"What else can we do? If we don't do this
  Nobody can borrow a grain of wheat from them!"
"If the people recognize you,
  They'll put you in jail, and kill you!"
"Kill me! Haven't they just stormed the government in the
          next town?
  There are too many poor people. Even if someone
          recognized me, he would not report to the police!"

                    . . . .

Black clouds steal the starlight from the sky,
Wind chimes rattle on the eaves;
He lies down in bed, pistol still in hand,
His frightened heart eagerly awaits the dawn in the east.

                              New Year's Eve, 1935
                              Winter in the City, 61–63

THE PORTRAIT OF A CHINESE SOLDIER

Before the Troops Start

He took a stack of paper money for the dead,
And wrote his name on each.
Facing the paddy fields and yellow rice crops,
Beautiful green water, and blue hills,
He lighted the paper money at a junction.
The west wind predicted his early triumphal return.
Their iron-like faces
Turned toward the vanishing smoke—
(That's the money for the dead.)
It went to slay the devils!
Nobody expected to return alive.
With tears in his eyes the regiment commander talked to
          the troops,
The spectators cheered, and sighed.
The willow trees waved good-by, a little sadly,
And the crickets played their songs of parting.

They left, without turning their heads once to look at their
        hometown,
A rolling wave of dust rose from the road.
A file of steel
Marched forward, braving the rising sun.

Torn Banknotes

The army paid them
The morning before they left.
In the autumn sky of September
White clouds sailed.
No time to drink a cup of plain wine,
Or to pack up a few needed articles,
They had to rush to the front, on the double.
Anger burned in their bosoms.
He held up his banknotes and shouted,
"This stuff is already useless!
We want to be real men to kill the enemy,
We must tear these to show our determination!"
"Tear them to pieces! He who does not is a 'Stateless Slave!'"
"Ya! The guy who is afraid of death and won't tear them is
        not a man!"
Everybody stared at the scraps of paper
Scattered on the yellow earth by the road.
"Why do we waste them?"
Chao Ch'eng shook his head.
"Damn it, are you still thinking of coming back alive?
You are a turtle's egg if you don't tear them."
"Stateless Slave! I'll let you have it if you don't tear them!"
Jeering and shouting surged,
And excitement whirled through everyone's heart.
Chao Ch'eng silently stared at his buddies,
Holding back his tears,
He struck a match,
The beautiful banknotes became ashes and smoke.
They called cadence and marched forward
The sun traveled across the cloud-adorned sky of September.

He Ended the Life of His Brother

The guns rattled
The bullets whistled,
The battle cries shook the earth.
In their hearts
Burned a hero's delight,
As they leaped from the protection of fortifications
To crawl forward.
The wind roared in from the immense wilderness,
Enemy planes thundered overhead:
The dance of blood,
The wail of death.
Guns churned the dust and smoke,
Cannon shells tore up every blade of grass.
Several birds, unknowing,
Proudly circled the sky.
The moment the comrades in front fell,
Those behind rushed forward,
Trying as they were to wrestle the land of the free
From the destiny of death.
After one of these assaults
He discovered his brother among a pile of bodies,
With his eyes half-closed
And blood gushing from his neck.
He picked up his brother's rifle,
Ready to carry him to the rear.
From behind came a spate of demanding gunshots
And the order to return and attack the enemy.
Save his brother? Or return to attack?
The dilemma
Twisted his heart.
He hugged his brother and cried
While bandaging his wound with a handkerchief.
"You cry! What's the use of crying!"
His brother opened his eyes a little wider.
He held his brother's hand for a moment,
Then stood up to walk away, silently.
"Brother, come . . . come back. . . ."

He returned and collapsed on his brother's chest
Agony robbed him of the last word.
"Brother! Use your gun, please
So that I don't have to. . . . You go back to the attack."
He listened to his brother's last heart-rending cry of pain,
In silence he clenched his teeth
The trigger clicked; he ended his brother's life,
And he held his rifle high to leap across the grassland.

Pawning an Arm

Fine rain sprinkled ceaselessly outside the window,
The blades of grass drooped.
He threw open his blanket
"What happened to my arm?" he shouted in anger.
And he struggled with pain to get up.
The nurse tried to hum a lullaby,
And even to tell him the fairy tale of the "White-robed
          Goddess."
His sad eyes
Held back wrathful tears.
With his left arm he pounded on the bamboo cot
Making it repeat his insistent demand.
The nurse brought to him his amputated arm
Soaked in chemical solution.
He seized it and laughed wildly,
"My sweetheart, so many devils have you killed,
Today I am going to pawn you!"
Deliriously he pushed away the nurse,
Jumped over the fence of the hospital,
And, like a jail breaker fleeing his pursuer,
Darted into a pawnshop.
"I want to pawn this arm, for five dollars!"
Tung! The arm was tossed on the counter.
The shopkeeper scurried away in fright
The chemical solution was splashed all over the window.
"Our shop only permits redemption, no more pawning,"
The proprietor explained nervously.
"Damn it, this arm is more precious than anything you name.
It's worth a thousand gold pieces
Or ten thousand suits of clothes.

Stupid dog, listen,
I haven't been paid for three whole damn months,
You and the whole lot like you just wine and dine,
And don't give a damn about the country and the war."
The proprietor lit a cigarette,
Trying to force a smile on his face.
He angrily grabbed the arm,
Darted back into the main street,
Still laughing deliriously
He threw the arm at the pedestrians.
Fine rain kept falling from the sky,
And the sky was so gloomy.

A *Disabled Shadow*

The back view of a disabled soldier,
Minus his right arm,
A sleeve dangling at the side,
Drew startled looks everywhere.
He went to the street from the hospital
And from the street he went to the countryside
And again returned to the city,
Bearing his bitter hatred in silence.
Liu Te-ch'eng: In the history of the war against Japan
There is his glorious name.
The Red-Cross sewn on his gray cotton-padded military
            jacket
Symbolized the grandeur of the man.
He walked forward, his chin up,
And laughed, in reminiscence of that struggle in blood and
      fire.
Yes, three months' toying with life and death,
Although one of his four limbs was gone
His robust life was spared.
Often on his face there protruded blue veins,
Anger locked his eyebrows
As he gazed at the rushing waves of the Ch'ien-t'ang River
That rolled and surged in a tide of blood.
The lush red fields on both banks
Were trampled under the enemy's iron hoofs.

Red clouds embraced the setting sun,
That retired slowly behind the blue hills.
He hated bitterly—when would victory be finally won!
The night wind blew on his wound
A sharp attack of pain, a shiver,
The feeling of loss prickled his heart.
No! If the country is gone, where is home?
Listen, the intense gunfire in the distance.
Battle cries in the dream . . .
Bayonets thrust at the dwarf enemies.
And when he woke up, the cool light of a sinking moon
Was kissing his thin blankets.
"Why didn't you let me die in the front line?"
Often he angrily shouted
And from his left and right heavily wounded comrades
Groaned sadly and in low voice, time and time again.
A morning breeze brought along the next dawn.
Guns and cannons howled on earth.
Our troops tough as steel
Marched toward a holy war.
From the supreme commander to the small shopkeeper
Banded together in an iron Great Wall
From the Ch'ang-pai Mountain to the mouth of the Pearl
        River.
The War of Resistance, a stupendous tidal wave of blood.
Four hundred and fifty million new sons and daughters
Struggled up from a blood bath, and shouted.
A new history of China
Must be revised according to a design sketched in blood.
Armless, legless,
So many shadows of the disabled,
Were the heroes who did the sketching.
Today a batch of them were carried back from the front,
Tomorrow perhaps there will be more.
On our immense territory
Thousands of shadows of the disabled moved about,
Into the bloody fire of a people's struggle
They cast a heroic sacrifice
To buy the dawn of freedom and liberation.

              1937–38
              The Portrait of a Chinese Soldier, 4–37

MAO TSE-TUNG (1893–   )

MAO TSE-TUNG's poems are prosaic, some say. This opinion seems to be justified when they are read in translation. What must be remembered is that he wrote in the classical style: the *shih* and the *tz'u*, and has demonstrated a mastery and control of these forms as well as of lively and forceful imagery.

Like most of the classical Chinese poets, Mao indulges in allusions and metaphorical expressions referring to a distant past. But few of his allusions really require annotation.

Reading his poems, one becomes unmistakably aware of Mao's admiration of such masters of poetry as Lu Yu and Yüeh Fei of the Sung Dynasty, both of whom were writer-statesmen and patriotic poets. One also notes Mao's familiarity with the entire range of heroes in Chinese history, including the controversial character Ts'ao, Ts'ao, who virtually usurped the throne in the Han Dynasty.

The man from a farmer's family in Hunan Province who rose to become the leader of Communist China is largely self-educated. Mao did his study mainly while a junior staff member of the Peking University library in the 1910s. During that period he read extensively both Chinese classics and Western works in translation.

Very authoritative in his tone when he writes on Marxist-Leninism, he is noticeably modest about his poetry. In the 1940s he allowed a small collection of his poems to appear. When the *Poetry Journal* was inaugurated by Tsang K'o-chia in 1957, Mao complied with a request to let some of his poems be reprinted in its first issue. He selected nineteen and sent them to Tsang with a note: "I have never wished to publish these pieces formally because they are in the old style which may, by setting a bad example, do harm to the youth. Furthermore they are not very poetic, nor are they unusual. . . . As to poetry, the new style must be the main stream.

One may write some poetry of the old style, but must not promote old poetry among the youth because the latter style restricts thought and is difficult to learn. . . ." (*Nineteen Poems*, 1–2)

Quite apart from his political stature and in spite of his own words about them, Mao's poems are worthy derivations from classical Chinese poetry, blending a pride in man's achievement with an admiration for nature's grandeur.

AT THE LOU-SHAN PASS

Sharp west wind,
In the immense sky a swan calls to the frosty morning moon.
     Frosty morning moon,
The hoofs of my steed fall at random,
And the bugle sounds choked.

Say not the dangerous defile and the long trail are hard to
       pass.
Now we have scaled the peak,
     Scaled the peak,
An ocean of blue hills
Bathed in the blood of sunset.

               Near the Szechwan-Kweichow border, January 1935
               Nineteen Poems, 11

SIXTEEN-SYLLABLE STANZA

What hills!
I sped my steed over them without dismounting.
Looking back with a start
I saw them only three feet three from the sky.[1]

[1] Author's note: A folk song says:
     The K'u-lou Mountain above
     The Pa-pao Mountain below,
     Only three feet three from the sky.
     Man passing over them must duck his head,
     And the horse must shed its saddle.

What hills!
Rising like angry waves in rivers and seas.
They rush by
As my horse immerses itself in the depth of battle.

> During the Long March, 1935
> *Nineteen Poems*, 12–13

ON THE LIU-P'AN MOUNTAIN

Light clouds on clear sky,
My eyes follow the southbound swan to the horizon.
He who fails to reach the Great Wall is not a man,
We have, as I count on my fingers, traveled 20,000 li.

The towering peaks on the Liu-p'an,
The banner unfurling in the western wind,
Today the long cord is in hand[2]
When shall I tie up the Yellow Dragon?

> During the Long March, September 1935
> *Nineteen Poems*, 15

THE SNOW

The land of the north
For thousands of miles sealed in ice
For ten thousand miles buried in snow.
Looking at the Great Wall and beyond
I see only an undifferentiated white,
And up and down the Yellow River
No longer is there any surging wave.
The mountains dance in silver snakes
The knolls dot the plain with waxen elephants
Trying to measure up to the height of the sky.
On sunny days
One sees the rouge of the sun against a gleaming purity—
Such extraordinary charm.

[2] "Long cord" refers to the petition received by an Emperor of the Han Dynasty from General Chung Chün for a long cord with which the general pledged to tie the chieftain of the invading "barbarians."—Ed.

So beautiful is the land,
That countless heroes bow their heads in tribute.
Pity that the first emperors of the Ch'in and Han Dynasties
Were lacking in literary achievement,
And the founding fathers of the T'ang and Sung eras
Fell short in artistic grace.
The man of an epoch, blessed by heaven,
Genghis Khan
Only knew how to shoot giant buzzards with arrows.
They are all gone now.
If we are to count the men of destiny
We have to depend upon today.

Nineteen Poems, 18–20

THE YELLOW CRANE PAVILION[3]

The nine rushing rivers flow through the heartland of China,
A heavy line links the north with the south.
In misty rain
The Snake and Tortoise hills guard the river.

Whither the Yellow Crane?
Only the site remains to greet visitors.
As I drink to the departed heroes
The tides in my heart surge high as the waves below.

Nineteen Poems, 6

[3] A historic structure on the river bank outside the city of Wu-chang near Hankow. The first line refers to the nine tributaries of the Yangtze River covering the general area of Hunan and Hupeh; the "heavy line" in the second line refers to the railroad crossing the Yangtze at Hankow; the hills mentioned in the fourth line stand facing each other across the Yangtze at Wuchang.—Ed.

ON THE PEI-TAI RIVER

Heavy rain on the northland
White surf surges toward the sky,
Fishing boats adrift beyond the Ch'in-huang Isle.
Only water in sight,
How does one tell directions?

The past has been gone for over a thousand years,
When the Emperor Wu of the Wei Dynasty ordered his army
        northward
To pass by the Chieh-shih Hill, as history tells us.
Again the rustling autumn wind now, but
What a changed world!

Nineteen Poems, 23

AFTER SWIMMING ACROSS THE
YANGTZE RIVER

Having just drunk the water of Changsha
Now I eat the fish of Wuchang.
Crossing the ten-thousand-li-long Yangtze River
A gaze at the unlimited sky of the southland.
Let the winds and waves batter me,
Still it is better than strolling in a quiet garden,
Now that I have found freedom in space.
Did not Confucius say when on a river:
"Such is that which passes and is gone!"

The sails stir
But the Snake and Tortoise hills remain still.
Here a grand scheme takes shape.
A bridge flying across
Turning into a broad road Heaven's Moat that used to
        separate the north from the south.

Building a stone wall to the west
Will cut off the rain fallen on the Wu Mountain,
To create a towering dam above a mirror-like lake,
The goddess of the Wu Mountain should be unchanged,
But only startled by the changed world.

May 1956
Nineteen Poems, 24–25

FENG HSÜEH-FENG (1906?–)

In 1922 a small collection of new poetry appeared under the title, *The Lakeside*. The authors were four young men who identified themselves with a beautiful spot on the side of the West Lake in Hangchow, Chekiang Province. All of the poems were short lyrics. One writer stressed youthful sentimentality; most of his words seemed to be drenched in tears. Another was bold, for that time, in his praise and worship of love. A third wrote very plainly, sometimes a bit too plainly. The fourth was Feng Hsüeh-feng whose verses were clear, concise, and refreshing.

The quartet did not last long as a group. Their collaboration produced only one other anthology, *The Songs of Spring*, published in 1923, before the four young writers drifted apart. Feng Hsüeh-feng was drawn to literary criticism and literary theories. He admired Lu Hsün and became his protégé; their association began in 1928 and lasted until Lu's death in 1936. Feng wrote essays in imitation of Lu Hsün's style with considerable success. Chinese readers today recognize him as a forceful voice in the literary polemics of the 1930s. Few still remember him as a "Lakeside" poet.

In support of Lu Hsün, Feng Hsüeh-feng expounded on the Marxist-materialist view of literature. He boasted of his prison experience, one quite a number of the leftist writers shared in those days—if they escaped death. *The Song of Ling Shan* grew out of his imprisonment.

His voice gained authority after he published a number of volumes of essays and remained active in the leftist literary movement. Then in 1957 when the "Hundred Flowers" incident occurred, he was among the disgraced, together with Hu Feng and Ai Ch'ing, accused of rightist leanings.

The incident started when the Communist Party chiefs declared that all schools of thought should be encouraged to contend with each other in order that a "hundred flowers could bloom" in competition. Shortly afterwards the party and the government reversed its policy in the face of the flood of adverse criticism thus released. Feng Hsüeh-feng was not among those criticizing the government, but his failure to refute the critics in defense of the Party line was interpreted as a rightist attitude. He wrote several "confessions" and "explanations," and silence followed. At the least, he partially lost his freedom. Toward the end of 1961 he was cleared.

THE CH'ING-MING FESTIVAL[1]

Ch'ing-ming
I strolled up and down the street in silence;
Under the willow branches pinned on the doorway,
There I seemed to see the shadow of my little sister with
    a cluster of bean flowers in her hair.

Hangchow, 1922
Compendium, 158

THE SONGS OF SPRING (II)

The sun in the east, the rain west,
The cuckoo calls desperately:
Gazing from faraway toward your home over there beneath a
    mountain in morning fog,
You pick a willow branch, gleaning a handful of the willow's
    tears.

1923 (?)
Compendium, 158

[1] Ch'ing-ming, a day to visit the graves of deceased relatives, roughly coincides with Easter.—Ed.

THE SONG OF LING SHAN[2]

We could see Ling Shan,
It is a strange mountain,
With sheer, craggy peaks in a towering array,
Its top is like the bony spine of a huge monster.
Below, a ring of supporting knolls form an iron castle.
Fields run along the side of a river before the mountain,
And behind stretches a sky of mysterious blue
          That no one can ever decipher.
People here said to me, "Ling Shan is a blessed place,
A great battlefield!
Many a great leader has gathered huge armies here,
Unfurling their banner of justice written in blood.
Ling Shan forever remains a landmark of victory."
And they said, "Sustained warfare, sustained victory, and
          sustained resistance!
Ling Shan, as a result holds the essence of the great earth."
Ling Shan, all year long radiates a grace that fills
          man's heart and lungs,
And we breathe the essence of that grace, day and night.

We could see Ling Shan,
A mountain never to be conquered.
It looks so magnificent.
With sheer, craggy peaks in a towering array,
It sometimes hides behind a dream-like haze,
And itself appears awe-inspiring and august.

[2] From the author's note: Ling Mountain is located in Kiangsi near Shang-yao. It is a beautiful, towering mountain ridge of over ninety li. After 1928, the Worker-Peasant Democratic Revolutionary Army under Fang Chih-min occupied this mountain and used it as its base of operations. Fang and the last of his men, were arrested and killed on this mountain in 1935. Legend grew about the place. . . . During the war, a concentration camp of the Third War Zone was located to the south of the mountain. [The author wrote this poem while imprisoned there in 1941–42.] We could raise our heads and gaze at it day and night. Among my fellow prisoners there were some who had fought as peasant-soldiers under Fang Chih-min about ten years before.

People pointed out to me also, "It was right here, at this
      Ling Shan,
The great fighters once again rallied huge armies,
Firmly gripping their banner of justice written in blood,
To overrun the entire southeast . . .
Right on this mountain, the last battle was fought, the last
      retreat made, and the last resistance staged!"
They said, "This mountain, a place of misfortune,
It was right here that they shed their last drop of blood.
This mountain tragically became such a grand shrine,
      A sacred place for all those following in their
      steps. . . ."
Ling Shan, the beautiful stance of the great unconquered!
Its aura reaches beyond several thousand miles.
We could see Ling Shan,
Ah, such a strange mountain!
From this mountain we learned the inevitability of history's
      tragedies.
From it we understood why we rush toward those tragedies
      without fear or retreat.
From it we understood that we were born for the realization
      of the world's ideals.
We understood where the beauty of all mountains and rivers
      came from,
And why there is a mysterious air of grace that appears
      from time to time here.
From this mountain I discovered the real soul of our
      generation.
It will move on, perpetually, by the great and unconquerable
      force of man himself,
It will seek the strange beauty of this force, as if it were
      thirsting for blood.

We could see Ling Shan,
Such a beautiful mountain.
In the morning it looks as tender and graceful as the morning
      cloud it wears,
In the evening it is twice as blue and imposing because of
      the setting sun on its back.

On a clear day, it seems to hide nothing under the bright
        sunshine,
But as dusk sets in, you look at it under the dim starlight,
      There seem to be thousands of troops and their mounts
        darting to and fro.
This is an unconquerable mountain!
It's the stance of this generation,
A sacred land, and a heart-rending sorrow,
But also a bugle call, and a milestone.

                  The Song of Ling Shan, 2–7

THE DESERTED VILLAGE

Why do her eyes suddenly light up, that little girl?
Is it not that in the flying yellow dust,
In the middle of a colorless countryside
Outside a deserted little village,
A cluster of pomegranate blossoms, bloody red pomegranate
        blossoms,
Appearing like a single touch of color,
      Suddenly is reflected in her eyes?

Isn't it?
Isn't this a violent odor,
A joy thirstily sought?

Ah, she, such a little life,
Has already had her fill of immense hardship.
Isn't it true that fatigue has already rendered her slow,
And the smell of blood has reduced her to simple-mindedness,
And yet her young but courageous heart, still drives her
Toward an unlimited devotion?

Isn't it so?
Ah, isn't this a beautiful
      And noble
Color?

                The Song of Ling Shan, 59–61

FIRE

Fire! Ah, if it is fire!
You cast yourself into the dark night,
You burn in the dark night.

There is a fire in my heart,
I want to fling myself into the dark night,
And let it burn there,
Let its flame rise higher, still higher.

The roaring fire,
The glowing fire,
The dark night swallows it,
And the dark night burns it!

The Song of Ling Shan, 19–20

HU FENG (1905?–   )

IN THE EARLY 1950S every reader in China knew Hu Feng as an authoritative literary critic personally trained by Lu Hsün, but few remembered his true name, Chang Kuang-jen. At the height of his career, Hu Feng's words contributed a great deal to the new literary trends. Through his volumes of literary criticism runs a persistent thread: literature is more than a superficial reflection of its social milieu; literature must be a penetrating revelation of the heart and soul of living people at a given time. Hu Feng does not believe that a poet can write good poetry if he only has sympathy with what he sees. A good poet must, says Hu Feng, merge himself with the people and their lives which he attempts to portray.

When the May Fourth Movement started in 1919 in Peking, Hu Feng was still a young boy in his native town of I-tu in Hupeh Province. Two years later he enrolled in a high school in Wuchang across the Yangtze River from Hankow. There he began to read the works of the "Lakeside Poets" Feng Hsüeh-feng and P'an Mohua which assert the importance of the individual human being's feelings. He also liked Wang T'ung-chao's *One Leaf*, which records the size of these young men after they had experienced disillusionment in real life. Ping Hsin's *Spring Waters* exerted a decisive influence on his style in those days. But Ping Hsin's verse was inspired by a feeling of gratitude to life, while Hu Feng was bombarded by the cries of anguish and discontent around him. The pamphlets circulated by the "Mutual Help Society" in Wuchang, and the radical essays published in the local *Wuhan Review*, further aroused his sympathy with the rebels, student demonstrators, and union organizers. He published his first story, admittedly juvenile, eulogizing them, and left Wuchang for Nanking where he felt the thunderous repercussions of the May 30, 1925, incident in nearby Shanghai. Soon afterward he went to Peking.

With his interest now clearly identified with literature, Hu
Feng in the late 1920s found himself torn between love and
art on the one hand, and the realities of life on the other. He
caught glimpses of the former ideal in Tolstoy's *Resurrection,*
and he was reminded of the latter by Lu Hsün with whom
he had developed a close association in Peking. He wavered
between the two, and gradually gravitated toward realism.
Thus we read in his *Wild Flowers and Arrows* (1937) de-
scriptions of his feeling of guilt about carrying on his shoulders
"a ghost of the past," while he longed for the light of the
future. We read his "Cold Night," that tells of his despair
and readiness to shrink back to a familiar corner of his mem-
ory, and his "To the Dead," which captures an outburst issued
from his other self—the one that evolved into the Hu Feng
of the 1940s.

The section he appended to *Wild Flowers and Arrows* is
clearly indicative of his later development. It includes several
poems he translated from English and Japanese, notably
poems by Langston Hughes, Frances E. Harper, and Claude
McKay on the life of the Negro in the American South.

Encouraged by Lu Hsün, he turned to literary criticism and
social essays which earned him the enviable position of a
favorite disciple of Lu. Indeed, after Lu's death in 1936, Hu
seemed ready to inherit Lu's prestige and leadership in the
literary circles. By 1947 he had published at least seven col-
lections of literary criticism and miscellaneous essays, in ad-
dition to his poetic works, and translations. In 1949 upon
the establishment of the new regime, he wrote his long
poem, *The Song of Joy,* heralding the "beginning of a new
era." He was near the peak of his career when suddenly to-
ward the end of 1954 the waves of "struggles against rightist
reactionaries" caught up with him. For one half year he was
assailed mercilessly in publications throughout the country.
He was accused of hiding behind Lu Hsün's glory in order to
sabotage the revolution; accused of withdrawing from the
Communist Youth Corps in 1925, after supposedly joining it
sometime around 1919, because he was afraid of losing his
life; accused of being instrumental in keeping the literary
leaders at loggerheads during the 1930s in Shanghai when the

Communists were trying to rally them under the red banner.

Hu Feng responded to the charges by publishing a series of self-criticisms, and has not been heard from since.

THE JOURNEY

I hold on to a faded dream,
Sauntering on a deserted road.
The chill sad call of the swan sweeps through the sky,
An immense cold bleakness all around—
I know it's evening.

I carry on my back a faded dream,
Strolling along in cold blurred twilight.
A belt of pine trees lies ahead,
Huge dark shadows lie ahead—
I sit down, all my courage gone.

I lean on a faded dream,
Among the clusters of withered weeds.
Gazing at the misty moon,
Hearing faintly the night watchman's gong—
I contemplate the blessed multitude of lives.

I prop myself on a faded dream,
And sleep fitfully.
When I wake up
The moon is already down,
Darkness reigns all around—
Ah, embrace me tightly
My good friend the dark night.

Late autumn 1926
Wild Flowers and Arrows, 20–22

TO THE DEAD[1]

You are dead,
Like fire, you lived:
And like fire, you died.

You are dead,
Your blood dyed their claws and fangs red;
Your blood also dyed red our hearts.

You are dead, and our hearts throb
For the cold, cold night kept by a lover,
And the fading twilight facing a mother.

You are dead, and our hearts are in anger
At the flesh and bones strewn around
And the blood soaking the yellow dust.

Our hearts throb:
Come on, come on,
Our brothers!

Our hearts are in anger,
Come out, come out,
Our enemies!

1926
Wild Flowers and Arrows, 14–16

FRUSTRATION

The center of the sky seems to be burning
The whole heaven is on the verge of tears.
Am I to be buried in the depth of bitter anger?
This boiling dead quiet,
This silent cry!

1 Author's note: When I arrived in Peking on March 20, 1926, it was already the third day after the massacre. I looked at the blood-stained clothes of the dead; I could not bear my sorrow and anger. . . .

The myriads of lives,
Moving,
Chattering,
While fiery clouds threaten immediate storm and
Cast immense black shadows.

The blurred, the unknown . . .
All in smoke, all in haze . . .
Even should my skin be slivered,
And my blood flow in all directions,
How can the burning heat in my heart be cooled?
Fly away! Fly away!
But even the gusty winds above the clouds
Cannot cool my burning cheeks,
Where shall I go?

Shall I use a hand of flesh and blood
To put out the flame in my heart,
Or remain in the orbit with all lives,
Trading pursuit for destruction?

June 1927
Wild Flowers and Arrows, 30–32

COLD NIGHT

No need to compare my feeling with an abandoned well,
Even less need to describe my life as a cool moon,
Vibrating in this cold night,
The rumbling roar of the town
Is enough to make me
Think of the declining years with a shiver.

Cannot I madly kiss the wounds of the past,
And shed some tears as Christ did.
When violence descends on me
—I shrink timidly and cannot raise my arms.
Only a pair of surviving legs
Drag on and on, aimlessly,
Step by step . . .

In the sky there may be a warm sun,
Or sobbing chilly winds,
Though the universe is immense
When did it ever give me
A smile of dawn,
And a sigh of dusk?

I wish to pour a cup of strong wine, crimson red,
Into my bosom split wide open.
I am hurt
I am dead drunk,
And in my confusion
I have found dear friends
And bitter enemies.

Or perhaps wearing tattered clothes,
To beg for food from door to door by day,
And at night, to curl up and sleep near Mother's neglected
    grave.
If ever I recall the stories heard in Mother's arms,
I shall hug the withered weeds under the cool moon, and cry.

> January 1928
> *Collected Works of Hu Feng*, 8–9

THE SONG OF THE SETTING SUN

The setting sun is almost below the horizon
Evening haze is about to rise;
Brother, let us go,
This is the most beautiful hour of the day.

A blossom of cloud, wine flushed in the distant sky,
Looks down with affection on the top of the woods.
In that silent, mirror-like pond beyond perhaps
There are rippling reflections, sweet as dreams.

Go through that gloomy forest,
Pass beyond this desolate, abandoned road;
Brother, let us go,
This is the most beautiful hour of the day.

On this side of the woods, only the rustling of the leaves,
Beyond the woods, the setting sun still lingers in the sky.
Over here, shadows grow, like black hair creeping out,
There, the afterglow still burns the blushing mountain tops.

The chain of mountains marches, link after link,
Leading your gaze on into infinite space;
The flame of the setting sun glows angrily red
Warming a trifle the dream of youth.

Youth that has gone is like petals withered and fallen.
They cannot be gathered, much less threaded into a garland.
Let us, then, warm up a bit the dream of last night,
While the setting sun remains a fiery red.

The afterglow lights the tops of the trees.
Listen to my song and hold my hand,
My brother, now let us go,
This is the most beautiful hour of the day.

> End of summer 1929
> *Wild Flowers and Arrows,* 74–77

from THE SONG OF JOY

Chapter I. *The Time Has Begun*

. . . .

Motherland
Our great motherland
In your bosom that has borne so much suffering
The little humiliation I have shared,
    And little sorrow
Are forever unforgettable.
But the day has finally arrived.

Today
For your new birth
I offer tears of joy:
For your motherly love
I offer tears of gratitude.

Motherland
My motherland
Today
At this sacred hour of your new birth
The entire world salutes you
The entire universe congratulates you.

A thunder roars,
Rumbling, rolling over your head.
The rain comes
Rustling, dancing on your head.
Motherland, Ah,
For you
The whole universe is singing joyfully
A symphony of nature,
Majestic yet tender
Drifting over the sea of life.
I feel your immense heart
        Stir and throb in excitement.

My eyes
Glance to the right
I see the profile of an old man
His hair like a bundle of autumn weeds,
His beard sticking out like iron wires.
In excitement he holds his mouth open
        Forgetting to move.

I feel
Hot perspiration start from his forehead,
I feel
In his eyes which I cannot see from here
        A fire is glowing.

My comrades at arms,
My brothers,
I have seen you
Dying in a dank and stench-filled prison,
Starving and freezing in a deserted village.
You—you and the peasants—have fed lice with your flesh,
Have drunk bloody water on the battlefield with your friends,
You have endured repeated hammerings, repeated trials.
You have conquered pain and death.
During these
Many, many years,
Your hope stayed alive
And your will stayed alive.

And today,
At this very moment that stirs you,
Forget all the past,
Except that the past
Has purified you, like a newborn child
Lying in a warm cradle
His untainted heart overflowing with the blessing of new life.

    . . . .

> Peking, November 11, 1949
> *The Song of Joy,* 13–18

FANG CHING (1913?–   )

Fang Ching, who grew up in a small town in West China, cultivated his writing quietly by himself and began publishing slim volumes in the early 1940s. The unpretentious elegance of his lines and a profound but undramatic sympathy with his fellow men make his works stand out among his generation. In 1948, he published his *The Songs of a Stroller* and *The Victory of Life*, a collection of essays which gives impressions of the people and scenes he encountered during his travels in Southwest China in the early 1940s.

NIGHT

When I wake up, suddenly, at midnight,
The fitful sad call of a cricket
Gently seeps through the earth,
A lonely feeling of immense space rises, hovering above.
And my searching heart
As immense as the night finds no limit.

Night, ah, your tangy flavor,
Lasts so long!
But the life of man, so short.
I gaze with sleepless eyes
At your passing immobility.

The impatient pelting rain drums a question
Asking you about an eternal mystery.
My faraway thoughts follow the raindrops, sinking into the
        earth,
Becoming seeds of silence.
The flickering fireflies,
My youthful joys!

Wild vines and brushes entomb a barren land,
Buried deep are youth and beauty.
Perpetual silence offers something,
Even bleached bones contain phosphorous that shines,
Hurry, then, to build life
With our blood-stained hands.

The long, long, weed-entangled night,
The night with chirping crickets, my night,
The night pierced by a prophet's eyesight, ah!

June 18, 1942 (?)
The Songs of a Stroller, 40–42

OVERNIGHT STOP

I slap the only bags I carry,
Some yellow dust of the road falls off, but new dust clings
    to them again.
Dust piles deep on the road, winds follow the trucks,
What an endless journey is the life of man
A road leading toward the infinite!
After a long stopover, I come to a roadside stop—
At which inns, their names unremembered,
Have I left behind my footprints?
The life I have walked through,
Has it left any trace at all?
Tonight I stay in this little village,
The lamps' soft light and the host's kind smile
Warmly comfort the heart of a traveler.
A night's sleep prepares me
For a new journey at dawn.

November 24, 1942
The Songs of a Stroller, 27–28

A SONG

Every day we discover, every day we create,
Every day we let our ideal
Lead us to adventure.
Let every day be
A patch of glittering sunshine.
We are all suffering children,
Our song,
On the wings of flying eagles,
On the tops of towering rocks,
Over the majestic and magnificent oceans,
And above the lustrous and lofty sun,
Pirouettes, rises, and soars away.
It firmly clings to, yet lightly flutters
On the flag that describes our will.

December 13, 1942 (?)
The Songs of a Stroller, 49–50

THE SONG OF A VAGABOND SON
To His Mother

Why this long silence?
Are you waiting for a clear answer?
Yes, I have already asked so many questions,
And there are still so many voices ready to burst forth from
my heart.

All the storms, travels, cold and heat, hunger and thirst,
My body must bear and my heart accept.
But in a land cold below zero,
I long for your warm, tropical eyes.

Snow covers the wide earth,
My emotions surge, limitless.
I am sad over the lost purity of my childhood heart,
And the vanished joy and fragrance of the dawning of life.

The warm fire in my mother's room,
And near the fire, the moving tales of winter days,
Could not detain my widespread wings,
Neither could her quivering, tearful words of blessing.

I have no lyrical tears
As I chew on the stony fruits of reality.
Relying upon my vision of truth and beauty
I drift along season after season.

I am not yet tired of searching
Though my youthful heart trembles so—
A living heart of China
Has ceased to care, ceased to feel.

The muzzle of a gun, the mouth of a man, and the voice of a
          heart
All are our prophets,
Declaring a solemn, sacred, message,
A revelation that flashes through the unconscious.

Snow covers the great earth.
Mother, you alone keep that little room,
Your hand halts with a needle and thread,
And in the corners of your eyes are tears of expectation.

You have grown old, so much older than before.
You murmur your feelings only to yourself.
Wearing out your heart never to be requited
Are time, travail, and the hardship of life.

I have asked none of many friends and relatives
To bring a greeting to you;
Neither have I in many years
Attended to Father's crumbling grave.

But we cannot soon return,
The end of our journey is nowhere in sight—
Only the *wu-t'ung* tree in the yard, like a loyal old servant,
Keeps watch over the house, never to leave.

Snow cannot cover my memory
My heart yearns to greet you, earnestly;
My warm finger thaws
The frozen paste to seal this message.

Let it bring, in this way,
My heart from a vagabond's road;
Let it light a fire in that chilly room
To warm and comfort your heart.

Snow covers our great earth
To prepare for the rich flowers and lush grass next spring.
This child-heart of mine longing for Mother
Is blessed as it forever kisses the smile in your eyes.

> Winter 1944
> *The Songs of a Stroller*, 55–61

A DIRGE

Ai, ai, why is our step so heavy,
What makes it drag?
Is it that old, long chain,
Or the slanted fetter and lock,
Or the road?
But the road leads us afar.
Slowly trudging on the road
Are the scattered shadows, all tired of walking,
All bending double, crawling along.
Why do they all bend their heads low?
Look, the innocent souls,
Of those starved to death, frozen to death,
Or killed by the enemy,
Or simply wasted away by their hard life—
All who should be living today.
Our hearts carry the burden of life,
And the overweight burden of death.
This is a solemn hour,
Dark shadows float on the road—
What is that black thing on our shoulders?

Ai, it's a coffin we are carrying,
Containing a heavy corpse—
The humiliation and error of a people.
In this most solemn funeral procession,
The most devoted pallbearers
Sing in subdued voices the last dirge:
Bury it, bury it deep
Bury a destiny full of sighs
In the grave dug from a ravaged land,
Then say your good-by resolutely to yesterday.
Let new love belong to our hearts,
A new road to our footsteps,
And a new world to our shoulders.

> January 10, 1945 (?)
> *The Songs of a Stroller*, 62–64

THE ROAD OF ALL LIVES

Who created illusions for you,
Brave young man?
You are an injured wild animal.
Licking your wounds at the edge of a forest,
Your eyes still search the wide horizon.

Bear our lives,
Let our dear ones drift apart. Still there are
Hunger, death, and despair to keep us company.
We keep our eyes wide open every day,
Why can we never see a ray of the sun?

Old man, who let the layers of anguish,
More than the accumulated years,
Bend double your waist?
The burden of the disaster this time
Overweighs the hardship of your entire life.

Child, in your mother's bosom
You are a stone weighing heavily on her heart.

The joy of your birth has long faded,
And the world greets you only
With the ugly sins of man.

We unfortunate travelers on the same road
Come together again tonight.
Let our feet carry us to the end of this winding dark road;
Let our eyes cling to that point of light;
Love, once frozen within our hearts, will flow again.

Tsun-I, January 13, 1945
The Songs of a Stroller, 65–67

JEN CHÜN (1912?–   )

JEN CHÜN admits that his poems are like "slogans and pane-gyrics," but claims that nothing except his own feeling has caused him to utter them. As a human being, he has to bow to the command of a number of external forces, but as a poet he defers only to the irresistible inner call. In his case the call is the urge to sing of the grandeur of the time. To be sure, it is the tragic grandeur of a tragic era, but it is also "a string of glowing years."

He wrote *The Glowing Years* before the Sino-Japanese War was over, in the temporary capital of Chungking. It was a time and place where he did not have to write such lines. The command, then, must truly have been his own.

He counters his critics with a reminder that Walt Whitman once upon a time had to face similar ridicule. He declares, in the poem prefacing his *I Sing for the Victory* (Chungking, 1943):

> Pretty poems,
> Let ancient mummies chant them;
> Elegant words,
> Let fossils appreciate them.
> We want to mount our war horses
>   Gripping our spears
> To sing our new songs aloud!

With a clear purpose in sight, Jen Chün polishes his weapon for mass agitation. He tailors his lines for recitation in public. His work was first read by a choral group in Shanghai in 1949 almost immediately after the city changed hands. Soon after that, the students of the Drama Institute in Shanghai arranged a 50-voice choral group to give readings of his "Smash the Blockade" accompanied, for the first time, by sound effects. Each reading drew an audience of over ten thousand. In this work, Jen Chün has acknowledged his debt to Mike Gold, whose "Strike" has his unceasing admiration.

THE GLOWING YEARS

History is smouldering,
Time burns your hand,
This is a string of glowing years!

Look!
Which city, which village,
        Or
Which river, which mountain peak
        Is not in flame?
Which pair of eyes
Or which one's heart
        Is not burning bright?

The light is intense and glaring,
Like the moon,
Only still more crystalline,
Like the sun,
Only still more brilliant.

This light starts from the will to revenge, hard as steel,
        And burns the hearts of love and hate.
It glows from the cross of Christ's martyrdom,
        From the forehead of the Buddha,
        And from the tip of Mohammed's sword . . .

It's the light of truth, and justice
Of freedom and democracy!

It has shone before
        On the great revolution of France
        On the liberation of American slaves.
It has shone before
        On the Chinese overthrowing the Manchus
        On the Russians ousting the Czar.
Now it is lighting the whole world,
        Helping it to free itself from the Fascists.

History is smouldering,
Time burns your hand,
This is a glowing era
That burns bright everywhere!
It will slash the thick dark night,
And bring to humanity
>   A sun, a moon, and stars, all completely new.
>   *The Glowing Years,* 95–98

THE TEMPERING OF STEEL

My friends, I say—
The enemy's bombs
>   Are just a big iron hammer
That pounds us, incessantly.

"It's up!"—[1]
Everybody
>   Like a soldier readying for action:
Nimbly prepares everything
>   Puts away everything
Gulps down as much food as he can hold,
Packs his little bag,
Fills his water canteen,
And brings along a snack . . .
>   Determined to carry out "Sustained Resistance War"
>   Against the so-called "Vicious" and "Exhaustive"
>   raids.

"Air raid!"—
Everybody smartly
>   Locks his door
>   Loads his bag on his back
>   And takes in hand a sack, of leather or cloth . . .

---

[1] Big lanterns were used as air raid alarms in most cities during World War II in China, with different colors designating the preliminary, the air raid, the urgent, and the all-clear signals.—Ed.

Under the direction and protection
    Of the police and Public Safety Corps
One after another
In neat order
    They walk toward the shelter.
A massive stream they are
    But without haste or panic.
"It's urgent!"—
Everybody harbors
    The same feeling
    The same faith.
Like members of one family
    They sit close together,
    They stand close together,
    Crowd together.
With patience, unity, and seriousness
    They deal with and resist
The brutal activities of the enemy!
"All clear!"—
Everybody picks up his sack of leather or cloth,
    Loads his bag on his back
    (Also loads a much greater mission and duty
      on his back)
    And walks back home,
    (If his home is yet undestroyed)
Walks back to his post.

Isn't it so, my friends?
The enemy's bombs
    Are just a big iron hammer,
We are already tempered steel
    More solid and resilient than ever.

                Chungking, June 1941
                The Glowing Years, 102–6

I SING OF MAY

Like a hurricane,
Like a flash of lightning,
May—
          The giant of the era
               Has arrived!
Piloting a three-engined
               High-speed plane,
Driving a streamlined
               Express train,
Breaking through the milky white fog,
               Singing songs of victory,
          Through the seal of ice and snow,
               Through the guard line of bayonets and spears,
Vibrating,
Rumbling,
          It has arrived!
It has come to the villages,
          Also to the cities,
To Shanghai, Peking, and Hankow . . .
          Also to New York, Paris, and London,
Bringing with it all fire,
          All heat,
               All force,
          And a body full of scars
Ah, scars!
Yes, in the past,
          In Shanghai, Peking, and Tsinan
          In New York, Paris, and Berlin,
You have been beaten,
          And shot
          And trampled under hoofs,
All bloody,
          Torn wide open!
But your tendons are of copper and your bones steel,
          Your immortal body
Can be wounded, but never fatally,
          And the wounds give you new strength.

When the time comes
        Once again you appear
Like a ferocious warrior with a hundred battles behind you,
        Leading an immense army
            Sweeping forward.
Never slow
        Never any hesitation!

When you arrive
        The sun gives light and heat especially for you,
            And presents a picture of total beauty,
Just as the peacock spreads
        Its gorgeous plumage.
Even cold-blooded worms
        No longer want to stay underground
But leap from their subterranean dwellings
        To offer themselves
            To the sun you have brought along!
The snow of Siberia
        Has begun to melt,
The solid ice blocks on the Yellow River and the Don
        Have started to thaw.
Cheer runs through the great earth
        And enchanting dimples appear on water.
On the trees, birds chime their songs of greeting;
        Red blossoms cover the countryside,
            Cover the cities . . .
And men,
        Although some at the sound of your footsteps
            Or at the sight of your shadow
Already
        Tremble in fear
As they suffer
        From extreme tension,
Afraid of seeing your colors bright and clear
        Afraid of hearing your sonorous roar.
These people, you see,
        Are an army of moles
Who know only how to hide underground,
        Being unaccustomed to the sun
            Especially the sun you brought along.

But there are people, many many more people,
>> Regarding you as a true brother,
>>> As an affectionate companion.
The moment you arrive
>> They'll be like those in a dream
>> Suddenly aroused by an insistent alarm.
They'll use banners and processions,
>> Sweat and blood . . .
>> As their most animated language.
In the streets,
>> On parade grounds
>> In buildings,
To you,
>> (And to the entire world)
They'll tell of their grievances,
>> Express their hopes,
>>> And ready their own strength.
The moment you arrive
>> They'll shake hands with you,
Kiss you
>> And hug you,
>>> And merge with you into one unity.

                                        . . . .

Now, May!
>> Once again you march with your majestic force
>>> On the old world.
We are the youngest generation of this era,
>> We are dead enemies to the old society,
>> We are the sons of the sun.
We want to be the vanguards
>> Shedding our last drop of blood
>>> To blaze a trail for you.
We shall gather all the red flowers in the world
>> To make a huge garland,
>>> And drape it on your neck,
So that you can soar everywhere,
>> Soar
>> And soar,
May!
>> You are bringing from the dark, dark night
>> To this world—a tomorrow.

I Sing for the Victory, 95–105

from SMASH THE BLOCKADE

O: indicates the sound of a gong, drum,
     cymbals, small gong, all struck
     simultaneously
SD: indicates the sound of a small drum
C: indicates the sound of cymbals
SG: indicates the sound of a small gong
     Each symbol represents a basic note which
     may be a ¼ note.
"–" represents prolongation of the basic note,
     making it a ½ note.
"/" represents a ⅛ note.

4

(*Male chorus*)	Forward!
(*Female chorus*)	The people of Shanghai! (O/)
(*Male chorus*)	Fight!
(*Female chorus*)	The people of Shanghai! (O, O)
(*Male voice*)	With your burning zeal
(*Female voice*)	And your courage like surging waves,
(*Male voice*)	And your determination like steel,
(*Female voice*)	With concrete action
	Respond to the enemy
(*Male chorus*)	Defeat the enemy. (SD, SD, O)
(*Female voice*)	Victory
(*Male chorus*)	Must belong to the people. (O–, O)
(*Female voice*)	Starting from "May 30th"[2]
(*Male voice*)	We have
	Struggled against imperialism,

---

[2] Refers to the incident in Shanghai on May 30, 1925 when labor
and student demonstrators protested against the killing of the labor
leader Ku Cheng-hung. There were many casualties.—Ed.

(*Female voice*)	Struggled against Sun Ch'uan-fang[3]
(*Male voice*)	Struggled against Kuomintang reaction-aries
(*Female voice*)	And finally we got Shanghai Back in the hands of the people.

(*Male voice*)	Since we had the power To recapture Shanghai
(*Female voice*)	We also have the power
(*Male chorus*)	To protect Shanghai
(*Female chorus*)	To rebuild Shanghai. (O, O, O)

| (*Male voice*) | Fight bravely!
The people of Shanghai! |
| (*Female chorus*) | Under the leadership
Of Chairman Mao and the Chinese
Communist Party |

(*Male voice*)	March forward without fail! People of Shanghai!
(*Female voice*)	We never stand alone—
(*Male chorus*)	All the people of China
(*Female chorus*)	All the peoples of the world
(*Altogether*)	All stand on our side. (O, O, O, O, O)

(*Male voice*)	Let the six million pairs of iron fists Reach up together like a forest,
(*Female chorus*)	Together, aiming at the imperialists,
(*Male chorus*)	At the Chiang gang of bandits,
(*Female chorus*)	Strike down without mercy:
(*Altogether*)	Smash the enemy blockade! Rebuild the people's new Shanghai!

(O, O–, O
(O, O–, O, C, SG, C, O, C, C, SG, C, O, O, O)

Shanghai, August 1949
Long Live New China, 22–26

[3] The military commander who occupied and ruled Shanghai in the 1920s.—Ed.

YÜAN SHUI-P'AI (1908?–   )

A FACILE command of popular tunes, folk songs, and the time-tested musical features of the Chinese language are the handy tools of Yüan Shui-p'ai, but it is a keen observation of the irony of life that gives substance to his poetry. Yüan was little known at the beginning of the second world war, but when his verses appeared in Hong Kong under the pen name Ma Fan-t'o toward the end of the war, recognition was instantaneous. They are humorous verses, often sharp enough to make the reader laugh with tears in his eyes. They are also—since the greatest irony of man shows up in his relationship with other men—political and social verses.

In these early works Ma Fan-t'o ridiculed the strange things going on in the middle and late 1940s: the birth of a pig billed as an omen of victory, the repeated efforts to clean up the cities in order to impress foreign visitors, the talk of giving uniforms to prostitutes, the soldiers dying of starvation while millionaires doubled their bank accounts in America, the streetcar that never came. . . .

Ma Fan-t'o skilfully burlesques popular songs and creates new ditties. Superb control and the use of local expressions and slang are the secret of his humor. The comic element is heightened by the ring of authenticity in his lines—the simple, down-to-earth expressions of the people. Ma Fan-t'o seems to have done nothing more than record them in such a way as to highlight their ironical and humorous character. The poems are funny in spite of their settings, which can be extremely pathetic.

In laughing at the follies of man, Ma Fan-t'o is also raising questions not easily answered. A pervading one is about the sense of the society in which he has found himself. When he takes in all that is going on at one glance, his attempt at a description of it in "Headline Music" is an admission of dismal failure. Life as it appears now, he seems to be saying in this poem, simply cannot be caught in rhyme, it is a cacophony.

THE CITY

The city waits for you ahead
With its smell of taverns,
With its smell of automobiles,
With its dust churned up by the wheels,
With its advertising and trades that tell lies.

It will entertain you with its noisy streets,
With the deception and indifference that lie among men,
With hearts that have become numb.
Like a crouching wild animal,
The city waits for you ahead.

> 1939 (?)
> Wen, *Complete Works, Hsin,* 461

HEADLINE MUSIC

Seven days and seven nights eating, sleeping, defecating
            on the top of a freight car
From 100 to 300 swept up at the entrance to the tunnel[1]
Big fire, Big fire, Big fire
Bodies, Bodies, Bodies
       The suggestive pictures on the walls
       Musclemen pushing their way forward
       Leg, Leg, Leg
       Curve, Curve, Curve
A pair of eyes protruding from the flames
And the flames shooting out from the eyes
City follows city, the rail line
From village to village, narrow trails and cavalries

[1] Refers to the tragedy that occurred in the early summer of 1941 when hundreds of people were suffocated or trampled to death in the air raid tunnel system in Chungking as the result of a panic and poor ventilation facilities.—Ed.

Infinite joy, when the moon is again full
Lots of people lose their hats in the thumping crowd
If the air raid siren sounds, full technicolor
First prize is definitely here, hurry up and get rich
Tense, Tense, Tense
Bullish, Bullish, Bullish
Four thousand million dollars tumble in the gold market
Change, No change, Don't discuss national affairs
Every tune grand, elegant, and elevating
Every scene full of exquisite music and dance
Sing in honor of schoolmates joining the army
Dance for benefit of the refugees
A queue tens of miles long, spending the night in the
cold wind
Peerless art on creamy artificial ice, spring color in the
palace of the moon
Every word is blood and grief, moving the audience to tears
They carried and supported their old and young, we were
deeply touched
Domestically produced great film, a tragedy with
costumes in the latest fashion
The plot touchingly sad, tender, tense
Ladies, old and young, are respectfully advised
to bring more handkerchiefs
Skylight, Skylight, Skylight. . . .

Chungking, December 14, 1944
The Songs of Ma Fan-t'o, 13–14

Author's note: These are almost all film ads, headlines of
all sorts, and certain commonly used expressions in news dis-
patches, thrown together. I can think of no appropriate name
for it, so I call it "Headline Music."

OLD WANG POPS THE QUESTION

They say that Old Wang has a girl friend, Miss Li,
For her, Old Wang's feeling definitely cannot be compared
with the ordinary.
First he invited her to see a spoken drama, four hundred
dollars a ticket,

Second, he sent her home later in a ricksha, costing another
    eighty.

The next day Old Wang started, no use beating about the
    bush.
"I'm studying accounting in the business school of the college,
    But I am not on the staff of any government agency,
    There is a little business of my own that I manage.

"Speaking of age I have only turned the twenty-sixth spring,
    However, on the roster of a certain bureau you'll find my
        name.
    Every month I receive the regular ten pecks of OPC rice,
    Thirty-one is the age in that registration I claim.

"The school chum of my sister's husband has a cousin
    Whose hometown relative is a maidservant in a certain
        mansion.
    Whatever happens you can always entrust to her,
    Then it's a cinch there will be absolutely no question.

"I have my ID card, salt coupons, special privilege cards,
    And a card that gets you things much cheaper at the Co-op
        store.
    And I still have put away a half bolt of blue cloth . . .
    Miss Li, I don't think I need to say any more."

Winter 1944
The Songs of Ma Fan-t'o, 15–16

INSCRIPTION ON A KLIM CAN

In the year A.D. 3000, a tin can was discovered in the ruin
of a big seaport near the Yangtze River delta. Upon examina-
tion by distinguished archaeologists, it was identified as a
precious antique dating back to the "People's Era." On the
can were twenty-four lines of inscriptions as follows:

Klim powdered milk
Inexpensive supply.
Chinese children's lives
On it rely.

Drink foreign milk
Recognize an alien parent,
How fortunate indeed
Are the children at present.

If the mother has no milk,
A dry nurse comes to the house.
There is no need
To trouble Chinese cows.

Simple and clear:
Everything needed daily
Is an imported item
From a foreign country.

Why develop industries?
That's too much ado.
Just open up your mouth
Let cakes come to you.

Living at others' mercy,
Be flexible, one's told.
This treasure must be kept
For generations to behold.

> January 18, 1946
> *The Songs of Ma Fan-t'o,* 142–43

A SONG OF REFORM

Speaking of reform, yes, we are going to reform;
We will get a haircut first, and then take a bath.
Remove our long gowns to put on Western suits,
And get hold of a walking stick to carry around.

Speaking of reform, yes, we are going to reform.
If you want me to be patient, I never can agree.
I'll bear all pains and make all sacrifices with teeth clenched,
To change all our sanitary facilities to the Western style.

Square table tops will be changed into round,
Porridge will be served before regular steamed rice.
Walking and driving will both keep to the right,
And all the stores will be renamed Corporations.

"Proprietors" will be replaced by "Managers,"
  The Spring Festival will be called Farmer's Day.
Don't say you're playing mahjong, say yours is a
          "Ma-ch'üeh"[2] game
Stop eating soybean sauce, use salt instead.

Tear down the seals on the gates, switch to locks.
Talk not too little, neither too much.
"Papa" has resigned in favor of "Father,"
  Bhikshuni returns to her lay life to become a "nun."

Open up the windows, but add a screen,
The ants are yielding their floor to the caterpillars.
Too much freedom is tyranny,
Nowadays democracy is so, so very different.

                              February 12, 1946
                              The Songs of Ma Fan-t'o, 166–67

STRANGE TALES, DOMESTIC VINTAGE

Trucks smash trains,
Skulls knock rifle butts.
Pandas ride on airplanes
Bandits are promoted to generals.
Ladies escort Mr. John[3]
Masters swap flies.
Land and sea forces join
To smash up a dance joint.
Hard to take inventory in liberated areas,
Get a copy from Tokyo.

[2] A more fashionable name for the same game.—Ed.
[3] It was considered chic in those days to go out with members of the foreign colony.—Ed.

Chennault is a foreign name
But Charlie has become a compatriot.
Let's welcome more garrison troops
So they can hit the Chinese.
Abolish the rickshas
The unemployed can join the army.
The moon is better abroad,
But civil war is our specialty.
The fat ones play mahjong,
The thin ones are stakes.
Prostitute roundup in the city,
Pressgang for men in the country.
Hats fly over the sky,
Tails follow everyone.[4]
Democracy is Communism
Progressive is anti-revolution.
Use gasoline to fight fire,
This is called "problem of face."
The victors are weeping sadly,
The vanquished chuckle with pride.
Traitors try traitors,
People kill people.
A mass of air of harmony
Ping pang ping pang ping.

> October 11, 1946
> *The Songs of Ma Fan-t'o*, II, 55–56

NEW YEAR

Some celebrate their New Year this way,
Some celebrate their New Year that.
New Year in the tall Western-style buildings, steam heat
   feels like spring.
New Year in the streets, men curl up on the sidewalk like
   dogs.

[4] Accusing someone of Communist affiliation was called, in those days, "giving someone a red hat to wear," and "tailing" referred to spying.—Ed.

The rich eat their dinners, lasting a half month,
Until their tongues are blistered, and their intestines start
    trouble.
The poor, ah, the poor have sweet potatoes for a meal;
They get sick, lose their jobs, and remain sad-faced.

Celebrate the New Year in the sound of firecrackers, gongs
    and drums, and drinking games,
And in the sound of guns and cannons, in the shadow of
    whips and gleam of swords.
Some celebrate by drinking champagne;
Others celebrate by drinking poison.

Some sleep the New Year in on a Simmons innerspring:
Others sleep the New Year in on a board full of nails.
It's Wang Hsiao-erh's New Year: Worse off year after year.
But the New Year of the Big Boss: Plenty of money, plenty
    of money.

> February 9, 1948
> *The Songs of Ma Fan-t'o*, II, 137–38

"VERY INTERESTING" DEATH

At a "very interesting" gathering,
The ladies and gentlemen brought up a "very interesting"
    question.
The gentleman had a Chinese name,
The lady, however, bore a name of alien origin.

Question: "Firecrackers are expressions of joy,
Why then are they used at funerals in China?"
Answer: "Because life is so hard for the Chinese, and to them
Death means a happy nirvana."

Capital! Capital! Very, "very interesting!"
The Chinese regard death as happy liberation.
Absolutely correct! Absolutely correct! Otherwise why while
    living in this paradise,
Do they still hang themselves, or jump off a tall building, or
    plunge into the sea, or take poison?

For example: A peddler "possessed by the devil" fell off a
    tall building, his head cracked wide open,
But to him, that could be only a "pleasant relief."
Or take the girl "teaching Cantonese" at a hotel, who "died
    on the spot,"
Naturally, "I died happily" must have been her belief.

So, why must you say that their deaths were "self-inflicted?"
If you say that they were "inflicted by others," wouldn't it
    earn someone merit?
Aid in someone's death—aid in someone's pursuit of happiness.
Why do you waste effort to absolve yourselves? The world
    should thank you for it.

Gentlemen, ladies, why don't you keep your dreams?
Ladies, gentlemen, why don't you keep your muddled heads?
Today you are looking down from the clouds, "very
    interestingly."
Tomorrow, don't tumble down and plunge directly in an
    outhouse.

> May 14, 1949
> *The Songs of Liberation,* 97–100

    The author's note to this poem gives the detailed back-
ground of a special conference billed as "Very Interesting"
by the intellectual and social elite in Hong Kong, including
both Chinese and British. The subject was a comparative
study of the Chinese and Western ways of life. The conver-
sation in the poem is a part of what transpired at the con-
ference. The reference to the deaths of a peddler and of a
young girl, whose body was found half-naked on the sidewalk
below a hotel, was based on two tragedies that rocked Hong
Kong earlier that year.—Ed.

JUNE WEATHER

June weather, too hot to bear,
I cook a meal in the kitchen,
Smoke fills the whole room;
Tears and sweat pour like rain.

Little Mao's heat rash is red all over;
His cry tugs at his mother's heart.
Not that Mother doesn't want to take care of you,
She just can't take time out from washing clothes.

June weather, too hot to stand,
Your dad works an extra shift at night.
There, even in winter he perspires in a thin shirt;
What will he do in weather like this?

When he comes home it's already daybreak,
He walks in, stiff and numb.
He drops in bed without a word;
Tears fall in silence; who dares to ask him?

                              The Songs of Ma Fan-t'o, II, 130–31

OLD MOTHER BLINDS HER OWN SON

It's snowing hard,
The river froze.
We finished the nation's war, but now we fight our own
        people.
Conscription could not reach rich men,
It only reached after my son, over twenty years old.

I entreated heaven, heaven did not respond;
I pleaded with the earth, the earth had no power.
I begged other people, but no one sympathized.
I cried my eyes dry, dreading the arrival of dawn
For at dawn my son was to report to the army camp.

While my son was asleep,
And the neighborhood lay in total silence.
"Ah, my son,
 Don't blame your mother for being too cruel,
 Don't blame your mother for being too cruel."

 I took needles.
 Two steel needles,
 And plunged them into my son's eyes.
 He screamed and blood spurted out.
"Ah, my son, they don't take a blind man in the army."

                        The Songs of Ma Fan-t'o, II, 105–6

Author's note: January 7, 1947 dispatch from Tan-yang, released in the *Wen-hui Daily* of Shanghai: A farmer of the Mei-chia Village was drafted. His mother stabbed his eyes when he was not looking. He lost his sight instantly.

CAN'T UNDERSTAND

Can't understand!
Can't understand!
Why can't you understand?
Why still can't you understand?

You take scolding,
You take beating,
Are you crazy or mad,
Or silly, or dumb?

Driven like a horse,
Slaughtered like a cow,
You wear out your bones, bear all hardships,
Having earned nothing, except a thousand years of debt.

They cheated you
They sold you!
They drained your blood
And ruined your family.

Not a single able-bodied man is left,
Even women and old men have to build fortifications.
Last autumn's battlefield still stinks in winter,
And a spring crop of corpses is to be buried in the same ditch.

Bitterness no end!
Tears never dry!
Who cheated us all our lives?
Who did us harm we could never redress?

Can't understand!
Can't understand!
You mean to tell me you really don't understand!
You mean to tell me you really don't understand!
                    The Songs of Ma Fan-t'o, II, 115–17

Author's note: A report entitled "Traveling in Northern
Kiangsu" in the *Wen-hui Daily* of April 14, 1947, quotes a
certain Division Commander as saying, "It is not advisable
to station troops along the Nanking-Shanghai line because
city life often has a demoralizing influence on morale. The
soldiers nowadays are all dumb. Frankly, if they understood,
how could they be willing to fight?"

KOWTOW

Give one kowtow,
Gulp a mouthful of rice,
Swallow a drop of tear,
Live one day less.
                    The Songs of Ma Fan-t'o, II, 76

CAN'T AFFORD TO LIVE

Have to eat, but can't afford to eat;
Have to wear clothes, but can't afford it;
Have to ride a ricksha, but can't afford to ride;
Have to rent a room, but can't afford to sub-lease.

A baby gets born, but we can't afford to feed it;
My parents are dead, but caskets I can't afford to buy.
Too hard to make a living in the country, but can't afford
        living in town.
Just can't afford to live, my friend, yet can't afford to die.

Half of my salary was deducted to cover an advance.
Half of my salary was paid back to Old Li.
Only a little small change was brought back home
To buy what, kerosene or rice?

The Songs of Ma Fan-t'o, II, 111

TO INDIA

It's a land of beauty and grace,
Everywhere green foliage spreads like umbrellas, and roses are
        big as bowls.
The peacocks' green feathers shimmer in the woods.
There the goddess of spring makes her perpetual home.

It's a land of beauty and riches
Watered by the blood of its people's heroes.
Yes, the people there are sturdy and brave;
They are like our own brothers.

It's an ancient friendship, two thousand years old.
Time cannot diminish it, nor high mountains block it.
We, nine hundred and sixty million people live together in
        peace,
Setting a new example for all the world.

Ah, north wind, please blow. Let our songs ride on your wings
To sail with the wishes and blessing of Peking
To the banks of the Ganges where soft breezes sway the
        willows,
To the land where flowers bloom all four seasons.

Selected Poems of 1953.9–1955.12, 456–57

I MEN (1915?–   )

I MEN, whose real name has not been ascertained, began publishing in the late 1930s under the initials, "S. M." His collection, *The Stringless Lute*, contains many successful attempts to free poetic expressions from old and new linguistic conventions. The proper rhythm for a theme, be it an old horse trudging on an ancient road or a string of boatmen pulling a huge wooden junk, is very well captured in his verse.

LONELINESS

Loneliness
The moon shines on a tree-shaded sidewalk
One listens to the sound of lonely footsteps vanishing into
      the immense quiet night.

Loneliness
The clock faces the candle's tears
One listens to the tick-tock marking the intervals between
      each winding and unwinding of time's axle.

Loneliness
Lying covered under a layer of clothes but with eyes wide,
      wide open
One listens to the rumbling waves from inside the heart.

Loneliness
It's not the window of night opening without winds,
It's not the side of a pond without the shadow of a man or the
      croak of a frog . . .

Loneliness
It's not the pain caused by a world deserted and desolate,
It's the inability to bear the human desert made of a
    multitude of men.

Loneliness
It's not a thought wandering afar either, casually leaving this
    world behind,
It's a burning love for mankind.

Loneliness
Ah!
Just because he is unwilling to bear loneliness.

> Chungking, spring 1941
> *The Stringless Lute,* 89–90

IF I KNOW

If I know (like the crystal blue sea near shore),
I am lucky:
If I don't know,
Still I am lucky. (The singing lark in flight and the swinging
    willows,
        They don't know anything about this at all.)

To know
And then again not to know, ah! . . .
Looking at the hazy days through the mist of this mountain
    city
One sees something, and then nothing at all.

The sun
Please come out, you, the Lord of light!
Let your burning rays
Be my eyes of wisdom that see all . . .

And let me, too,
Open my eyes wide like the sunrise dispelling the clouds,
Let me have enough clear wisdom,
And enough strength to control the gloom of sorrow (like a
        sturdy line trimming a full white sail)

Thus my own eyes become
Two new suns
Rising from the myriad of glittering dewdrops in
        the wilderness. . . .

Chungking, spring 1941
The Stringless Lute, 85–87

from BOATMEN

IV. One Cable

Their steps in cadence (like a column of seasoned soldiers
        answering a "Fall in" command),
Their steps solemn (like the crisp rhythm of the morning
        frost on a sandy beach),
Their steps firm (so firm that they almost cease being
        human),
Their steps silent (everyone of the men being as silent as an
        iron statue):
One cable ties up all—
The huge wood junk and the men pulling it,
The grain and the seeds on board and the men pulling them,
The force and the direction and the men exerting force,
And the men themselves, each individual and the entire
        group,
One cable unifies the steps,
Organizes the force,
And organizes the group,
Together with the direction and the road—
Only one of those flaxen ropes, long and thin, looking so
        fragile.

Forward,
Forced march forward.
The road for this march,
Mind you, my friends,
Is not covered mile by mile,
Not even step by step,
But only inch by inch.
Every inch like that in a turtle's race,
Every inch like that covered by a snail at its highest speed.
And every inch has its obstacles,
A shapeless rock
Or a stone itself already so ironically broken,
Or a half-rotten rusted nail dug out accidentally by a rabbit
        from an ancient grave . . .
But one inch forced forward, is, after all, one inch advanced,
And one inch advanced is one inch of victory.
With one inch's force,
The force of man and the force of a group,
They move one inch closer
To the morning sun, the disc that spits fire in the sky.

> Chungking, February 5, 1942
> Wen, *Complete Works, Hsin,* 569–70

OLD SOLDIER

An old soldier
On a lean horse
Emerges from the morning mist,
A blurred image approaching the woods,
And again receding into the blurring mist,
He has
A dirty service cap pressing on his furrowed brow,
A beard frozen in thick frost,
And a nose spouting warm vapor.
His sunken eyes are closed,
His wrinkled cheeks drooping,
His hands hidden in the depth of his padded jacket sleeves.
The reins lie unattended on the horse's shaggy neck.

The outline of his back
Hunched in fatigue
Lets the sluggish, rocking steps carry it to an unknown
      destination,
Day after day,
Carrying a sword
That has a bit of dust
A gleam of metallic light,
A touch of rust,
A layer of frost,
And a trace of blood reflecting the rising sun.

The Stringless Lute, 10–12

LU LI (1920?–   )

Lu Li was a young student when the Japanese began a shooting war in northeastern China. He drifted in and out of Japanese-occupied areas and found himself in the "border zone" living with the guerrillas who fought under the Communists against the Japanese. In his poetry he records his prison experience, battlefield experience, and his experience of working for the Communist party and later for the Communist regime. In one of his earlier collections, *When He Wakes Up*, there are examples of his shorter lyrics, cast in a style very different from his later works; his "Wild Flower," written in 1938, shows a sensitive response to minute suggestions from the outside world:

> Wild flowers grow in the bush,
> Like visions coming to life in prison.
>
> We walk on the riverside;
> The wild flowers nod to us from the shore.
>
> Gazing at the wild flowers,
> We no longer fear the difficult road ahead.
>
> Wild flowers are about to bear fruits,
> Our visions are also about to bloom.

Yet even the earlier short lyrics embody a view of life that later finds more eloquent expression in a longer poem, "Life," written in 1950. Lu Li, together with I Men, Chang Chihmin, and a number of others, belongs to a group, that bridges the gap between Pien Chih-lin and the latest folk-song writers. Lu Li's works reveal a path of growth, but no trace of any dramatic inner struggle or traumatic emotional experience, such as Hu Feng's works seem to indicate.

A MIDNIGHT'S MEMORY

Moonlight seeped in over the threshold.
I thought it was the sun,
Opening the door, I found it was still midnight.

Soon, wind blew in from the north,
Strumming the string of the bow—the moon.
And I heard the sound of daybreak.

The rivershore weighted down under the mountains' shadows,
And a star flashing across the immense wilderness:
Everything lingered in a sound sleep, I felt.
I alone was the first awake.

When He Wakes Up, 87–88

from LIFE

. . . .

One day, a lady comrade said to me,
"You are a busy man, you seem to enjoy yourself."
Thank you for your unenjoyed compliment.
At a time like this
Of course we are busy.
Many things are beginning,
For many other things we need to prepare fully.
Yesterday we dissolved the old system,
Today, we must, from the warp and woof of history,
Discover the thousands of threads
With which we'll weave a backdrop for the new era.

. . . .

If you feel that our life is meaningless,
That's because you haven't plunged yourself into life,
Nor have you dedicated your life,
Nor have you embraced this world with your flesh and blood.
You have your small world of liberty,
That winds around your neck like a woolen scarf.

We, I'm sorry to say,
We are stupid, not as clever as you.
We know only how to dig dirt,
Placing the heavy yoke of the world on our shoulders,
And laboring like bullocks.
And every day, we are very happy.
You can hear us laugh aloud any day,
And any day you can hear us sing.
When our arms are hooked in our comrades' arms,
We walk out of our workshops, our factories' gates.
We, young men and women,
In our laborers' steps,
Dance our *Yang-ko* toward a new era.

. . . .

Poets of our time
Please write this kind of poetry,
Write this kind of daily life of ours.
Write down the details of our life,
Write how we collect chips of coal to warm up a winter,
Write how we collect scrap iron to build a world of steel,
Write how we polish our machines, handling them like
      sweethearts,
Write how we are chagrined because a piece of glass was
      accidentally broken,
Write how we save on power and yet produce more,
And how we repair our dormitory, and how happy we
      are . . .
Just write about us, ordinary people,
About our happiness and sorrow,
About how we conclude a day's work
And how we march toward tomorrow.

. . . .

1950
I Sing of Mao Tse-tung, 114–19

CHANG CHIH-MIN (1918?–   )

ONE OF THE newcomers in poetry, Chang Chih-min began publishing his verses in the late 1940s. He described himself not as a poet, but "a worker with a mouth and a pair of hands": his mouth, "To curse as well as to sing," and his hands "to hit as well as to comfort." He wanted no sadness or despair but rather shouts of protest, and he got them.

He went to live with the peasants during the political transition and sat in on their "Speak-bitterness" sessions when they accused the landlords of crimes. Chang wrote down these narratives in the folk-ballad style, and then read them back to the peasants to see if they understood them. He maintains that he changed every word that was not a part of the peasants' true language.

The folk ballad is particularly suited to story-telling. Its rhymed couplets lend themselves to easy recitation, sometimes accompanied by simple folk musical instruments. The stories Chang has recorded (some of them undoubtedly true) are usually life histories from the birth of a peasant child, to the climax of his triumph over the landlord and other social vices with the approach of Communist liberation. Many passages have a sweeping and galloping flow which, sustained by the feeling of the characters involved, can be very moving. His "Can't Kill Him" is a fine specimen.

Chang's shorter poems are also cast in the folk-song style.

AFTER THE RAIN

The rain halts,
The wind ceases.

The girls
Again spread out their colorful clothes in the sun:
The children
Chase a rainbow on the lawn.

Look!
Who has painted another coat of fresh color on the blue hills?
Listen!
The cornstalks are talking in their crackling voice.

Summer 1957
Personalities in the Commune, 128

from CAN'T KILL HIM

The Reminiscences of a Fifty-seven-year-old Peasant Who Has Changed His Lot

Part I. Fifty-seven Years Passed in Hell

My Name Is "Can't Kill Him"

My mother said: "You and Lai-hsi were born on the same
    day,
But Lai-hsi's family was a rich family."

For the rich family a new baby is a great joy!
The poor cannot afford feeding another boy.

His family bought wine and weighed in flour,
My mother lost her eyesight shortly after she delivered me.

To be born with lots of money is always lucky,
So they called him "Fortune comes" to a good family.

Fully six months had passed after I came,
No one had yet given me a name.

"What shall we call our child?" asked Mother;
Father said, "Call him 'Can't Kill Him'; the King of Hades
　　must have made a mistake."

Strangle My Sister

Mother gave birth to a little sister
There was not even rice gruel to feed her.

My sister was strangled to death,
So Mother could work for others as a nurse.

Father would give me to the Li family,
Mother said: "Before you take my son away, first take me."

This was hard for him, for I was his only son;
His tears fell like pearls from a broken string.

All my blue veins showed, I was so thin;
Deep as wine cups my eyes sank in.

One day I saw Lai-hsi in the street, white steamed bread in
　　his hand,
He called me to stop me, "Hi! Can't Kill Him!

"You crawl on the ground like a dog;
I'll give you a piece of bread; you snap at it with your
　　mouth."

I crawled on the ground, hunger had killed my pride;
Right in my chest, he gave me a kick.

"Why don't you slap yourself when you are dying for food;
When did you last eat things so good!"

· · · ·

Sell My Mother

Two pecks of rice we owed Lai-hsi;
Hard as we tried but we could not repay his family.

On New Year's Eve, we had nothing to eat.
Lai-hsi's father came; he was burning mad.

"I came to collect, not to beg, today.
Sell your wife, if you can't repay."

He forced us on the spot to sell Mother for money,
And at midnight he brought over a black donkey.

Mother saw it, she clawed her own face;
Blood streamed down her cheeks.

Father knocked his head against the wall;
I hung on the donkey's tail, and wouldn't let go at all.

"Mother, Mother, you mustn't go, you see,
If you go, who's to take care of me?"

. . . .

Part II. I've Come Back to Life

Speak-bitterness

A thunder rocked heaven;
Along came the Communist Party.

Under a big tree, Lai-hsi and his father were hung;
One whip flew up as another came down.

"You drove my whole family to ruin;
You forced my father to death and my mother to marry
     again.

"You, heartless wolf who sought only the death of the poor,
Even for cash you wouldn't sell your grain to us hungry
     folks.

"I've tended your sheep for over three years;
  You figured again and again and said I still owed you more.

"You've beat me in the past, now I'll beat you;
  Even after eating your flesh I still won't be through!"

. . . .

September 5, 1947
The Sun Has Come Out, 12–27

RENDEZVOUS

The little creek gurgled
On its bank a girl sat washing clothes.
Never, it seemed, could she finish washing her clothes,
As she kept at it from dusk till moonrise.

But she was not just washing clothes,
She looked to the east and to the west.
Clearly she was waiting for someone on the riverside,
She was waiting for the shepherd, little Wan-ch'ang.

Had Wan-ch'ang really forgotten their appointment?
The more she waited the more anxious she became.
A spell of anger followed a spell of worry,
Finally Wan-ch'ang arrived at her side.

"As I was just herding the sheep this way,
  The ditch in our commune broke a lock.
  The water in the vegetable patch was rising higher and
      higher,
  Which do you think I should take care of first?"

Seeing that Wan-ch'ang was drenched through and through,
  Her anger took flight, all in all.
"Quick, let's make some hot soup to help you perspire,
  There is still a piece of ginger at our house. . . ."

Autumn 1957
Personalities in the Commune, 62–63

SEWING

The dawn is breaking
And the roosters call.
The lamp is still shining in Third Sister-in-law's room,
Why has she stayed up all night?

Ah, so Third Brother is going out to work,
To build irrigation ditches along the Yung-ting River.
She finished mending his trousers and started on his bedding
And sewed his jacket after doing the socks and shoes.
Because Third Brother had a bout with dysentery early in
        spring,
She made him a quilted apron.

She thought to herself as her fingers moved on the stitches:
When water comes down along the canals
We'll fill the northern reservoir first, then the southern.
To soak the several hundred acres of dry field.
No longer need we worry if the Old Heaven does not rain.
This fall the yield is going to be twice as high.

The bags that he needs are packed and ready now,
Third Sister-in-law gently calls Third Brother
"Hey, hey!
It's time to get up!"

> Autumn 1957
> *Personalities in the Commune*, 73–74

WHAT KIND OF TROOPS ARE THESE

Listen! The thunder! The rumble that rocks the sky.
Look! A wave of smoke spanning mile upon mile.
What kind of troops are these,
Every one of them in full combat dress?

Carrying picks, hoes, hammers, and rakes . . .
And baskets for dirt, for manure, for other things to be
         moved . . .
They drive in front of them horses and bullocks
Pulling carts large and small.

A boisterously surging river!
A roaring and rolling river of humanity!
This is an army corps formed upon a will,
They move toward their battlefield.

> Summer 1958
> *Personalities in the Commune,* 127

VERSE ON THE WALL

The People's Speech

"Let's attack here!
  Drive away the mountain gods,
  Break down the stone walls
  To bring out those 200 million tons of coal.

"Let's strike here!
  Let the Dragon King change his job,
  Let the river climb the hills,
  Let us ask it for 8000 acres of rice paddies.

"Let that valley open its bosom
  To yield 500 catties of oats every year.
  Cut down that knoll
  To make a plain over there . . .

"We want flowers and fruits all over the mountain,
  We want fat sheep and pigs to fill up the pens.
  We want electric lights to shine in every house,
  And every cart, large or small, to go uphill."

Challenge the Great Earth

Let's wage war against the great earth!
Let the mountains and rivers surrender under our feet.
March on nature,
Let's take over the power of rain and wind.

We shall tolerate not a single inch of unused land!
Nor a single place harassed by disaster.
Make wet rice, wheat, and yellow corn grow on top of the
mountain,
And beans, peanuts, and red kaoliang rise on sheer rocks . . .

Break It

Which generation left with us "No strong man can control
a flood?"
Break it! We must control floods,
Making them listen to our command.

Why must New Year's Eve be spent at home?
Break it! Bring your ration
And let us keep vigil over the year's passing at our place of
work.

Who said: "Even Old Man Heaven cannot plug all rat
holes?"
Break it! Under our hands
The rats are to disappear totally and return no more.

Who said: "No good farm can raise three crops of vegetables
a year."
Break it! Under our hands
The vegetable leaves will stay green on the farm all year
round . . .

(An inch of time is worth ten thousand pieces of gold.)

The sky shakes, and the earth trembles!
Our warm blood boils day and night without stop.
By day we chase the sun,
At night we pursue the stars.

"An inch of time is an inch of gold,"
  That's the value of yesterday.
Time's worth today
Is "An inch for ten thousand pieces of gold."

> Summer 1958
> *Personalities in the Commune*, 149–52

I'M A NEWCOMER
BY CHUNG HSÜAN

I'm a newcomer.
There are young girls gathering shells on the beach.

I'm a newcomer,
And I'm seeing for the first time:
From the other shore of the immense sea
Rises a beautiful dawn with peerless warmth.
Its pure white light
Shines on the bent, naked bodies of the young girls.

I'm a newcomer,
And I'm seeing for the first time:
All the fishermen who live on the beach
Carry guns to go fishing in the sea.
They love the sea so dearly:
They are prepared to kill every enemy invading it,
The mother who has nursed them for generations.

I'm a newcomer.
And I'm seeing for the first time:
The dawn breaks on the young girls,
And on the fishermen.

> 1939
> *I'm a Newcomer*, 80–81

YEN HSI-SHAN'S TAX AGENT
BY LIU CHIA

Yen Hsi-shan's tax agent
Came to the village.
Immediately he got hold of the village chief,
"In three days the rice levy must all be in.
If one grain is missing
We'll use your head to make up the balance."

He rode away as soon as he finished speaking.
Behind his horse
A rope led a cow and two sheep.
The villagers peeped from behind their doors,
Tears glistened in their eyes.

The village chief struck his gong
The villagers' hearts sank.
They went home,
Searched every basket and every urn;
Even the rice already in the kettle was taken, dripping,
And household articles were sold for rice to be given to the
        military governor.

The Japanese
And Governor Yen,
Six and half-a-dozen, they were the same.

The tax man came again.
His horse was chewing corn at the stable,
He himself sat half-drunk in the big house.
Before the village headquarters
Gathered a huge crowd in tatters.
They watched their food hauled on the scales;
Their hearts, like rocks, plunged.

He who scampered over the wall in flight
Was roped back,
And those hiding in haystacks,
Or sick in bed,
All were dragged out.
The tax man's whip was raised higher and higher,
The rope on the villagers was drawn tighter and tighter.
Lockers, beddings, clothes, pots and pans . . .
Everything was carried away.

From down the road came a woman running.
She rushed forward, her hair flying.
Pushing the crowd aside,
She threw down a sack:
"This is the tax grain, ah!
To be handed in to Governor Yen. If not enough . . .
Take me to the Governor."

The village chief was stunned.
Opening the sack he poured out the contents.
Everyone fell back, horrified—Good Heavens!
There were two children's heads, still dripping blood.
One head with a pigtail
Was the woman's child,
The three-year-old, Little Silver.
"Murder, Murder!"
The crowd scattered.
The woman turned around:
"I am the murderer.
I killed them with my own hands
To pay my tax to the Governor."

The tax man smiled.
Coldly he urged the village chief
"Hurry up!"
Those remaining stood motionless.
The northern wind was whistling in higher notes.

On the Western Front, November 20, 1945
Lin the Tenant, 15–17

NIGHT
BY AI MU

Night

The miserably wet long night of the northwest . . .
The wolf's
Fiery red eyes
Are lighted in the wild underbrush of the northwest.
Countless stars
In the depth of the night
Hang like ripe lemons.
In the forest—
That pitch dark
All-embracing tent—
The hunters leap forward in the thicket.
Greedy fire snakes are their guns,
Spitting their explosive flaming tongues.

And four of us
Panting
Groping toward a faraway place.

> From "Leap Forward," in
> *I'm a Newcomer*, 103–5

THE GREEN SPRING
BY SHAN MEI

When spring comes
I see the woods turning green,
The water in the river turning green,
The hills turning green,
The fields turning green,
The little beetles turning green,
And even the white-bearded old man turning green.

The green blood
Nurtures the fatigued earth,
And from the earth bursts forth
A green hope.

I'm a Newcomer, 82–83

from LOVE SONG OF TURFAN
BY WEN CHIEH

Young lad under the apple tree,
Please don't, don't sing any more;
A girl is coming along the creek,
Her young heart throbs in her bosom.
Why is her heart throbbing so,
So violently, even skipping beats?

Springtime, she works in the orchard,
The songs pass by her ears softly,
The buds on the boughs are not yet open,
The young lad already hopes for fruit.
She cannot understand his strange ideas,
She says, "Don't bother me with your songs."

The young man spends the summer in the orchard,
Gazing at her all the time while working.
The fruits are only as big as grapes,
In his songs he already urges their picking.
She cannot guess all his thoughts,
She says, "Don't stick to me like a shadow."

Pink fruits weigh low the green branches,
Autumn is a season of ripening,
Night after night she cannot sleep.
Is she thinking of the tree full of good apples?
These things he should understand, she says,
"There is something, why don't you say it?"

. . . Young lad under the apple tree,
Please don't, don't sing any more:
She is coming, treading on the meadow,
What is she hiding behind her smiles?
Say it out, what lies truly in your heart.
It's time to harvest the love sown long ago.

1954
Selected Contemporary Chinese Poems, 202–4

NEW FOLK SONGS

CONFUCIUS, it is said, preserved *The Book of Poetry* for us because the folk songs therein teach moral and political lessons. The "music academy" of the Han Dynasty was an official bureau to collect folk songs not only for the enrichment of poetry but also as a mirror of the people's feelings about the government.

The Communists have encouraged the collection of folk songs since 1949. A concerted drive to encourage the laboring masses to write verses reached its height in 1958. The campaign was conducted with the same efficient organization and total mobilization as that used in all other major movements sponsored by the new regime in Peking. "Cultural workers,"—teachers, writers, and students—descended on the countryside, the factories, and the collective farms to arouse interest in verse writing and several types of mass activity were instituted. In the "poetry contests" the bards mounted a makeshift platform in the village square to compete in extemporaneous verse writing. The challenger would say the first line or couplet and demand that the contestant complete the quatrain, which seems to have been the stanza form exclusively used in these contests. The winner, chosen by popular applause, would replace the challenger and occupy the platform until he in turn was defeated by a more resourceful minstrel. At "poetry fairs" model verses were posted and broadcast over a loudspeaker. Poetry booths offered aspiring "poets" an opportunity to win recognition by completing an incomplete stanza posted on the wall. A writer or a group of writers from a factory might challenge another individual or another production unit—from farm or factory. These challenges were also posted.

The participants in these contests and fairs were all sorts of people, boys and girls, old and young, literate and semiliterate. An old factory worker, Ts'ao Wen-ming, received an invitation to take part in the "poetry fair" in the Wu-hua district of Yunnan Province toward the end of November 1958. He was too excited to sleep that night. He had been singing folk songs and making songs all his life for his own entertainment, but now he was to challenge other folk-song singers and he wondered if he could write down half of the words he could sing. The next day, as he stepped down the "poetry lane" where an infinite number of songs, complete and incomplete, decorated the floats and sidewalk booths, he waxed courageous and completed four poems in his clumsy child-like handwriting before the day was over. During the five or six days of the fair, over 60,000 visited and took part in the contest, netting a total of over 10,000 verses.

No accurate statistics are available on the total result of the 1958 poetry movement throughout the country, but these figures will serve as an indication of its general scope: national publishers collected over 700 volumes of folk songs, while on the local level the figures were astronomical—3733 volumes were printed in 141 cities and villages in Szechwan Province; some 600 pamphlets of verses were published in one city alone, Ku-ling in Fukien Province; and there were 23,000 poetry clubs in the province of Hupeh.

Out of the flood of new folk songs have emerged quite a few verses which demonstrate the resourcefulness of the participants. An old peasant wrote:

> Three feet deep I dug and there the crop grew more.
> One stalk rose to pierce the sky.
> Colorful clouds tied a sash around the corn's waist;
> That scared the moon into taking a low bow.

And another:

> An illiterate like me takes a pen to write poetry,
> Joy fills my heart as water fills the river.
> For a thousand years the tip of my pen never talked,
> Now I have more to say than I can ever finish.

Some of the songs in print may have been subjected to slight editorial polishing, but these are few. Most of them are recorded as they were first heard. Through them one can hear the quality of the Chinese voice—untrained, unsophisticated, but always proud, robust, and stirring.

WOMEN TRANSPORT CORPS
A FOLK SONG OF TIENTSIN, HOPEI PROVINCE

The stars have not yet retired, and the sky is still dark,
From down the road comes the women transport corps.
Pushing small carts and pulling large carts.
They have a load of laughter for every load of coal.

She pushes her cart, fast as flying,
Crushing the pearly dewdrops on the grass.
That big sister, she has picked a twig of flower,
Wonder to whom she wants to give it.

"Speaking of yesterday's labor hero meeting,
The hero of steel production is named Wang K'uei.
If you, big sister, have him in mind,
I'd be glad to deliver the message, without charge."

She wets her hand with dewdrops and wipes it on her friend,
Scolding her: "You and your nasty mouth.
Wait until our steel output has risen,
If you want to marry him, I can be your go-between."

They push their carts, fast as flying,
With a load of laughter for every load of coal.
With stars on their shoulders and the moon above they keep
    busy running,
One more drop of their sweat, one more drop of molten
    steel.

The Songs of the Red Flag, 325–26

WITH ONE STROKE I DIG THROUGH
THE CRYSTAL PALACE
A SHENSI FOLK SONG

Iron hoe, two catties and a half heavy,
With one stroke I dig through to the crystal palace.
The dragon king can't stop trembling when he sees it,
He kowtows, and he pledges:
"I'll give water, I'll give water, just as you say."[1]

The Songs of the Red Flag, 194

MANY, MANY ARE THE SONGS
OF GOOD HARVEST
A FOLK SONG FROM TSUN-I, KWEICHOW PROVINCE

Many, many are the bumper crop songs
We pack them on horses.
The first horse has already reached Tsun-i,
The last horse is still on the Erh-lang River.

The Songs of the Red Flag, 209

A BIG MOUNTAIN IS MOVED AWAY
A SZECHWAN FOLK SONG

A roar of songs,
Ten thousand people start at once.
Under blows of spades and hoes,
A big mountain gives way.

The Songs of the Red Flag, 92

[1] Legend says that the dragon king controls rainfall and water and lives underground in a crystal palace.—Ed.

IT CAN BEND THE HUGE RIVER

A pole, three feet three inches long,
Carries dirt when we build a dike or dig a pond.
Even a high mountain it can carry off;
Even a huge river it can bend.

The Songs of the Red Flag, 94

TOMORROW WE TAKE OVER
THE HEAVENLY PALACE[2]
A FOLK SONG FROM TAN HSIEN, SHANTUNG PROVINCE

Patches of white clouds float on the sky;
On each cloud unfurls a red flag.
Are they heavenly soldiers arrayed in battle?
Why do the red banners flutter on the clouds?

Look at them carefully, again and again
Hey, they are the members of the commune working half way
  up the mountain.
With the blue sky on their heads and picks in their hands,
They run over the mountain, riding on the clouds.

They are competing with the gods,
Their shouting pierces the ninth heaven.
They raise the five grains on hard rocks
And plant the sacred peach trees on the clouds.

The sun, emerging from the sea, becomes alarmed,
Tigers and wolves are frightened, fleeing in all directions.
Tomorrow we'll take over the heavenly palace,
And seize the heavenly river to water the sacred peach trees.

The Songs of the Red Flag, 89–90

[2] Heavenly palace refers to the higher realm where at one time the legendary Magic Monkey intruded, insulted the gods, and in general turned things upside down. The sacred peach trees were said to be in the private garden of the queen mother of all the gods.—Ed.

OUR SONG MAKES THE YANGTZE RIVER
FLOW BACKWARDS
A FOLK SONG OF SU HSIEN, ANHWEI PROVINCE

Our songs now fill baskets;
Basket upon basket, they fill storehouses.
Don't say that they are but colloquial words,
Once broadcast in the field they turn into grain.

There are twice as many folk songs this year,
A large baleful of them rolls off our tongues, casually.
Don't leave them to be sung next year,
No one can use last year's calendar.

If you walk, walk the long, long road;
If you sing, sing forty songs at a stretch.
Think about our prospects of happiness,
We laugh until midnight, unable to go to sleep.

It takes good hoes to till the land,
It takes good singers to sing songs.
Now that everyone is a singer,
Our songs make the Yangtze River flow backwards.

The Songs of the Red Flag, 57–58

PLEASE TAKE GOOD CARE OF MY HOME
BY A RED ARMY SOLDIER

Taking off my insignia, handing in my ID tag,
I can't hide my ten years' feelings.
To leave my outfit, ah,
Is like leaving home.

I left home, still talking in a child's high-pitched voice.
Though young, my determination was firm,
Leaving my father and mother behind
To pick up a rifle, to change our fortune.

In heavy snow my company commander gave me his cotton-
        quilt jacket;
Late at night my platoon leader mended my socks and shoes.
No amount of words or time is enough to tell
Of the comradely affection I have felt.

In seven days I learned to shoot the old 38;
In half a year, to ride a war horse.
Neither heaven nor earth did I fear,
In following the Communists to conquer the country.

Never have I straggled in the marches of ten thousand li,
Never have I heeded the forest of guns and the shower of
        bullets.
I wrestled Maxims from the enemy with my bare fists;
On foot I caught up with the tri-axled trucks.

Cooking wild greens, swallowing burned rice flour,
We tightened our belts to pursue the Hu's and the Ma's[3]
With the blue sky as our blanket and the grass our mattress,
We camped at the foot of the T'ien Mountain Range.

We fortified the hilltop, defending it to the last,
Calluses piled thick on our hands,
We forgot life and death to cross the rivers,
Covering ourselves with battle scars.

I joined the Party under a canopy of gunfire,
I studied without going to school.
From a buffalo-herding lad to a soldier in uniform,
It is the army that has fostered and raised me.

Taking off my insignia, handing in my ID tag,
I can't hide my ten years' feelings.
To leave my outfit now, ah,
Is like leaving home.

[3] Hu Tsung-nan and Ma Pu-fang, two Nationalist generals.—Ed.

This afternoon I'll go back to the country to work in the
    fields,
This morning I am polishing my rifle for the last time.
A well-polished rifle I shall hand over to my leaders,
So that a new comrade may use it.

I seize the hands of my comrades at arms, so difficult to let
    go;
I hug my leaders, long and hard:
"Ai, leaders and comrades, please
  Take good care of this outfit—my Home."

The Songs of the Red Flag, 363–64

MONGOLIAN PASTORAL

Marching beyond the Great Wall,
Beautiful is the northland.
The grass is tall,
And the horse, strong,
And Mongol lads herd their cattle
On the bank of the Yellow River,
Or at the foot of the Yin Mountain
As the brave ones ride across the waterway.
In solitude they gaze at the setting sun,
Listening to the camel steps in cadence with a bell,
In cadence with a bell.
Still more lonesome
Is the long, long road leading to a deserted river crossing.
Gray sky
And infinite wilderness,
The brave ones ride downhill from a knoll.

Chinese Rhymes and Songs, 2-B, 162

from ASHIMA
A Ballad of the Sa-ni Tribe in the Yunnan Province

[Ashima was a beautiful girl who rejected a wealthy and influential suitor of her tribe, Ah-chih of the Je-pu-pa-la family. The latter gathered a strong group of armed men and kidnaped Ashima. Her brother, Ah-hei, was the best horseman and archer in the community. Upon hearing the bad news, he sped to the kidnaper's family in anger . . .]

Ah-hei jumped on his horse
And whipped his mount savagely.
Following the direction given by the old woman
He took off in flying pursuit of Ashima.

The sun could not bear to shine,
The bluebirds hovered on the road.
The house of Je-pu-pa-la was dank and dreary,
Where Ashima was suffering.

"Why is this dungeon
So very, very dark?
The rocks, damp and cold,
Are chillier than ice.

"Ah, wind, why can't I hear you sing?
Ah, birds, why can't I watch you fly?
And sun, why can't I feel your warmth!
And moon, why can't I see your light!

"What is that calling outside?
Is it not the voice of my father and mother?
But when I listen carefully,
It's only the chirping of the crickets.

"What is that running outside?
Is it not the happy noise of my playmates?
But when I listen carefully,
It's only the throbbing of my own heart.

"What is that blinking beyond the wall?
Is it not the eyes of the flying dragon horse?
But when I look carefully,
It's only two fireflies darting by."

The dark dungeon may be as strong as rocks
But Ashima's will can break it;
The dark dungeon may be as cold as ice.
Ashima's heart can melt it.

The bluebirds call in the sky,
The sun shines above,
Ah-hei, soaked in sweat, pressed on
With anxiety gnawing his heart.

Two days' journey he made in one day,
And in two days he covered five days' distance.
You could see only the woods flying backwards,
You could see only the mountains fall away from him.

[Finally Ah-hei arrived at the kidnaper's house. The kidnaper
resorted to the tribal custom of a series of contests whereby
only the winner could have his wish. Ah-chih and Ah-hei com-
peted in singing and in strength. Each time Ashima's brother
emerged the winner. Ah-chih tried a number of tricks without
success, and in desperation he plotted to kill Ah-hei by letting
three vicious tigers loose on him. Ah-hei shot all three to
death. As the victorious Ah-hei and his sister were setting off,
the Je-pu-pa-la family broke a dike to drown them . . .]

As they arrived at the foot of the Twelfth Cliff,
As they approached the river,
Suddenly a flood roared down from above,
In a minute the small stream became a huge river.

If the brother walked ahead,
The sister could not cross the river.
If the brother walked behind her,
The sister still could not cross it.

Ah-hei held on to the hand of Ashima,
And Ashima grabbed Ah-hei's hand,
Braving the flood water
They walked ahead together.

. . . .

The flood water rolled down,
Along came a whirlpool
The lovely Ashima
Was swept away in the waves.

Only her voice
Kept coming back
"My brother Ah-hei
Hurry and help me!"

[Ashima was saved, according to the legend, by a fairy named
Shih-ch'ia-tu-le-ma, who had once been a mistreated girl and
had committed suicide, and whose spirit remained on the hill
as an echo . . .]

From then on
Ashima became an echo.
Whenever and however you call her,
She'll answer you exactly.

. . . .

Her voice
Remains forever in the ears of the Sa-ni people.
And her shadow
Is forever printed on their hearts.

A *shih ma,* 45 ff.

WATER FLOWS AROUND OUR VILLAGE
A FOLK SONG OF HO-CHIEN, HOPEI PROVINCE

At sunset the day before yesterday,
Water stayed in the river to the west.
This morning under the red rising sun,
Our ditch led water to the east
By noon the sun moved to due south,
Our ditch already guided water around the village.

The Songs of the Red Flag, 182

I STAND ON MOUNTAIN HIGH
A FOLK SONG OF TSAIDAM, TSINGHAI PROVINCE

I stand on mountain high, looking west,
There a white belt winds its way through the hills.
No, it's not a belt,
But a newly cut highway climbing the peak.

I stand on mountain high, looking west,
There patches of white cloud float over the hills.
No, it's not white cloud,
But the shed of oil drills built on the peak.

I stand on mountain high, looking down,
Black waves churn in the water flowing over the wells.
No, it's not water,
But crude oil gushing forth through an opening in the
    reservoir.

The Songs of the Red Flag, 320

I'M A LONGSHOREMAN
A Folk Song of I-ch'ang, Hupeh Province

I'm a longshoreman,
My power controls the ten-thousand-li course of the Yangtze
      River.
My left hand brings in the city of Shanghai,
My right hand moves away the city of Chungking.

I'm a longshoreman,
My drive shatters the ninth heaven.
I've loaded thousands of suns,
I've unloaded thousands of moons.

I'm a longshoreman,
I fight and I produce on the river.
With a shout I lower a load of iron into the hold,
The dragon king falls off his throne in the crystal palace.

I'm a longshoreman,
A fighting vanguard on the production front,
In order to outdo the British
We load and unload, fast as the wind.

The Songs of the Red Flag, 323

MONKEY SUN DESCENDS TO EARTH
A Folk Song of Feng-jun, Hopei Province

Sun the Magic Monkey descends to the earth,
He transforms himself into a sparrow to appear among men.
Before he plants his feet firmly on a branch
A shotgun blast roars close by.
In a hurry he transforms himself into a fly
And lands near the stove of the Chang house,
But a swatter instantly looms up to greet him,
He has to flee the Chang household.

Summoning the local god he asks:
"Why do people hit me?"
The local god answers with a smile,
"Now that everybody is bent on removing the four evils,
Shooting sparrows or swatting flies is no news."

The Songs of the Red Flag, 249

ONE STEP COVERS TEN THOUSAND LI
A Folk Song of Chungking

The hall is full of red "flowers of production,"
Index arrows shoot up piercing the sky.
The worker's one step covers ten thousand li,
He dares to challenge the Monkey King, Sun Wu-k'ung.

Red flowers bloom in technological revolution,
The workers clap their hands in glee
Their laughter rides on the wind to reach the river
The river laughs with them, turning up whitecaps.

The Songs of the Red Flag, 272

THE ELECTRIC LIGHTS SHINE
IN EVERYBODY'S HEART
A Nursery Rhyme of Ts'ao Hsien, Anhwei

Big stars and little stars in the sky,
Electric lights upon electric lights in the commune.
Look, so many stars there are in the sky,
Look, so many lights there are in the commune.

The many stars in the sky light up the earth.
The many lamps in the commune light up our eyes.
Now when Grandmother wants to do sewing
She no longer needs me to thread the needle.

The stars in the sky give twinkling light
The lights in the commune are burning bright.
Sister embroiders flowers, so colorful,
No longer need she hurry during the day.

The stars in the sky are crowded as sesame seeds
The lights in the commune shine on our family.
Mama carries little brother in her lap,
Under the light she learns reading and writing.

Stars face stars in the sky,
Under the beam of every house hangs an electric lamp.
The stars are dim against the lamplight,
The electric lights shine in everybody's heart.

The Songs of the Red Flag, 233–34

BUILDING PUMPKIN TRELLIS
A HOPEI FOLK SONG

Young pumpkin leaves
Large as rice bowls,
Two lovers are building a pumpkin trellis.
One ties the cornstalks into poles
The other ties the poles to make frames.
Just don't let the young lad step on the flowers.
Ah, pumpkin seedlings,
Hurry up and grow.
Vines grow long,
And leaves grow big,
To climb along the cornstalks
To cover the whole trellis,
So the pumpkins can hide themselves under the arbor
To have a tête-à-tête cheek to cheek.

The Songs of the Red Flag, 224

THE RHINOCEROS MOUNTAIN
A SZECHWAN FOLK SONG

A Rhinoceros Mountain in front of the door,
That Rhino had slept for thousands of years.
Suddenly it woke up, blinking its eyes in surprise,
To find wide, wide highways winding all over its body.

An electric wire spans the space,
Loudspeakers are now mounted on the Rhino's back,
The Rhino had never made any noise before, but now
Its resounding roar vibrates through the sky.

The Songs of the Red Flag, 232

HAYSTACK
A FOLK SONG OF TSUNG-YANG, SHENSI PROVINCE

The haystack rises, round and round,
On top, a haying comrade of the commune reaches the sky.
He tears a piece of white cloud to wipe his perspiration,
And he leans over to light his cigarette on the sun.

The Songs of the Red Flag, 218

A SWEET POTATO ROLLS OFF THE HILL
A FOLK SONG OF KWANGSI

A crystal river flows to the east of our commune,
From its bank rises a gentle slope.
On the slope the communers are digging sweet potatoes
In a happy hum of laughing chatter.

Suddenly I heard a noise in the river.
Water splashed up over ten feet high.
And I heard my own frightened voice shouting,
"Who is the careless one that fell down?"

Everybody heard me and roared and roared,
One girl answered:
"Nobody fell off, nobody at all,
It's only a sweet potato!"

The Songs of the Red Flag, 223

CHINESE SOURCES CITED

—English translation of title, author,
Chinese title (publication place, date)—

About Hsü Chih-mo, Liang Shih-ch'iu, *T'an Hsü Chih-mo* (Taipei, 1958).

All-out Attack, Tsou Ti-fan, *Tsung kung chi ling* (Shanghai, 1949).

The Analects, Lun Yü (a journal published by Lin Yutang in Shanghai in the 1930s).

Annotated T'ang Poetry, Hsü Wen-yü, *T'ang shih chi chieh* (Taipei, 1954).

Ashima, Yunnan jen min wen kung t'uan, *Ah shih ma* (Peking, 1954).

Before Death, Wang Tu-ch'ing, *Ssu ch'ien* (Shanghai, 1927).

Before the Image of the Holy Lady, Wang Tu-ch'ing, *Sheng mu hsiang ch'ien* (Shanghai, 1926).

The Black Hands of Sin, Tsang K'o-chia, *Tsui o te hei shou* (Shanghai, 1936).

The Brand, Tsang K'o-chia, *Lo ying* (Shanghai, 1934).

The Canal, Tsang K'o-chia, *Yün ho* (Shanghai, 1936).

The Carpenter Shop, Tsou Ti-fan, *Mu ch'ang* (Shanghai, 1940).

Chinese Ballads, T'ien Chien, *Chung kuo mu ko* (Shanghai, 1936).

Chinese Rhymes and Songs, University of Peking, *Chung kuo ko yao tzu liao* (Peking, 1959).

Chung shu chi, Chu Hsiang, *Chung shu chi* (Shanghai, 1937).

Collected Poems at Forty, Hsü Hsü, *Ssu shih shih tsung* (Shanghai, 1948).

Collected Works of Hu Feng, Hu Feng, *Hu Feng wen chi* (Shanghai, 1948).

Compendium, Chao Chia-pi (ed.), *Hsin wen hsüeh ta hsi* (Shanghai, 1935).

The Complete Works of Hsü Chih-mo, Hsü Chih-mo, *Hsü Chih-mo ch'üan chi* (Tainan, 1961).

The Complete Works of Wen I-to, Wen I-to, *Wen I-to ch'üan chi* (Shanghai, 1948).

The Crescent Monthly, Hsin Yüeh (a literary journal, Shanghai, 1928–32).

The Cycle, Hsü Hsü, *Lun hui* (Hong Kong, 1951).

Dead Water, Wen I-to, *Ssu shui* (Shanghai, 1928).

Discipline, Wang Tu-ch'ing, *Tuan lien* (Shanghai, 1927).

Experiments, Hu Shih, *Ch'ang shih chi* (Shanghai, 1920).

The Flower of Man, Lü Ying, *Jen te hua to* (Shanghai, 1948).
The Flowerlike Sin, Shao Hsün-mei, *Hua i pan te tsui e* (Shanghai, 1928).
Forty Poems, Tu Yün-hsieh, *Shih ssu shih shou* (Shanghai, 1946).

The Glowing Years, Jen Chün, *Fa kuang te nien tai* (Shanghai, 1948).
The Goddess, Kuo Mo-jo, *Nü shen* (Shanghai, 1921).

The Han Garden, Pien Chih-lin and others, *Han yüan chi* (Shanghai, 1936).
Heaven and May, Shao Hsün-mei, *T'ien t'ang yü wu yüeh* (Shanghai, 1927?).

I Sing for Happiness, Li Chin-fa, *Wei hsin fu erh ko* (Shanghai, 1926).
I Sing for the Victory, Jen Chün, *Wei sheng li erh ko* (Chungking, 1943).
I Sing of Mao Tse-tung, Lu Li, *Mao Tse-tung sung* (Tientsin, 1950).
I'm a Newcomer, Hu Feng (ed.), *Wo shih ch'u lai te* (Shanghai, 1941).
It Is Not Yet Dawn, T'ien Chien, *Wei ming chi* (Shanghai, 1936).

The Lakeside, Feng Hsüeh-feng, *Hu p'an* (Shanghai, 1922).
Leaves of Three Autumns, Pien Chih-lin, *San ch'iu yeh* (Shanghai, 1933).
Light Rain, Li Chin-fa, *Wei yü* (Shanghai, 1922).
Lin the Tenant, Wang Hsi-chien and others, *Tien hu Lin* (Shanghai, 1949).
Literature, Wen hsüeh (a journal, Shanghai, 1933–37).
The Lonely Country, Wang Ching-chih, *Chi mo te kuo* (Shanghai, 1927).
Long Live New China, Jen Chün, *Hsin Chung-kuo wan sui* (Shanghai, 1950).
The Long-term Visitor and Hard Times, Li Chin-fa, *Shih k'e yü hsiung nien* (Shanghai, 1927).

Miscellaneous Poems, Wang Tu-ch'ing, *Ling luan ts'ao* (Shanghai, 1927?).
The Mud Puddle, Tsang K'o-chia, *Ni nao chi* (Shanghai, 1939).

A Night in Florence, Hsü Chih-mo, *Fei-leng-ts'ui te i yeh* (Shanghai, 1926).
Nineteen Poems, Mao Tse-tung, *Shih tz'u shih chiu shou* (Hong Kong, 1958).
Noctural Songs, Ho Ch'i-fang, *Yeh ko* (Shanghai, 1950).

Northern Travels and Others, Feng Chih, *Pei yu chi ch'i t'a* (Peiping, 1929).
Northward March, Tsou Ti-fan, *Tsou hsiang pei fang* (Peking, 1954).

On Poetry, Ai Ch'ing, *Hsin shih lun* (Peking, 1952).
One Leaf, Wang T'ung-chao, *I yeh* (Shanghai, 1922).
Orchid Winds, Wang Ching-chih, *Hui te feng* (Shanghai, 1922).

Personalities in the Commune, Chang Chih-min, *She li te jen wu* (Peking, 1958).
The Poems, Cheng Min, *Shih chi* (Shanghai, 1949).
The Poems of Chih-mo, Hsü Chih-mo, *Chih-mo te shih* (Shanghai, 1925).
The Poems of Meng-chia, Ch'en Meng-chia, *Meng-chia shih chi* (Shanghai, 1931).
The Poems of Ping Hsin, Ping Hsin, *Ping Hsin shih chi* (Shanghai, 1942).
The Poems of Yü Ta-fu, Cheng Tzu-yü (ed.), *Ta-fu shih tz'u chi* (Hong Kong, 1954).
Poetry Journal, *Shih k'an* (a literary supplement to the Peking *Morning News*, 1926).
The Portrait of a Chinese Soldier, Wang Ya-p'ing, *Chung-kuo ping te hua hsiang* (Chungking, 1938).
The Precious Horse, Sun Yü-t'ang, *Pao Ma* (Shanghai, 1939).
The Prophecy, Ho Ch'i-fang, *Yü Yen* (Shanghai, 1954).

Recovery, Kuo Mo-jo, *Hui fu* (Shanghai, 1928).
Reminiscence, Yü P'ing-po, *I* (Peiping, 1925).
Returning West, Yü P'ing-po, *Hsi huan* (Shanghai, 1924).
Roaming in Clouds, Hsü Chih-mo, *Yün yu* (Shanghai, 1931).

Selected Contemporary Chinese Poems, Li Ts'ai-mi (ed.), *Chung-kuo hsien tai shih ko hsüan* (Hong Kong, 1959).
Selected Modern Chinese Poems, Tsang K'o-chia (ed.), *Chung-kuo hsin shih hsüan* (Peking, 1956).
Selected Poems of Ai Ch'ing, Ai Ch'ing, *Ai Ch'ing shih hsüan* (Peking, 1955).
Selected Poems of Liu Ta-pai, Liu Ta-pai, *Liu Ta-pai shih hsüan* (Peking, 1958).
Selected Poems of 1953.9–1955.12, The Association of Chinese Writers, *Shih hsüan 1953.9–1955.12* (Peking, 1956).
Selected Poems of Tsang K'o-chia, Tsang K'o-chia, *Shih hsüan* (Peking, 1956).
Selected Poems of Wang T'ung-chao, Wang T'ung-chao, *Wang T'ung-chao shih hsüan* (Peking, 1958).
Selected Short Poems of T'ien Chien, T'ien Chien, *T'ien Chien tuan shih hsüan* (Peking, 1960).

Selected Works of Chu Tzu-ch'ing, Chu Tzu-ch'ing, *Chu Tzu-ch'ing shih wen hsüan chi* (Peking, 1955).

Selected Works of Feng Chih, Feng Chih, *Feng Chih shih wen hsüan chi* (Peking, 1955).

Selected Works of Hsü Chih-mo, Hsü Chih-mo, *Hsü Chih-mo hsüan chi* (Shanghai, 1936).

Selected Works of Wang Tu-ch'ing, Wang Tu-ch'ing, *Wang Tu-ch'ing hsüan chi* (Shanghai, 1947).

Selected Works of Wen I-to, Wen I-to, *Wen I-to hsüan chi* (Shanghai, 1951).

The Short Story Monthly, Hsiao shuo yüeh pao (Shanghai, 1924–29).

Sketches of Dreams, Ho Ch'i-fang, *Hua meng lu* (Shanghai, 1936).

The Snowy Morning, Chu Tzu-ch'ing, *Hsüeh Chao* (Shanghai, 1922).

The Song of Joy, Hu Feng, *Huan lo sung* (Peking, 1950).

The Song of Ling Shan, Feng Hsüeh-feng, *Ling shan ko* (Shanghai, 1947).

The Songs of a Stroller, Fang Ching, *Hsing ying te ko* (Shanghai, 1948).

The Songs of Ma Fan-t'o, Yüan Shui-p'ai, *Ma Fan-t'o te shan ko* (Hong Kong, 1946).

The Songs of Ma Fan-t'o, II, Yüan Shui-p'ai, *Ma Fan-t'o te shan ko, hsü chi* (Shanghai, 1948).

The Songs of Spring, Feng Hsüeh-feng and others, *Ch'un te ko chi* (Shanghai, 1923).

The Songs of the Red Flag, Kuo Mo-jo (ed.), *Hung ch'i ko yao* (Peking, 1959).

The Songs of the South of the River, Wang T'ung-chao, *Chiang nan ch'ü* (Shanghai, 1940).

The Songs of Yesterday, Feng Chih, *Tso jih chih ko* (Shanghai, 1927).

The Sonnets, Feng Chih, *Shih ssu hang chi* (Shanghai, 1949).

The Sound of War, Kuo Mo-jo, *Chan sheng chi* (Shanghai, 1938).

Spring in Edo, T'ien Han, *Chiang hu chih ch'un* (Shanghai, 1922).

Spring Waters, Ping Hsin, *Ch'un shui* (Shanghai, 1922).

The Stars, Ping Hsin, *Fan hsing* (Shanghai, 1921).

The Starry Sky, Kuo Mo-jo, *Hsing k'ung* (Shanghai, 1923).

The Stringless Lute, I Men, *Wu hsien ch'in* (Shanghai, 1942).

The Sun Has Come Out, Chang Chih-min, *T'ien ch'ing le* (Tientsin, 1949).

The Sunken Bell, *Ch'en chung* (a journal edited by Feng Chih, Peking, 1925).

This Age, Wang T'ung-chao, *Che shih tai* (Shanghai, 1932).

Three Memoirs in Chinese Literature, Ts'ao Chü-jen, *Wen t'an san i* (Hong Kong, 1954).

The Tiger, Hsü Chih-mo, *Meng hu chi* (Shanghai, 1931).

The Traveler's Heart, Mu Mu-t'ien, *Lü hsin* (Shanghai, 1927).

The Trip to the West, Li Kuang-t'ien, *Hsi hsing chi* (Shanghai, 1949).

The Troubled Years, Tai Wang-shu, *Tsai nan te sui yüeh* (Shanghai, 1948).

The Turmoil, Kuo Mo-jo, *T'iao t'ang chi* (Shanghai, 1948).

The Vanguard, Kuo Mo-jo, *Ch'ien mao* (Shanghai, 1928).

The Vase, Kuo Mo-jo, *P'ing* (Shanghai, 1927).

Venice, Wang Tu-ch'ing, *Wei ni shih* (Shanghai, 1927).

The Victory of Life, Fang Ching, *Sheng te sheng li* (Shanghai, 1948).

The Wen-hui Daily, Wen hui pao (published in Shanghai and Hong Kong since the 1940s).

When He Wakes Up, Lu Li, *Hsing lai te shih hou* (Shanghai, 1943).

Wild Flowers and Arrows, Hu Feng, *Yeh hua yü chien* (Shanghai, 1937).

Wild Grass, Lu Hsün, *Yeh ts'ao* (Peiping, 1927).

The Wind Chimes, Ch'en Meng-chia, *T'ieh ma* (Shanghai, 1933).

The Wind of Spring, Tsang K'o-chia, *Ch'un feng chi* (Peking, 1959).

The Winds of the Universe, Yü chou feng (a journal published by Hsü Hsü and others in Shanghai and Hong Kong, late 1930s and early 1940s).

Winter in the City, Wang Ya-p'ing, *Tu shih te tung* (Shanghai, 1935).

The Winter Night, Yü P'ing-po, *Tung yeh* (Shanghai, 1922).

The Works of Kuo Mo-jo, Kuo Mo-jo, *Mo-jo wen chi* (Peking, 1957).

The World of Man, Jen chien shih (a journal edited by Lin Yutang, Shanghai, 1934).

The Wuhan Review, Wu han p'ing lun (a journal published in Wuhan in the 1920s).

The Zero Degree of Life, Tsang K'o-chia, *Sheng ming te ling tu* (Shanghai, 1947).

INDEX OF TITLES IN
ENGLISH TRANSLATION

INDEX OF CHINESE TITLES

(Romanized according to the Wade-Giles System)